Black Women Shattering Stereotypes

Black Women Shattering Stereotypes

A Streaming Revolution

Kay Siebler

LEXINGTON BOOKS
Lanham • Boulder • New York • London

Published by Lexington Books
An imprint of The Rowman & Littlefield Publishing Group, Inc.
4501 Forbes Boulevard, Suite 200, Lanham, Maryland 20706
www.rowman.com

6 Tinworth Street, London SE11 5AL, United Kingdom

British Library Cataloguing in Publication Information Available

Library of Congress Cataloging-in-Publication Data

Library of Congress Control Number: 2021932272

ISBN 978-1-7936-3600-3 (cloth)
ISBN 978-1-7936-3602-7 (pbk)
ISBN 978-1-7936-3601-0 (electronic)

Dedicated to the women whose coattails I ride every day, those who I can name (Gwen Siebler and Sandy Starks) and those I can't. These women— and so many others—showed me that women can be smart, outspoken, determined, and full of spirit, regardless of the barriers put in their path. They taught me that there are sometimes hard consequences for speaking out and up, but the alternative life is not worth living. To use one's voice for social justice and equity is the only good reason to speak. To Adrienne Rich, who said, "Those of you who teach, teach women writers" and to Audre Lorde who wrote she was "a Black woman warrior poet doing my work—come to ask you, are you doing yours?" I have read deeply and with passion these women's work since the 1980s. And every day I try to do the work Lorde and Rich charged me with. This book is part of that work.

Contents

Acknowledgments

To Dahja Ward and Janae Boykins: two of the most powerful young women I have ever known. To be Black and female in the United States at this point in time is to be a daily warrior in a culture that is destined to destroy you. They are surviving and thriving against all odds. This project would not have been possible if Dahja and Janae didn't inspire me through our office conversations, their classroom brilliance, and the engaged ways they move through this world. Dahja and Janae, I thank you for the hours in my office, under the poster of Audre Lorde, attempting to solve all the world's problems. I am deeply in awe of your spirits, your hearts, and your minds.

To all the generous and smart women who agreed to be interviewed, who added their brilliance to the work of Black women I am trying to shed light on here. Thank you for your insights and thank you for speaking the names of the women we need to study and absorb. Your voices matter; their voices matter. Here is to a deep gratitude and celebration of all the Black women: creators, bright stars, powerful and enduring spirits, and also rulers of the world.

I also would like to acknowledge my partner, Yipsel, and my son, Zephaniah, a.k.a. Boots, a.k.a. Starfish Baby, a.k.a. Snooks, for giving me the space and time to write. They left me alone whenever I needed. They listened when I needed to talk. They fed me and allowed me the space to put this project together.

The cover art for this book is the phenomenal work of Katharen Wiese of Lincoln, Nebraska. She is a powerhouse. You can find more of her work at www.katwiese.com. Support Black women artists, y'all.

And finally, I would like to thank the editor at Lexington Press, Jessica Tepper, who read an article I had written and saw a book project there. Thank you, Jessica. I owe the physical reality of this project to you.

Introduction

Black Women Shattering Stereotypes: A Streaming Revolution

In the summer of 2020, at the height of marches and protests regarding horrific and systemic racism in the United States, *Netflix* posted a "Black Lives Matter" list of offerings. Of the forty-two films/series chosen for their list, twelve featured the stories of Black women/girls and seventeen were produced, written or directed by Black[1] women. That same summer, the Academy of Motion Picture Arts and Sciences (host of the Oscars) implemented new eligibility requirements for films with an eye to increasing diversity ("Oscars to set best picture"). Perhaps these two examples are evidence that we are slowly creeping forward in recognizing and celebrating the work of Black women in media. More importantly, the work of Black women behind and in front of the camera allows all of us to consume stories that defy the tired and troubling stereotypes that have plagued Black women for centuries. When Black women are behind the camera, writing/producing/directing, the harmful stereotypes created by the white supremacist capitalist patriarchy (WSCP) are not only confronted but often shattered. But we need more Black women behind the camera critically and consciously working toward change, telling the stories of their lives and characters in dramatic juxtaposition against stereotypes. Those women being hired are wrecking those ratchet, trifling images of mammies, jezebels, sapphires, and sisters with an attitude. They may express anger, but they are not Angry Black Women: they carefully articulate the justifiable reasons for their anger: systemic oppression in the form of racism, sexism, classism, and homophobia.

Thirty years ago, *Daughters in the Dust* (1991), a gorgeous arthouse film by Julie Dash, received attention from the (primarily white) film critics. The film offered a decidedly Black female perspective, a worldview largely missing from the film canon. Dash's film was "not about explaining Black history to white people" (Scott 2020, 89). It was about celebrating the rich

1

and beautiful culture of Black women from a Black woman's perspective. *Daughters in the Dust* felt revolutionary (it was), but it was limited to art-house releases, small venues, and university classrooms. In 2000, *Love and Basketball* by Gina Prince Bythewood became a major Hollywood release, again from the perspective of a Black girl and her love of a sport she wanted to *play*, not watch. She had to fight to follow her passion. Just as the protagonist of that film, Monica, had to fight systems of race, class, gender, and sexuality to pursue her dreams, so did Bythewood and Dash. These films were messages of perseverance, hope, and love. That was decades ago. In 2000, Dee Rees offered us *Pariah*, another independent film, but this one featured a young lesbian protagonist. The film propelled Rees into the mainstream industry and she has continued to produce/direct shows and films such as *Mudbound* (2011) and *Bessie* (2015) that feature the stories and perspectives of Black women. Since *Daughters in the Dust*, *Love and Basketball*, and *Pariah*, Black women have been building a body of work that deals with all these issues: community, history, love, family, and culture. That is not to say that their work is recognized. The canonical list of films entitled "The Criterion Collection" is notoriously tone deaf when it comes to anything other than films by whites and males. If there are films about the Black experience on Criterion's list, they are directed/produced/written by whites. In fact, as of 2020, there was only *one* Black female director on the list: Euzhan Palcy's *A Dry White Season* (1989). The list's white male selection committee can't seem to identify with Black films, especially those by Black women. Yet Black women filmmakers keep waiting for the call, like jilted prom dates. Bythewood, director of *Love and Basketball*, said, "Every month, they (Criterion) put out an alert about their films coming out, and every month, I open it to see if they're going to highlight any Black filmmakers. And it never happens" (Buchanan and Ugwu 2020, AR6).

The Criterion list, and the white guys who keep it, may be ignoring Black women writers, directors, and producers, but consumers are not. Today as we look at the landscape of what Black women are offering us, what they are writing, directing, and producing, it feels like a revolution. Instead of one or two films every ten years by, about, and for Black women, we now have so many that it is difficult to keep up. That is a good problem to have. This book offers a small beginning, a select few to examine closely. After doing so, I feel hopeful. After talking to Black women, I can testify that they are ravenous for these representations. They are not only watching, but they are also thinking and talking about what these representations mean. There is so much more to come from Black women, both producers and consumers. Black women's voices and perspectives have been squelched and silenced for too long. Now is their time and they are taking it.

In 2013, *Being Mary Jane (BMJ)* aired on Black Entertainment Television, featuring a strong female character. Unlike *Scandal* (2012–2019), produced by Shonda Rhimes, a celebrated Black female writer/producer who made a name for herself in the popular series *Grey's Anatomy* (2005–present), *BMJ* (2013–2019) represented an Afrocentric perspective of being young, college-educated, and professional. Simultaneously, a young woman named Issa Rae began self-producing her own series entitled *Awkward Black Girl*, posting her episodes on YouTube. Although these shows all featured educated, professional, unmarried Black women dealing with issues at work and in their personal lives, Mary Jane Paul and Rae's character, J, unlike Olivia Pope on *Scandal*, confronted issues of Black family, Black community, and Black culture in every episode. *Awkward Black Girl* was picked up and produced by HBO and renamed *Insecure*. Issa Rae renamed her protagonist Issa Dee, but the themes and thrust of the show remained similar to *Awkward Black Girl*. These shows offered a feminist, Afrocentric perspective. From the shows' soundtracks to book references to topics of systemic racism, sexism, and homophobia, Mary Jane and J/Issa offered viewers a dynamic and complex Black view of the world from a female perspective. Inversely, *Scandal*'s protagonist, Oliva Pope, was a lonesome island unto herself, figuratively captured by a white president to be his mistress (a stereotypical Jezebel), and often held hostage by her damaged Black parents. There was no community or culture for Pope, only dysfunction and drama. In contrast, *BMJ* and *Awkward Black Girl/Insecure* felt revolutionary in the way they represented contemporary Black womanhood and empowerment.[2] Although *BMJ* and *Awkward Black Girl/Insecure* were likely written for an assumed Black female audience, both series were picked up by popular streaming services (Netflix and HBO), proving an appeal to a wider demographic.

Whereas one could see Olivia Pope manifesting tired Black female stereotypes such as the Jezebel and Sapphire, one would be hard-pressed to put Mary Jane Paul or J/Issa Dee in such boxes. Mary Jane and J/Issa defied and disrupted the stereotypes of Jezebel (Black seductress of white men) and Sapphire (a Black professional woman who uses her sexuality to get ahead in the WSCP[3]). Newer productions, particularly those by Black women, disrupt these stereotypes. As recently as 2014, research showed that Black adolescents, when asked about the Black female characters they were watching on television, found largely negative representations. According to Adams-Bass et al. (2014), "[Black adolescent] respondents generally agreed that there were few positive or uplifting images of black women in the images they viewed. Overall, perceptions and meanings of black women imagery could be placed in the following categories: black women are unusually sexual, black women take care of others, black women are strong, and black women are angry" (87). Perhaps there has not been a total *revolution* since 2014. I am not arguing here that we exist in a post-racial culture. However, when Black women are behind the camera, there are distinct and important differences in how Black womanhood is portrayed, deviating from these one-dimensional stereotypes.

In this introduction, I offer Mary Jane Paul and J/Issa Dee as examples of a heartening trend, one away from stereotypes of Black women to one towards complex and interesting Black female protagonists that mainstream audiences are drawn to. Mary Jane Paul and J/Issa Dee, when held up against Olivia Pope, represent two extremes. Paul and J/Dee are a new type of Black female character who defy stereotypes and are operating within a Black community/family; Pope manifests old stereotypes that may be interesting to some white audiences, but perhaps less than before. Within the past few years, an important trend is emerging in films and streaming services: the offering of Black female roles that defy sickening stereotypes. I posit that this trend is the result of two shifts in the entertainment industry. The first is that the entertainment industry offerings change when Black women are given the opportunity to produce, direct, write, and create characters, which is happening more. The second is that streaming services and social media such as YouTube open up avenues for Black women to write/produce/direct and gain an audience in ways that Hollywood and traditional television did not. In conjunction with opportunities available for Black women through pushing product on streaming services, audiences of streaming services may trend young and more diverse, creating a bigger demand for this diverse programming. These newer, younger, more diverse audiences are not as interested in stereotypes of Black women as the typical television viewer of yore.

When looking at the offerings on popular streaming services such as Hulu, Netflix, and Amazon Prime, programming featuring Black women in complex and interesting roles is easy to find and trending as popular: *Little*, *Blackish*, *Grown-ish*, *Mixed-ish*, *Girlfriends*, *Good Girls*, *Insecure*, *High Fidelity*, *Girls Trip*, *For Colored Girls*, *If Beale Street Could Talk*, *Nappily Ever After*, *Bessie*, *Self Made*, *Dear White People*, *The Chi*, *Lovecraft Country*, and *Twenties* are just a few offerings produced between 2018 and 2020. These shows/films not only portray Afrocentric female characters who are complex and authentic, but this programming is popular enough to garner the attention of mainstream audiences.

WHERE WE HAVE COME FROM: RACIST STEREOTYPES ON TV AND IN FILM

Mammy, Jezebel, Sapphire, Welfare Queen, Diva, Gold Digger, Gangsta Bitch, Baby Mama, Angry Black Woman: These historical stereotypes of

Black womanhood have emerged from slavery and evolved to contemporary times. The "welfare queen" stereotype, which emerged after the Moynihan Report (1971) and was codified by the Reagan Administration (1981–1989), was a central character to Reagan's Welfare Reform Policy. The "updated" stereotypes, typically generated by hip-hop music and reality programs, emerged during the past twenty years. Programs such as *Real Housewives of Atlanta* (2008–2020), *Teen Mom* (2009–2020), *I Love New York* (2007–2008), *Basketball Wives*, and *Flavor of Love* helped codify the Diva, Gold Digger, Gangsta Bitch, Baby Mama, and Angry Black Woman stereotypes. "Tabloid talk shows" such as *The Maury Povich Show, The Montel Williams Show, Bill Cunningham Show, and The Jerry Springer Show* also contributed to perpetuating and codifying these stereotypes of Black womanhood (Hudson 1998). According to Ward, editor of *Real Sister* (2015), a book about Black women on reality TV:

> Reality TV has become a battleground of stereotypes, respectability politics, and ratchet capitalization, and in this ever-expanding genre, Black women are playing increasingly prevalent roles; however, the portrayal of Black women on many shows consistently presents negative and stereotypical images (5).

Even as reality and tabloid television are reinforcing old stereotypes or inventing new—just as harmful—stereotypes of Black womanhood (Hudson 1998, Ward 2015, Giannino & China 2018), there are also hopeful trends. Since 2016, there is evidence of films and series writing new and refreshing scripts of what it means to be Black and female in a WSCP. Primarily because of streaming services that open up avenues of delivery and consumption for smaller projects outside of network television and Hollywood, viewers can avoid stereotypical characters and feast upon the new offerings of Black writers and directors. Shows/films such as *Girlfriends, Queen Sugar, Twenties, Chewing Gum,* and *High Fidelity* demand the viewer disregard the stereotypes and see Black female characters as complex, interesting, dynamic, even if they are flawed. In these programs, we see Black female characters of various ages, educational levels, and social classes working, loving, and living outside of the tired stereotypes. In Hollywood films such as *Girls Trip, Little, Self Made, Hidden Figures, Black Panther,* and *The Photograph,* we can access complex and varied versions of Black womanhood.

This book, instead of focusing on media that codifies old or invents new stereotypes, examines texts that offer up complex and interesting Black female characters. The argument here is not to suggest that these characters or the shows are not flawed, but these characters and shows are not perpetuating negative stereotypes. They offer critically conscious viewers entertainment that can be enjoyed and discussed. The shows/films analyzed in this book give us reason to hope that audiences are interested in complex characters and thoughtful portrayals. Although there are still stereotypes of Black women being depicted (often by white or male directors), we have enough offerings to see the real possibility of creating shows/films that not only draw Black female characters in compelling ways, but that those offerings are attracting a general audience, educating against stereotypes. The focus on Black women in the context of this research is important because of the underrepresentation of Black women's lives and perspectives in scholarship (Robinson 2011). This book attempts to remedy a small part of that ignored perspective and celebrate a hopeful trend in current entertainment media.

To change stereotypical depictions, the WSCP must allow Black women to write and direct. When Black women are behind the camera, creating the words that bring the characters to life, the results defy stereotypes. When these shows are offered to the mainstream (re: white) audiences, they have the potential to shift minds and culture. This may not always be the case, but when examining the directors and writers in the shows that offer complex Black women protagonists, the writers/directors are often women of color. Other scholars have noted a similar dynamic of Black females finding an outlet to define complex Black female representations in the entertainment and music industries (Roberts 1991, Kahn 2008, Jeffries & Jeffries 2015, Baker 2018). Of course, creating films and series is a money-making venture. If there is no money to be made, it is likely that the show will not see the light of day. Yet even in the WSCP some women manage to create films and series that offer a different gaze than that of the typical white male. Often series begin as self-produced YouTube (or other social media) offerings that are then picked up by major production companies (e.g., *Broad City*, *Twenties*, and *Awkward Black Girl*). There are also key Black women with financial capital who are now funding and encouraging other Black women (Issa Rae, Lena Waithe, Oprah Winfrey, and Ava DuVernay to name a few). When Black women are given the opportunity to create, their characters generally defy "respectability politics" because the characters are flawed, complex, and not "models of respectability." Rather these characters represent a realness that defies both stereotypes and squeaky-clean perfection.

Respectability politics refers to the policing of Black writers/directors/actors by others in the Black community so that Black characters created by Black writers/actors must always reflect excellence that is beyond white critique. Shonda Rhimes' Olivia Pope could be seen as an example of this "respectability politics" in play: a white-like assimilated Black woman who the white audience is drawn to and can root for. The underlying belief of "respectability politics" is that one Black character stands in for all black people and so they must represent social uplift and respectable behavior to the white viewers (Pickens 2015, Cooper 2017). Contemporary films/television written and directed by Black women and featuring Black protagonists often defy these respectability politics. The characters are not models of "good" womanhood; rather they are complex characters, flawed yet struggling to be better. They often confront racism, sexism, classism, and homophobia—sometimes in conflicted ways—but they are confronting these complex issues. They are refreshingly human. That is not to say characters and shows that reify the stereotypes of Black womanhood do not exist, only that there are popular, readily available alternative offerings. Because Hollywood is driven by the white male gaze (and his pocketbook), we cannot hope for much from that media source. However, even from Hollywood we see movement: there are films driven by Black women (producers, writers, directors). A few years ago, the representation of Black women in Hollywood productions were fraught and even depressing. Regarding Halle Berry's role in *Monster's Ball* (2001) and Lupita Nyong'o role in *Twel Years a Slave (2013),* Jeffries & Jeffries (2015) wrote, "It is notable that the two Black women whose performances are recognized for excellence among the Academy are sexually objectified by men, in particular White males, expounding the race and gender conundrum" (130). Hollywood may still be abhorrently lacking in Black female characters or stuck in the zone of "trauma porn" when Black women are featured, but we can see progress. *Hidden Figures* (2017), *Little* (2019), *Girls Trip* (2017), and *The Photograph* (2020) are Hollywood productions that deviate from the stereotypical narrative of Black woman as traumatic victim. On streaming services, we have even more reason to celebrate: one can discover a panoply of shows featuring dynamic Black women in a wide range of genres, including *Watchmen* (2019), *Hair Wolf* (2020), *Bessie* (2015), *Dear White People* (2017–2020), *High Fidelity* (2020), *Twenties* (2020), and *Lovecraft Country* (2020) to name only a few. Whether one is looking for psycho-thriller, rom-com, biopic, satire, or comedy, one can fill up one's queue to binge on various genres, all featuring Black female characters that defy stereotypes. And most of the time, when checking the credits, these offerings are brought to us by Black women directors and writers.

Some might argue that although these characters/shows may not abide strictly by the previous stereotypes of Black womanhood, they are still wedged into stereotypes. Shawna Hudson (1998) argues that even if a character is not strictly, say, a Jezebel, if she has enough Jezebel-like characteristics, she will be assigned that label and the rest of the ways in which she defies that stereotype are ignored by the consumer (253). Perhaps. Perhaps the white consumer who already holds onto racist stereotypes will see those stereotypes in these characters and disregard the rest (Entman & Rojecki 2000). Or perhaps not. That question I leave to other researchers. My research focuses on what Black women see. How do the Black women viewing these new texts perceive the characters and how do they respond to these characters? Do they see the characters as defying the stereotypes and reflecting an authentic persona? For these Black women in the audience, my research found that Black female characters created by Black women writers/directors/producers are seen as existing refreshingly outside stereotypical representations, offering Black women audience members entertainment sources that affirm who they are. The issue of audience is central to any discussion of how Black womanhood is portrayed and consumed.

A racist white person might watch one of Tyler Perry's Madea movies and see a Mammy figure (a large Black mother who is the warm, bosomy caretaker of the domestic sphere), whereas a Black audience member might see something entirely different. A Black viewer may see in Madea a comic foil, a man dressed up as a woman, an exaggerated domineering mother correcting and directing family members' behavior, and a matriarch holding the family together through tough love and no-nonsense unfiltered speech. Either way, Madea's traits are very un-Mammy-like as Mammies are passive, smiling caretakers of *white* people. When considering whether a character is stereotypical or not, harmful or not, one has to examine these complex issues of audience and purpose. Scholars such as Christopher Sewell (2013) might argue that Madea is a racist Mammy caricature, but Black viewers may not see the character that way (Sewell 2013). Or they may be able to laugh at the character as a stereotype, but become uncomfortable imagining a *white* audience laughing at the racist stereotype (Ward 2015). EJ[4], a single nineteen-year-old college sophomore who is studying at a rural Midwestern university, said of Perry's film *Incognito*,

> Tyler Perry [portrays stereotypical female characters] a lot and I don't know why. . . When we [Black female audience] are watching, we know, we can laugh because we know we aren't like that way. We know Black women aren't crazy. Black women aren't like that. But then I go to school and I hear white people and men talking and they are talking as if it is a reality. After watching [*Incognito*] I hear men say, "That is why I don't want to be with a Black woman." Those movies give them a reason to believe what they believe.

EJ's astute insights complicate the portrayal of entertaining Black female characters. The concern of respondents such as EJ is not so much that the character reflects negative stereotypes of Black women, but that these stereotypes matter when the audience is white or even Black men. Through talking with Black women like EJ, I understood that there are lots of films and series they are watching that make them uncomfortable because of the stereotypes that are on display for white people/Black men; but there are also many films and series these viewers offered up as positive representations of Black women, characters they identified with and championed as interesting and important. It was these films/series that I focused on for my research. But I am doing so through the lens of a white woman. I attempt to mitigate that whiteness at every turn, seeking to foreground the voices and perspectives of Black women, acting as the journalist compiling their perspectives for the reader. But my whiteness may have been a barrier and it may continue to be a barrier for those reading this work.

Within the context of this book, I am examining these films/series as a white female academic, a feminist, a self-identified queer, a teacher who teaches against racism and as someone who is interested in roles and narratives that defy and break stereotypes of Black women, Black families, and Black communities. Although my lens is through the location of educated white privilege, I am attempting to examine texts that I believe defy stereotypes and put Black women at the center of an Afrocentric narrative. In addition to my scholar's eye, I bring to my analysis of these texts the interviews I conducted with Black women that directed my analyses. In interviewing Black women, I asked them about their media preferences and which characters or shows they felt affirmed them or represented Black womanhood in complex and interesting ways. For the women I interviewed, I asked them to think critically about what attracts them to a show or a Black female character. I found most of my participants were already critical consumers of their entertainment. They had taken up hooks' (1992) and Boylorn's (2008) charge that "Black women must be willing to critique and challenge popular media images in contrast to their lives and experiences so that what is presented as an authentic or 'real' experience of Black womanhood is not based on the most exaggerated stereotypes" (Boylorn 2008, 415). Through the participants' responses, I found that not only are Black women willing to critique images of Blackness, but they are also vocal advocates for the shows and films they believe reflect complex Black female characters.

Some may bristle at the fact that is my glaring whiteness: what right do I have to do this work? In answer to that critique, a real one that needs to be interrogated, I offer that I am answering a call laid out by Adrienne Rich and Audre Lorde in the 1980s. As an undergraduate student at that time, I entered into a curriculum devoid of Black and female voices, a silence that was profound but one that I didn't hear until I took a women's literature class in 1985. In that class, Professor Barbara DiBernard opened a world to me. The texts we read, by women, by queers, by Black women queers, by those perspectives and ideas that had been traditionally locked out of my education, blew the top of my head right off. In that class, I read Adrienne Rich who, at a conference presentation, challenged academics, "Those of you who teach, teach women writers" (1986, 18). Nearly simultaneously, Audre Lorde wrote, "Perhaps for some of you here today, I am the face of one of your fears. Because I am woman, because I am Black, because I am lesbian, because I am myself—a Black woman warrior poet doing my work—come to ask you, are you doing yours?" (1984, 41–42). In teaching her women's literature class, Professor DiBernard was answering that call, doing her work to teach Black women's voices. From the moment I read those words, I have been attempting to answer those twin calls of Rich and Lorde my entire life. This book, this research, is just another way I am trying to answer those challenges set down by Lorde and Rich. My whiteness cannot, should never, give me an excuse to say, "Well, someone ELSE has to write/talk/teach about Black women." Yes, my whiteness is a problem, a barrier I cannot shrug off; my whiteness clouds my perspective and denies me the opportunity to truly understand the lived realities of what it means to be Black and female. But that can't be an excuse for me to leave the work of giving voice and light to that perspective to others. We *all* must engage in this work. The white supremacist patriarchy will not fall if whites don't do this work. Racism is not for Blacks and other Traditionally Marginalized People (TMP) to dismantle. It is for whites to dismantle. This book is just one small way in which I attempt to do this anti-racism work every day of my life.

RESEARCH FOCUS AND PROCESS

In order to examine roles in contemporary films and series, I had to make choices. I limited my focus of analysis to film and streaming/television series featuring Black female characters who defy stereotypes and reflect complex female characters. In order to focus on shows/films that had female protagonists offering complex realities, I devised a rubric to determine whether I would include a film/series for analysis. Similar to the Bechdel Test (1985), invented by Alison Bechdel in her comic strip *Dykes to Watch Out For*, I included films/series that fit the following criteria, dubbing my version "Black-del Test":

(1) The writer/director/producer is a Black woman.
(2) There is a main character who is a Black female and she has a name and interacts with other Black females who also have names.
(3) The Black female character is not focused on getting/keeping a man (the narrative is not driven on WSCP ideals of females obsessing over males), but if there is a love interest, they are Black.
(4) The character interacts with a Black community, she is not "a fly in the buttermilk," or speck of Black in a sea of white.
(5) Issues of race/gender are addressed in the storyline (a white-washed version of Black identity is *not* perpetuated).

For those unfamiliar, the Bechdel Test outlined similar criteria. Alison Bechdel invented her criteria after feeling frustrated by the lack of dynamic and interesting female characters in Hollywood films. The Bechdel Test asks three questions of films: Are there at least two female characters with names? Do they talk to each other? Do they talk to each other about something other than men? Even if a film passes the Bechdel Test, it does not mean the film is necessarily feminist, but the Bechdel Test makes one aware of how limited Hollywood film offerings are that pass this bare minimum of females on screen who aren't there for the male gaze. In some films that "pass" the Bechdel Test, the exchange between two female characters with names may be limited to sixty seconds in a ninety-minute film. An example of a film that features a female character but which *barely* passes the Bechdel Test is *The Post* (2017), a bio drama about Katherine Graham, the publisher of the *Washington Post* who helped break the Watergate scandal. Meryl Streep's character, Katherine Graham, has a brief exchange with her daughter that lasts less than a minute; otherwise she is talking to other men the entire film.

Similar to the Bechdel Test, I wanted a list of criteria that would create a rubric for the portrayal of Black female protagonists. Before I could consider the production worthy of analysis, it had to pass the test. I did this because I wanted to focus my research and analysis on what is being produced for/about/by Black women. In the "test" I used to select films/series, I wanted to focus on more rigid criteria than The Bechdel Test to ensure I was looking at roles that could be refreshingly complex, female-centered, and Afrocentric. I also wanted to make sure I was examining and celebrating the work of Black writers/directors, particularly females. For example, films such as *Charlie's Angels* directed by Elizabeth Banks (2019) and *Ocean's 8* by Gary Ross (2018) may feature Black female characters, but they fail to measure up to my criteria because the Black women featured never talk to other Black women and they are devoid of any Black community or cultural connection. The popular series *Empire* (Fox 2015-2020) featured an almost exclusively Black cast, but Cookie—the main female character—rarely interacted with other Black women. Her focus was primarily the men in the show and gaining access to power through men or by taking down men. I wanted to examine media that was not only presenting new and dynamic ways of portraying Black womanhood, but media that was created/written/directed by Black females to analyze how these Black women were creating female characters. Also, I wanted to focus on the most contemporary productions, those produced between 2015 and 2020. What I found is that not only are women creating more complex and "real" female characters, but that Black female audience members note this and are drawn to these shows/characters.

In my research interviewing Black females from a variety of socioeconomic backgrounds, geographic locations, educational levels, sexualities, and ages, I found that they were very attuned to which films/series reflected positive and complex versions of Black womanhood. They were drawn to these films/series and wanted to talk about them. Likewise, they were quick to point out films/series by Blacks (primarily by Black men) that they felt did not do justice to the lived realities of Black women or girls. And they were often very uninterested in talking about films that represented Black women in ways that, if not stereotypical, were one-dimensional. These representations, in films such as *Django Unchained* by Quentin Tarantino (2012), *The Help* by Tate Taylor (2016), *Ghostbusters* by Paul Feig (2016), and *Charlie's Angels* by Elizabeth Banks (2019) offered uninteresting female characters often drawn by whites and hinting at or fully embodying stereotypes.

I limited my analysis to films/series produced since 2015. I did this to answer the question, "Are tired stereotypes of mammies, jezebels, sapphires, and Welfare Queens still prominent in the most recent film/series?" I quickly found the answer to this question to be "No, if the film/series are directed/written/produced by Black women." In examining the offerings available on streaming services and from Hollywood in the past five years, I also wanted to test a theory that political conservatism at the national level often creates a backlash of progressive representation in the entertainment industry. During the Reagan years (1981–1989) and continuing through the George H. W. Bush presidency (1989–1993), there was a full-on political, racist assault against Black individuals and communities ("the war on drugs" was institutionalized in national politics, primarily affecting Black and poor communities; "welfare queens" lore was created and perpetuated in national policies regarding public assistance to poor mothers; "three strikes you are out" laws created mass incarceration for Black men, particularly of poor communities). As a response to this racist cultural shift, filmmakers and television producers were fighting back with Black-centric, positive, and complex views of being Black in the U.S. Shows such as *The Cosby Show* (1984–1992), *Family Matters* (1989–1998), *A Different World* (1987–1993), *The Fresh Prince of Bel Air* (1990-1996), *Living Single* (1993-1998), *Moesha* (1996-2001), *Reading Rainbow*, and *Oprah*, aired to great reception for both Black and white audiences. These shows offered counterarguments to the daily racism spewed by the leaders of the country in policies and news cycles. Also, in the 1980s through the 1990s, films such as *Do the Right Thing* (1989), *Boyz in the Hood* (1991), *New Jack City* (1991), *Menace to Society* (1993), *Poetic Justice* (1993), *Malcolm X* (1992), *Waiting to Exhale* (1995), and *She's Gotta Have It* (1986) told complex stories of Black community, Black identity, and Black womanhood in the United States.

Similarly, as I wrote this book, we were in the throes of the most racist presidency in our recent history. Following on the heels of a political moment that celebrated the First Black Family, and much revered and adored presidential couple of Michelle and Barack Obama, the WSCP culture delivered a president to the highest office who openly articulated racist ideologies, crafting policies to match. Michelle Obama, simply by living in the White House, offered a new definition of Black womanhood: capable, strong, smart, "Mom-in-Chief" (Henderson 2019). In the racist backlash cultural moment of 2016–2020, even as the administration was openly engaging in racist language and policies that demonized and stereotyped Blacks, some in the entertainment/art industries were fighting back. When the conservative and racist Trump administration took hold of political power, entertainment outlets seemed to counter it with shows featuring Black women and families that defied the stereotypes. Series and films such as *Black-ish*, *Empire*, *Atlanta*, *Hair Love*, *Queen Sugar*, *Insecure*, *The Chi*, and *A Black Lady Sketch Show* provided alternative narratives of complex Blackness.

When racism reemerges with a vengeance in the dominant culture, there is often a just as adamant swing into Black pride from the non-dominant cultures. In a *New York Times* opinion piece, Tiya Miles (2018) connected a racist turn in the dominant culture with the election of Trump to emerging Black hair pride. "Despite and perhaps because of a surge in white supremacist language in the United States, a wave of Black cultural resistance is flooding the arts as well as the streets. And with it, Black hair in its natural state of sublime uprightness has returned as a symbol of political consciousness and visionary imagining," Miles wrote. She offered up the example of the *Black Panther* female characters who tore off their wigs and declared them "stupid" (Miles 2018). In the pre-Trump era, when the country was enjoying a strong Black identity in the highest position of power, there seemed to be a broader celebration of Blackness. The Obama administration set the stage for films/series that reflected resistance to white supremacy. For instance, while in office, Obama celebrated Lin-Manuel Miranda's *Hamilton*, awarded the Kennedy honor to the Queen of Soul, Aretha Franklin, and invited to the White House performers such Stevie Wonder, Mavis Staples, Queen Latifah and many, many more ("Music and arts" 2016). After Obama left office in 2016, film/series featuring Black women or produced by Black women emerged, but perhaps his administration and the resulting cultural shifts set the stage for these offerings. Regardless of how they arrived, the explosion of Black women creating today acts as an obvious counterpoint against a racist backlash brought on by Trump and Republican lawmakers/policy makers.

RESEARCH PROTOCOL AND RESULTS

In order to answer my questions about what characters, films and series were speaking to Black women, I interviewed over 100 Black women between the ages of eighteen and sixty-five. These women were selected with attention to diversity regarding socioeconomic class, educational level, age, geographical location, sexual orientation, gender identity, and family type. Each woman was asked a series of questions regarding what she was watching and what films, characters, and series featuring Black females appealed to her. My focus was exclusively interviewing Black women because I wanted to hear from that demographic what texts and characters they found to be complex, interesting and authentic. I wanted to see whether the women perceived stereotypes (Mammy, Jezebel, Angry Black Woman, etc.) as still manifesting in the media they consumed. I wanted to limit my focus to contemporary films and series after 2015 for reasons stated earlier. Interviews typically took one hour and were conducted in person or over video live streaming. In two cases, due to technical difficulties and geographic location, interviews were conducted over the phone.

As a white queer woman in her late fifties, my white privilege would be a barrier in this research. Who was I to question Black women on their media preferences? Who was I to even contact them to ask them to take time for an interview? How could I indicate to them that I was attempting to check my inherent racism and white privilege in not only my conversations with them, but within the context of the book that I was writing? There is no way to know whether the women I interviewed were as honest with me as they would have been with a Black woman interviewer. There is also no way to know how they self-edited their comments or language or ideas because I was a white woman asking questions. I am certain my race had some effect on these interviews. How could it not? What I attempted to do was to put the interviewees at ease, assuring them that I wanted to hear their thoughts—good and bad—about images of black women that they were seeing and consuming. I also attempted to communicate with every participant that my perceptions would be clouded by my whiteness and their insights were, therefore, all the more valuable to me. In many contexts, I would insert asides to point out racist or misogynist dynamics in films or series that featured Black female characters, offering the women I interviewed examples of my critical eye that might show them I was moving beyond a white-washed viewing. For instance, I often pointed out my discomfort with how Shondra Rhimes drew her female characters when juxtaposed against other Black women directors whose characters seemed much more complex and less of a white-drawn version of what Black womanhood is. Or I would comment regarding my frustration that Black women are never allowed to be angry on screen because of the fear of manifesting the stereotype of Angry Black Woman. Or I would point out my frustration with "trauma porn" featuring Black females or "the white savior" character that tended to show up and save the Black people, a gross revision of history.

I would also follow-up my asides with "What do you think about that?" indicating I was genuinely interested in different perspectives. The women I interviewed were not hesitant to disagree with my assessments. One woman came to the defense of Rhimes, strongly disagreeing with my critique of her work where Black women, from my perspective, seem isolated and alone. When an interviewee disagreed with my assessment or analysis, I backed off of my opinion and listened. As a white woman, who was I to critique any of these films/series? But especially, who was I to critique one of the most famous and well-regarded Black female writers/directors on television? When I did insert comments, my comments were intended to communicate that even if I was unaware of some dynamics of racism in media, I was attuned to others, a white ally.

There is such a tricky and uncomfortable dynamic between a white researcher and a Black participant because of the generations of exploitation and misrepresentation that have occurred. In approaching participants, I always approached with the utmost respect. They were the experts. I was collecting the data. When I began my research, I started by interviewing female students I had worked within my classes. They knew me as a white woman, a professor, who deliberately and intentionally worked and taught against racism, trusting me on that level. Because I used the "snowball sampling" technique for gathering participants, these women led me to other women who led me to other women. In each context, I would ask the interviewee if she knew of anyone else who might be interested in talking with me. If the answer was "yes," I asked if she could forward those women my name and contact info. I never asked participants for names/emails/phone numbers directly; rather, I would ask if they could forward my information to other women who might be interested.

If I received an email or phone message from a potential interviewee, I would then forward her the questions I wanted to ask, to ensure she was clear on the direction of the conversation. If she agreed at that point, I would ask her to sign the IRB "consent to be interviewed" form and we would schedule a meeting or video call. By using the snowball sampling technique, I was riding the coattails of the women I had spoken with before, allowing their relationships with other women to get my foot in the door. Nearly all the women I interviewed reached out to friends, family, and coworkers. With each email/phone call I received, I followed up personally and was met with enthusiasm and eagerness on behalf of the potential participant.

Although I am certain the dynamic and relationship between researcher and participant would have been altered had I been a Black women asking the questions, I also feel confident in saying that the participants who agreed to be interviewed seemed clear on their opinions, uninterested in what *my* opinions or agenda might be regarding the shows or films they were talking about. In every conversation, I allowed the woman I was interviewing to steer the topics. I would ask follow-up or clarification questions, but she directed the interview. There were many shows/films about which the interviewees provided fascinating insights, but they were outside the focus of this book (science fiction, psycho-thriller, reality television, children's programming). I found that, without exception, the women I interviewed were keen critical consumers of media and were fully attuned to the representations of Black womanhood (or girlhood) they saw.

The interviews focused on three open-ended questions that I forwarded to each participant before the interview:

(1) In the past five years, what television, films, or streaming programming have you watched that featured Black female characters? Were these characters portrayed in complex and varied ways? How would you describe each character?
(2) If you were to identify a Black female character from the past five years that you feel represents a positive and complex way of being Black and female, which character would you point to (ask this as many times as they can identify) and why do you find this character interesting or important?
(3) If you were to identify some Black female characters from the past five years that you feel represent Black women's stereotypes, which characters would you point to, and why do you find these characters to be stereotypical?

As the women talked, I asked follow-up or clarification questions. I found that the interviewees were extremely specific and analytical in answering the questions, offering much insight and fodder for further analysis. Although I chose which shows and films to focus on for this book, the beginning analysis of these shows and characters came from the interviews and the insights and analysis provided by my participants. The only exception to this is the analysis in *Chapter 4: Black Feminist or Tired Jezebel*. This chapter, a version of which was originally published as an article in *The Journal of Television and Film* (Fall 2019), served to launch my book project. In that article, I examined the differences between two popular female protagonists from serialized dramas, both directed by Black women. The drama series were *BMJ* and *Scandal*. For the chapter here, I added an analysis of *Insecure*. Beyond these three shows, my participants drove which shows/films were the focus of their discussions with me. My hope is that their voices and perspectives drive this argument to avoid a white, privileged woman from doing so.

After compiling and coding the interview transcripts, I found that stereotypes such as Mammy, Jezebel, Sapphire, and Welfare Queen were rarely, if ever, mentioned by the participants in my study. However, the stereotype of "Angry Black Woman" emerged in these conversations as the dominant stereotype the interviewees were concerned about and aware of. Upon my own evaluation of contemporary films and series depicting Black female characters, I found the Angry Black Woman stereotype was often *discussed* in shows, but in ways that illuminated the stereotype and what it meant for Black women (the Catch-22 of having to choose between being a doormat or expressing anger at racism/sexism and suffering the label "Angry Black Woman"). Episodes of *BMJ, Black-ish, A Black Lady Sketch Show, Grown-ish,* and *Insecure* all confronted the stereotype of the Angry Black Woman in storylines. My participants were quick to point to the discussions of the stereotype in these shows as reflecting their own experiences. Participants spoke about feeling caught between expressing anger and being called an Angry Black Woman. They felt their identity as a Black woman within the WSCP gave them real reasons to be angry every day, yet they were denied the right to express that anger. Therefore, these women celebrated open conversations among characters on these shows addressing that very tension of being denied the right to express anger.

The participants were also deeply interested in telling me about Black female characters they noted who defied common stereotypes. Stereotypical characters were more likely to be noted on "reality shows" that tend to rely on staid stereotypes of most demographics to drive the dramatic narratives. My research, however, was outside the genre of reality shows. There are several compelling books and articles that address not only the representation of Black female characters in reality shows but how audiences (both Black and non-Black) perceive and internalize the stereotypes portrayed there (Giannamo & China 2018, Jackson 2006, Ward 2015, Boylorn 2008, Wiltz 2004). These authors and their ideas are worth reading.

Streaming and Social Media Benefits Black Women Creators

The population I interviewed were more likely to watch a program upon a peer recommendation than they were to seek out shows or watch those "recommended" by streaming services. Similarly, the population I interviewed were more likely to stream their media from sources such as YouTube, Amazon Prime, Netflix, and Hulu than they were to go to a movie theatre although many respondents said they would go to a movie theatre to watch a film featuring Black actors. Ninety-eight percent of respondents went to the theatre to watch *Girls Trip*, for example, because they were interested in a comedy featuring Black women, something that many described as an anomaly. Many respondents pointed out that Hollywood films seemed to feature Black women in historical dramas of struggle (*Hidden Figures, Harriet, Selma*) or "trauma porn" (*Twelve Years a Slave, Precious, The Hate You Give*), whereas streaming services gave a wider selection. With the move to streaming services, participants could pick and choose specific shows that featured Black women in authentic ways rather than being limited to Hollywood-sanctioned views of Blackness. In addition, algorithms of those streaming services then fed the viewers more "Black female-centric" choices to sample.

In examining the texts (films, series) that emerged as some of the most popular shows being consumed, and in exploring the shows offered via the "recommended for you" algorithms on sites such as YouTube, Hulu, Prime, and Netflix, I discovered a wide range of programming featuring positive and complex representations of Black female characters. As I began exploring these offerings more closely, I found that there was a direct connection between the shows that were creating Afrocentric storylines and dynamic characters that defied stereotypes and the race/gender of the writers and directors. In many series with several directors and writers involved, it was not uncommon for a series featuring Black leads to have writers/directors who reflected the diversity of the storyline. In this book, I offer up some of those programs for deeper analysis, weaving throughout the analysis the voices and perspectives of the women I interviewed. The underlying through-line is that there are reasons to hope. The stereotypes of the past are more difficult to be found. When Black women are in charge of the texts, the characters and communities they create for their audiences defy and destroy those old stereotypes. Because of the Digital Age technology, allowing new talent to post their own work, and streaming services that can offer more diversity with less financial investment, Black women's stories are getting play. Through the gaze these contemporary filmmakers, script-writers, directors, and actors offer—most of them Black women—we can find reason to hope for better forms of entertainment media, a diversity revolution.

CHAPTERS' OVERVIEWS

In interviews with participants, the politics of Black women's hair emerged repeatedly as a marker of authentic or real representation. Chapter 1 "Natural Hair: A Marker of Black Female Resistance and Empowerment" documents the representation of natural and processed hair and what that says about a female character to her audience. Black women's hair was a marker of racial caste in the United States, even more than skin tone in some contexts. And the politics of Black women's hair has a long history. The way a character wears her hair matters. A lot. Especially to Black female audience members. Hair rituals and the bonding female experience over hair care was a topic of discussion among my participants. The women I interviewed paid attention to how Black women's hair was treated in the shows they watched, often connecting to their own stories and their lived experiences around hair. These women articulated that authenticity of a character is regularly related to how her hair is styled or not styled, how her hair is wrapped (or not wrapped) in bedroom scenes, and whether there are images of her or her female friends/ family attending to their hair. This chapter weaves the politics of hair into the portrayals of Black females in contemporary media. The chapter also offers up participants' own hair stories and how they felt their experiences were reflected accurately in the shows they consumed.

In conjunction with the politics of hair in the Black community, and even more specifically in the community of Black women, colorism and hierarchies of skin tone was also a regular topic of conversation in the interviews. Chapter 2 "#TeamLightSkin versus #TeamDarkSkin" discusses this issue of skin tone bias. The women I interviewed readily addressed the issue of colorism in the Black community, with younger participants articulating this issue as #TeamLightSkin and #TeamDarkSkin, a social media phenomena where two camps have been drawn, each posting pride in their skin tone grouping. Respondents expressed frustration with this colorism within the Black community. Participants noted female actors with darker skin as a refreshing addition to the light-skinned actors of previous years, Halle Berry being the "model" Black female actor of the light-skinned Hollywood preference. In contrast to Berry, many pointed to Viola Davis as a counterpoint in nearly every regard. Whereas Berry is described as light, thin, tiny with "good hair," Davis was described as darker, bigger, with natural hair. Chapter 2 examines many of the popular program and film offerings, making the argument that one can see a broader range of skin tones for female characters in the past five years as well as overt discussions of colorism on some shows.

Chapter 3 "All the Single Ladies: Sex and the Single Woman" examines contemporary portrayals of Black single women and how these characters disrupt rather than reinforce the Sapphire and Jezebel stereotypes. Historically the role of the single Black female was one of hypersexualized Sapphire or Jezebel stereotypes tempting white men. A Sapphire differed from a Jezebel in that the Sapphire was often a professional woman and a Jezebel was not. A Sapphire put her professional life first and used her sexuality to get what she wanted. A Jezebel was simply a "loose woman" whose function in the plot line was usually to be the object of desire, an irresistible and unavoidable character who was the downfall of the "good [white] man." The Jezebel and Sapphire characters were never the main characters; they were always the evil, conniving demise of the men, cautionary tales of seductresses who were using their sexuality to access power through men. In contemporary shows such as *She's Gotta Have It*, *BMJ*, *Insecure*, *Twenties*, and *High Fidelity*, the characters, although sexually active and empowered through their sexuality, are different from Jezebels and Sapphires in significant ways.

First, these characters are the center of the story; their narrative is the one that counts. Their lovers—who manifest as both male and female in many of these shows—are the secondary characters. These protagonists are seeking relationships and sex as one part of those relationships, but there are also emotional elements to the relationships. We see the characters as liberated in their sexuality, yet they are not always confident. Or they may be confident, but they are not always making the best choices. Or they are making good choices, but their partners are not as invested as they are in the union. These characters offer complex and complicated ways of being sexually active Black women seeking meaningful connections and relationships with their chosen partners. They offer frank discussions of contemporary sexuality and the messiness of embarking on relationships, negotiating the nuances of how to be with another person concerning emotional and sexual intimacies.

In chapter 4 "Black Women Are Not Always Womanist: The Politics of Empowerment", I examine relationships beyond sexual/romantic ones to include friends, families, and communities. In analyzing *BMJ* (BET, 2013–2019), *Insecure* (HBO, 2016–2020) and *Scandal* (ABC, 2012–2019), I look at the differences between an Afrocentric series (*BMJ/Insecure*) and one intended for dominant white audiences (*Scandal)* and how that changes the portrayal of the Black female protagonists. I argue that the contemporary version of womanist—Black feminist—characters create a complicated juxtaposition between a white supremacist rendering of Black feminism (*Scandal*) and an Afrocentric, female-centered rendering of a womanist (*BMJ* and *Insecure*). Through an analysis of contemporary representations of Black feminist/Womanist protagonists, we see ongoing themes of racism, misogyny, classicism, and intersectionality that, in one context, (*Scandal*) are uninterrogated and foundational to the show's narratives and, in another context (*BMJ/Insecure*), are regularly addressed, complicated, and questioned. The post-racist/post-feminist *Scandal* serves the white producers/audiences, whereas the primary audience for shows such as *BMJ* or *Insecure* are "woke" African-American women who are hungry for honest and open discussions of race, class, and gender as they relate to contemporary realities of Black professional women.

One way that characters on these shows communicate the complex issues of racism, misogyny, homophobia, classism and intersectionality they are facing is through direct address to the camera. In series such as *High Fidelity*, *Grown-ish*, *Mixed-ish*, *Insecure*, *She's Gotta Have It*, and *Chewing Gum*, we not only see women grappling with these complex issues, but we see the characters talk directly to the audience about them. Chapter 5 " 'I'm Talking to *You*': Breaking the Fourth Wall," investigates the contexts and effects of these female protagonists who take control of the narrative by speaking directly to the audience as a confidante or intimate. Often these moments of "breaking the fourth wall" and looking at the camera, talking to the viewing audience as a friend or confidante, allow the audience in on internal struggles or problems that the characters is trying to parse through. When these characters turn to the audience, they draw the audience in, creating an intimacy with the character and the issues she is facing. We are positioned as a trusted friend, an intimate, a person in whom the character confides. By addressing the audience in these ways, the characters allow the audience to see more complex and dynamic female characters, a way to authenticate her as a "real" person to the viewers. In allowing the audience into the character's psyche, we have a chance to understand the complexity of the issues she is facing, often regarding racism, sexism, and sexuality.

In many contexts, these audience-directed asides not only deepen our understanding of the character but also provide a comedic element. We see the character become snarky, sarcastic, biting, or irreverent even as she is making a point to the audience about a complex social or personal issue. These asides make us smile, but they make us think, too. The element of levity and humor is one part of contemporary films and series that felt revolutionary to some of my participants.

In talking about these moments of levity with Black women, it became apparent that the humor felt significant. Many women articulated that they wanted to laugh and celebrated the films and shows that allowed them to laugh. Laughter is not only cathartic, but it feels revolutionary when for so long Black women have been the butt of the jokes, being laughed *at* instead of laughed *with*, or portrayed as the defeated, traumatized victim. Certainly there are still plenty of places where a Black female character is the object of derisive laughter. On tabloid talk shows or reality shows, Black women are often still featured as Baby Mama (a woman who has multiple children with different men in order to entrap men) or Sister with an Attitude (S.W.A.; "perpetually perturbed, tooth-sucking, eye-rolling, finger-wagging, harpy, creating confrontations in her wake and perceiving racial slights from the flimsiest of provocations. She is all sharp edges and raw nerves, an angry, aggressive know-it-all, presenting a one-sided view of black womanhood" (Wiltz 2004, C01) or Gangsta Hoe (women who are hip-hop groupies, posing only as a sexual prop for men). These harmful and stereotypical representations are real and pervasive. However, there are also Black women comics (writers, actors) who are presenting smart and biting satire to make us laugh *with* the outrageous indignities of racism and sexism, much to the delight of their audience. Chapter 6 "Funny Women: Laughing with, Not Laughing At" analyzes films, series, and stand-up routines written by, directed by, and starring Black women. Whether it is the stand-up shows of Tiffany Haddish, Leslie Jones, Michelle Buteau, and Wanda Sykes (Netflix offerings), Hollywood films such as *Little*, *What a Man Wants*, and *Girls Trip*, or streaming series such as

Chewing Gum, Insecure, Social Distance, A Black Lady Sketch Show, 2 Dope Queens, and *Good Girls*, the humor featured allows Black female audience members to engage in a type of laughter that includes them and their experiences, specifically regarding racism, sexism, and homophobia. The ensuing laughter is cathartic and delightful.

As there has been a surge of Black female comedic offerings in the past five years, there has also been a surge in the offerings of historical dramas featuring Black women, telling *their* stories, teaching a herstory lesson that has heretofore been literally and deliberately hidden by the WSCP. Films such as *Hidden Figures* (2018), *Harriet* (2019), *Bessie* (2015), *Self Made* (2020), *Respect* (2020), *Roxanne, Roxanne* (2018), and *The Immortal Life of Henrietta Lacks* (2019) offer biographical dramas of Black women who have made herstory, educating their audiences not only on the importance of Black women to our nation's narrative of determination and grit, but illuminating the nuanced realities of battling racism and sexism in a culture that is determined to prevent Black women from becoming who they are determined to be. Whether it is retelling stories that we think we already know (Harriet Tubman's life in *Harriet*, Aretha Franklin in *Respect* and Bessie Smith in *Bessie*) or illuminating women who many did not know about (Katherine Johnson, Dorothy Vaughan, Mary Jackson, Henrietta Lacks, Madam C. J. Walker), these films offer us a way to see the importance of Black women and how systems of racism and sexism work in tandem to not only prevent Black women from succeeding but then hiding their stories, their lives from all of us. Chapter 7 "History Lessons, We Are Strong, Independent Women" analyzes these biopics that affirm and celebrate Black women in ways that are revolutionary, forcing the viewers to confront the many ways in which we erase and minimize the contributions of Black women to our collective history.

The final chapter of the book examines where these various cultural texts featuring Black women are leading us. Conclusion "A Reason for Hope" speculates that we are on a trajectory, especially with the diversity of programming offered through streaming services, that will allow Black female writers, directors, and actors new ways to educate us all—both the population within that demographic and those outside that demographic—to an alternative definition of Black womanhood. The hope is that these new portrayals that defy and disrupt historical and contemporary stereotypes of Black womanhood will shape the narrative of our current culture. When we look to the work that Black women are doing in media, in politics, in education, we can see that given the time and resources, these women can educate both other Black women and the dominant WSCP in important and affirming ways, addressing the realities of sexism, racism, homophobia, classism, and colorism. By addressing these complex issues through the entertainment media we consume, we are taught difference, we are taught complexity, we are educated *against* the stereotypes that for so long have shackled us all, but particularly Black women. There is reason to hope if the entertainment industry continues on this trajectory of giving space and voice to Black female lived experiences. The more we, the viewers, watch, proclaim and celebrate these Black women creative artists, the more the industry will open its purse strings and give these perspectives and voices financial support. By becoming critical consumers of media created by Black women, by spending our time and money supporting their work, we can shift the perspective of the dominant WSCP to include these alternative viewpoints that have been locked out for too long. It is up to us. As we view, like, share, post, and push these shows and films for, by, and about Black women, we have the ability to encourage company executives in investing in more program offerings. In the digital age of streaming services, the revolution is in our hands, literally at our fingertips. We can be part of this streaming revolution that pushes content shattering the stereotypes of Black womanhood, giving Black woman writers, producers, and directors a chance to create.

NOTES

1. When referring to a specific political/social identity of race, I use the term "Black" (a historical reference to Black Power movement, Black Pride, Black Panthers, and Black Lives Matter). When quoting from secondary sources, I use the term "African American" if those sources use that term.

2. I would like to clarify that I am focusing on popular/mainstream streaming series and Hollywood productions. There is amazing work being done by Black feminist filmmakers such as Kebo Drew, one of the major forces behind and within QWOCMAP [Queer Women of Color Media Arts Project], and Sangodare Akinwale, a.k.a. Julia Roxanne Wallace, who is the cofounder with Alexis Pauline Gumbs of the Black Feminist Film School. QWOCMAP and the Black Feminist Film School are doing important work training and supporting queer women of color in making their own films.

3. The white supremacist capitalist patriarchy is the dominant culture in the United States. Throughout I will use WSCP to designate this dominant culture, one that subjugates Black women (and other women of color) to maintain systemic power. Traditional stereotypes of Black females such as Mammy, Jezebel, Sapphire, Welfare Queen, Video Hoe, Ghetto Bitch, Baby Mamma, and Angry Black Woman are created by the WSCP to keep Black females disempowered. These stereotypes are created and reproduced by media created by and for the dominant culture but have real-life consequences through social and political policies that are based on these stereotypes.

4. Some participants chose to use their authentic name; others chose to use a pseudonym. I do not distinguish between a participant's real name or pseudonym in the text. However, in Appendix I, participants who chose a pseudonym are identified

with an asterisk (*) next to their name. When a pseudonym was desired, the partici-pant provided it. The first time I use a participant's identity by quoting her, I will give basic demographic information (age, relationship status, occupation, and location). After the first reference, I will not give detailed demographic information about that participant. For a list of all quoted participants and their demographic information, see Appendix I.

Chapter 1

Natural Hair: A Marker of Black Female Resistance and Empowerment

"Hair is beauty. Hair is emotion. Hair is our heritage. Hair tells us where we were going. Hair is power. You can't imagine what it is like to lose it." This voice-over opens of Netflix's *Self Made*, the fictionalized biography series about Sarah Breedlove, most famously known as Madame C. J. Walker. Walker built a beauty empire on products designed for Black hair. Nappy, Afro, straightened, box braids, weaves, sew-ins, locs, twists, curls. A Black woman's hair is her statement to the world of who she is. She is judged by her hair. She is marked by her hair. The WSCP judges her natural hair, calling it "nappy." Whether it is braided, twisted into dreds, or an Afro, "natural" black hair is often seen as unacceptable. Black hair, particularly on a woman, is critiqued as being "too ethnic." Even within her own community, a girl or woman is regularly judged by her hair. "A woman's hair is her crown," more than one woman told me. Her status is shown in her hair and a Black female character's strength, authenticity, and appeal is often reflected in the way she wears her hair. When it comes to a Black female character's hair, there is no such thing as an apolitical or neutral do.

HAIR AS AN ACT OF RESISTANCE

Whether untamed Afro or straightened, styled, braided, or woven, a Black character's hair says something about who she is. Black female characters' hair is noted and noticed, whether consciously or unconsciously, by the audience. Perhaps white audience members are oblivious to the more nuanced politics of a Black female character's hair, but Black audiences are not. For Black women audience members, the hair says something not only about the character, but about the respect (or lack of respect) afforded that character by the director. "Tyler Perry is the worst," one of my respondents told me. "There was no need, *no need*, to put those women in such ratty wigs. You are making a movie (*Acrimony* 2018) and you can't even afford a decent wig? Come on!" (Coretta, in her sixties, grandmother of six, retired bus driver). Another woman told me, in regard to Tyler Perry's films such as the Madea series, "Your hair is one thing you can control. It is very disrespectful to not pay attention to his characters' hair. [Perry] is making us look raggedy" (Shayna, in her forties, divorced mother of a teenage daughter, stay-at-home mom). For these women, the disrespect evident in what they see as a cheap wig or bad hairstyle on a Black female character was a sign that Perry was disrespecting Black women, being sloppy and lazy with his care of Black women. Another respondent, however, defended Perry's choice of cheap wigs for some of his female characters. "That's just the truth. Some women, they put on ratty wigs. That's not him [Perry] disrespecting. He is just telling it how it is," Drayah, a twenty-one-year-old college student from a Midwestern university, said. Yet even this Perry fan admitted to noticing the bad quality of the wigs. Respondents may have disagreed on what statement was being made by a wig or a hairstyle, but they were pointing to hair as an indication of whether a Black female character was authentic or respected. There was meaning inferred from the politics of a Black female character's hair.

The importance of hair makes sense. When marginalized groups are denied access to white power structures, most of the time they are denied access based on appearance, how they *look*. In a WSCP, the dominant culture values females based on their sex appeal (as defined by the patriarchy), passivity, and their usefulness as status symbols for men. For Black women, the WSCP not only expects them to be sexually available to men, but Black women have to ascribe to white beauty aesthetics. This ideal of white beauty aesthetics has traditionally meant, especially for female actors, being light-skinned with straightened, flowing hair. If she was darker-skinned with natural hair, she was a character of lower status, unacceptable, and unimportant.

These stereotypes are changing and how hair is coiffed is one way we can see these shifts, a movement from conforming to white standards of beauty to seeing beauty in Black aesthetics. Sure, a character might have straightened hair, but does she wear a scarf/bedtime bonnet and avoid the sauna/swimming pool to protect her hairstyle, both markers of authentic Black female experience? Are there scenes that show her in kitchens, living rooms, and on front stoops between the knees of a beloved friend or relative, having her hair done? Is love between women (mother and daughter, aunties and nieces, sisters and friends) demonstrated through fingers styling hair? When such moments appear in shows and films, chances are the director or writer is a Black woman. These scenes cue the Black female audience to identify another layer of authenticity and intimacy of the characters on screen.

Hairstyle choices are a way that a Black woman either assimilates to the white supremacist patriarchy (straightened hair or wigs that mimic white hair), or resists the WSCP with natural styles. And either way, she spends lots of time and money to achieve the look she is going for. There is status with hair. If she chooses to subvert, either by going natural or *not* investing time and money on her hair, there are consequences. Will she get hired? Will her colleagues respect her? Will she have access to systems of power? Hair matters. "Many Black women opt to alter their hair and wear Eurocentric hairstyles, not because they have internalized Eurocentric standards of beauty, but because they seek to minimize the perception that they are different from their colleagues or because they see it as an economic necessity for employability, recognizing that some view natural Black hair as less appropriate in the workplace" (Dawson, Karl, and Peluchette 2019, 391). Her hair can be an act of resistance, a statement, a fascination, an impeccably crafted wearable art. Or it can be an action of assimilation to white standards of beauty: long, silky, styled. For Black female actors, their character's hair is the purview of the director or stylist. And if these people are white, they are often oblivious to the politics of black hair. However, Black women audience members and Black female actors are anything but oblivious. They look to how Black females' hair is treated as cues of respect and acceptance or as markers of assimilation or resistance.

Many of the woman I interviewed, when I asked them what films, television shows, and streaming series they felt reflected positive representations of Black womanhood, offered the Oscar's 2020 best animated short *Hair Love* as an example of a revolutionary commentary on hair and black love. *Hair Love* references the social media subculture of hair vlogs—or video blogs—posted on sites such as YouTube where Black girls and women share "sisterhood and supported wellness" through hair tutorials (Neil and Mbilishaka 2019, 156). The affirmation *Hair Love* revealed about Black women's relationship to their hair ran deep. A poet in her twenties who publishes a zine and lives in Kansas City told me, "The first time I saw [*Hair Love*], I cried" (Janae). This particular day that I interviewed Janae, she wore her hair in luxurious ropes of braids, edges smoothed into intricate swirls, ends carefully styled. "[The narrative in *Hair Love*] was totally my experience growing up. I lived with my dad for a while and he had no idea what to do with my hair. He would part it and try to comb it and put it in piggy tails, but mostly he would fuss and give up and call one of my aunties or cousins. 'Get over here and do something with her hair!'" (Janae). In the film, the little girl has instructional videos of how to create a beautiful hairstyle, but she can't do it herself. We later learn the videos are made by her and her mother, now sick and in the hospital. The little girl gives up after several attempts and turns the comb over to her father who approaches her head as if it is a wild bramble, a thing to be tamed. And he does tame it; he creates the hairstyle the little girl wants with determination born of love for his child. This film touched the hearts of many of the Black women I interviewed because it showed a man loving on Black female hair, putting in the time and energy to create the style, offering up his hands and heart to the craft of creating a perfect hairstyle, a testimony of love for his daughter. Love is manifested through his hands. He loves his daughter, therefore he wants her to have a perfect hairstyle, a statement beyond style to status: this girl child is loved and cared for.

The nuance that love of Black girls is imbedded in hair care can be seen in several films and series. Often these moments are fleeting with an older sister, friend, aunt, or mother caring for a girl's hair such as in *BMJ* (Season 3, Episode 9), *Black-ish* (Season 3, Episode 8), *Mixed-ish* (Season 1, Episode 3), *Little*, and *Good Girls* (Season 2, Episode 6). In some series/films, there is at least one episode or scene devoted to these moments of intimacy, care, and bonding over a young girl's hair (*Hair Love,* 2019*; Nappily Ever After,* 2017*; Mixed-ish*, 2019*; Jezebel,* 2019). Similar to the affection and care the father in *Hair Love* shows through fixing his daughter's hair, these intimate moments of Black mothers and aunties, friends, and relations emerge in films and series as code for enduring affection and sisterhood. The love runs deep when we see a female—be she a small girl or a grown woman—nestled between the knees of another woman, her hair being pulled and twisted, braided, and combed. In *Insecure*, we see a mother working braids into her bowed daughter's head, as the mother converses with Issa's love interest, Daniel. In *BMJ*, we see Niecey working Mary Jane's head; and we see Mary Jane working her niece's braids. In "Let's Go Crazy" (Season 2, Episode 7), we see Mary Jane with her natural hair and the tender moment when she sits between Niecey's knees so Niecey can sew in her weaves. In *Good Girls*, we see the mother braiding her daughter's hair while talking through boy problems with her preteen. All these scenes reflect small moments of sisterhood or motherhood where girls and women, sisters, mothers, and daughters talk about love, life, and problems to solve. Each of these hair bonding moments communicates tenderness, intimacy, care, and the love within the family and community between women/girls. To work on someone's head is to love on them.

LOVE THE CHILD; LOVE HER HAIR

Nappily Ever After (2018) is a film about a woman's (Violet Jones) journey to natural hair. Early in the movie, we see Violet as a little girl at a pool party. But she can't play in the pool because of her hair. The film cuts to a kitchen scene with Violet and her mother attending to Violet's hair. Her mother is wielding a hot comb that has been heating on a gas stove burner. Violet is playing with a blonde Barbie, stroking its hair. Grown Violet narrates the scene. "Once a week: wash, conditioner, and hot comb. Until my hair was straight enough to run her fingers through it without one snap, crackle or pop. . . .Only then was I perfect. But for an 11-year-old girl, perfection was no fun." The next scene shows her jumping into the pool despite her mother's warnings and her hair relaxes; white children mock her for it, calling her a Chia Pet. No matter how hard her mother tries, the child's hair will never be perfect enough. She will not be accepted by the white culture with natural hair; but her processed and straightened hair comes at a cost. The movie is segmented into different hair stages of Violet's life, a trajectory from assimilation (processed, straightened) to ownership of self (natural): straightened, weave, blonde, bald, new growth. During her bald stage, Violet befriends a motherless child whose hair reflects her wayward and unruly life. On the child's porch, the girl nestled between her knees, Violet braids her hair. "I always wanted braids when I was younger, but my mom wouldn't let me," she tells the child. The child smiles, feeling loved. Black girls who have styled hair with barrettes and braids and nappy ends smoothed out are seen as loved and cared for. Black girls with wild and uncombed, untamed locks are often seen as waifs without someone in their life willing to take the time. "Black hair takes time," one my respondents, Courtnee (in her thirties, trans, partnered/no children, social worker in Arizona), told me. And that time is often expressed as love for the girl.

The scene in *Nappily Ever After* of a girl being subjected to straightening and processing is replicated in other productions. In *Mixed-ish*, Aunt Dee Dee takes the girls to get their natural hair straightened and styled, even under the protests of the girls' mother. In films by director Behn Zeitlin such as *Beasts of the Southern Wild* (2012) and *Wendy* (2020), a girl child's un-styled hair a signal that she is wild, uncared for. The difference between the young girl's (Diane's) hair in *Black-ish*—featuring an upper-class Black family—and the representations of the young girl's (Santamonica's) hair in *Mixed-ish* are stark. Whereas Diane's hair is always carefully processed and coiffed, Sanitmonica's is natural, ends untamed, often pulled back in a basic pouf with nappy edges around her face. These differences tell us about class and care. Small girls who are cared for, especially of upper social class, have processed and styled hair; natural, untamed hair on little girls indicates lower class or even neglect.

These images of girls and hair rituals ring true to the Black women I interviewed. In talking about the media they consumed, many marked authenticity of the Black female experience in these hair care moments, one woman doing another's hair. They shared stories of unruly hair that was tamed by female friends and relatives, the bonding time spent in the kitchen or in front of the television while another woman did their hair. The interviewees spoke of the hard discomfort of pulling, burning, and tugging under the quick hands of a mother, an aunt, a cousin, a friend. These moments of someone bent over a woman's or girl's head, as reflected between Black female characters on the screen, spoke to these women of their own experiences of female bonding over hair. These scenes of hair care were not just about pride in appearance or love manifesting as presenting "prettiness" to the world, but of deep female connection, from the screen to the space of lived experiences of Black women. Michele, in her twenties, a college senior and social justice activist on her campus, spoke about the moments of female bonding through hair care on one of her favorite programs, *Good Girls*. "In that *[Good Girls]* you see so much blackness; granted they are doing a bunch of crazy stuff. But you see the momma braiding her daughter's hair and then you see her with the bonnet on. Those moments feel real. They are so *REAL*," Michele told me. In *Little*, there is a moment similar to this where the girl is sitting between the legs of her assistant, April, getting her hair braided (badly) (2019). The two are talking about things that matter, discussing intimacies they are not able to talk about in other contexts. But between the knees of another Black woman who is running her fingers through one's hair, the characters share vulnerability, love, and tenderness.

THE BEDTIME BONNET

For many viewers, another marker of authentic Black femaleness is the bedtime bonnet. Black women know that no woman will spend hours on her hair, dropping lots of time and money, and then go to bed without carefully covering. When a Black female character is portrayed either getting ready for bed or in bed and there is no hair wrap involved, the viewing audience knows someone other than a Black director created the scene and someone other than a Black woman is the intended audience. In a sketch on *A Black Lady Sketch Show*, friends are aghast when one admits she doesn't put a scarf on before going to bed; the scene ends with the deviant sitting, exasperated, with a colorful scarf tied loosely over her unruly curls; her friends victorious (Season 1, Episode 2). Bedtime bonnets signify a small moment of Black female authenticity and these moments are noted, however brief they are in the context of a thirty-minute episode or a two-hour film.

Grown-ish (2019–2020) is narrated by Zoey Johnson, a first-year college student. In morning or nighttime scenes, Zoey sports a head wrap to protect her curls, her braids, or whatever her do of the episode is, all of it natural Black hair. In addition, the peers who drift in and out of Zoey's room in the morning often sport hair covers: scarves, nylon caps, and wraps. This is also true of *Black-ish*, the show in which Zoey was the older sister, spinning off into

Grown-ish. In *Black-ish* (2016–2019), the younger daughter, Diane, is often seen in her pajamas either going to bed or getting up. In each context, her hair is wrapped. As with *Black-ish* and *Grown-ish*, *BMJ* features many scenes where the title character, Mary Jane, is seen in bed with her hair carefully covered. Similarly in *Good Girls* and *She's Gotta Have It*, pajamas always include a scarf or other bonnet for the Black female characters. When Black women direct shows, the audience sees the females wrapping or wearing bonnets for bedtime. Regardless of the program, bedtime turbans, wraps, and bonnets are the norm for Black women. In the *BMJ* episode "Purging and Cleansing" (Season 3, Episode 9), Mary Jane reads the memoir of Malala Yousafzai to her niece who is on a sleepover; later the niece comes in to Mary Jane's bed, both of them in their pajamas and night head scarves. Mary Jane asks her niece, "Is that [scarf] too tight?" The girl nods and Mary Jane takes off the scarf, loosens the girl's braids and says, "Be free, my child, be free." They laugh and Mary Jane says "I love you" before turning off the light and snuggling in with the child. The scene offers a moment of tenderness and love around the ritual of bedtime hair bonnets. In another episode, Mary Jane is talking with her mother on the phone. Mary Jane is pictured in bed with her head scarf on, holding her sister's baby while the toddler plays on the bed. She is having a phone conversation with her mother who is also in bed wearing a brown turban while styling her wig that is in her lap. These everyday moments and the centrality of Black female hair rituals are important. These intimate moments communicate quiet authenticity of Black women's lives and how intertwined hair and hair care is to those moments of love and relationship between females. The centrality of hair, the intimacy of relationships between women, and the care of one another through the daily rituals of hair care offer a connection between the characters and the lived experiences of Black viewers.

Normalizing the bedtime bonnet becomes a way to normalize Black hair and all it represents. In 2020, a children's picture book, *Bedtime Bonnet* (Redd), was published featuring the ritual of wrapping and tucking a little girl's hair for bed. The arc of the story revolves around anxiety the girl feels when she can't find her head covering. The book portrays the bedtime ritual between the girl and her mother, between hair and Black pride/identity (every person in the family has their own bedtime hair cover). The book's narrative twines together love and hair care. It is rich with Black cultural references to hair. This children's book emerged nearly simultaneously with the short, animated film *Hair Love*, another story that features a small girl child wrangling with and then feeling pride and love in rituals of hair care unique to Black females.

Ten years before *Hair Love*, Chris Rock produced and directed the documentary *Good Hair* (2009). Rock explored Black women's desire to engage in hair styling practices that are painful, time/money consuming, and potentially harmful (toxic chemicals for perming and straightening) with the design to mimic white hair culture. Rock was drawn into the issue when his young daughters asked for their hair to be straightened. As a Black man, he approached the topic of how Black women relate to their hair as a relative outsider. And one of the things he discovered was the time and financial investment that Black women put into their hair, manifesting in their extreme care to maintain the do (no swimming, no athletics, and no man better touch her hair during love making). The elaborate hairstyles involve chemicals and expertise to get the hair to look, many times, as "white" (long, flowing) as possible. But more than that, these non-natural hairstyles limit physical activities for the Black women and girls who choose them. These hairstyles not only have a financial cost (hundreds of dollars to create the style, thousands over a lifetime) but also a physical cost, sharply curtailing how a woman moves and acts in the world, down to the activities in which she can engage. The filmmaker implies that Black women are hobbling themselves both physically and financially, perhaps even putting their health at risk, in pursuit of "white/good" hair. As a film created at the height of the "flowing mane" period of Black female hair aesthetic, there are few women interviewed who argue for natural hair; it is the age of processed dos.

Fast forward ten years and the tide has shifted. The politics of hair have moved to natural. There are more Black women writing and directing films/ shows that are either including or focusing on the politics of natural Black hair. These films/shows are typically focused on care and pride in natural Black hair rather than processed Black hair (although there are scenes in various shows and films that address the complexities of processed hair). Natural hair tells a story about the character and the story it tells reflects an authentic reality for the Black females in the audience. Hair is never neutral; it is coded. It is love, resistance, community, power, sisterhood, and righteous indignation. It is a statement against the WSCP. Natural hair speaks volumes.

THE HISTORY OF HAIR

Black hair has a deep cultural history and much of it is rooted in racism, as hair texture, not skin color was a way to determine who was Black and who was not in white supremacist U.S. culture. Collins (2000) wrote about Orlando Patterson's theory regarding hair texture, not skin color, being the primary marker of race and status. Journalist Lisa Jones (2004) published a book of essays on the politics of hair, noting "Hair is the be-all and end-all. Everything I knew about American history I learned from looking at black people's hair. It's the perfect metaphor for the African experiment here: the price of the ticket (for a journey no one elected to take), the toll of slavery, and the costs remaining. It's all in the hair" (11–12). When interviewing Black women about the films and streaming series they watched, the hair of the female characters typically came up, particularly when a female character wore natural hair; her hair cued to the audience to see her as authentic, powerful, and righteously Black.

In contemporary films and series directed and written by Black women, hair is examined and discussed by the characters. Barely one minute into the first season of the HBO series *Insecure* (2016), Issa Rae's character, Issa Dee, is called out by a middle school girl because of her natural hair. Dee is standing in front of a classroom of what appears to be pre-adolescent children. "What's up with your hair?" a little girl calls out. "My cousin can put some tracks in it, unless you *like* it like that" (Season 1; Episode 1: Insecure as F**k, 2016). The message in that opening exchange is clear: Dee's hair, in its tight-curled flat-top, is unacceptable, a site of critique. Although the children laugh at her hair, Dee stands strong. She may be "insecure," but she is unwilling to compromise her authenticity. This exchange between Dee and the schoolchildren establishes the tone of the main character: she is strong; she won't back down; she is sure in herself; she is proud of her Black identity and Black femininity. These traits are reflected in her consistently natural hairstyles throughout the series.

In the film *Nappily Ever After* (directed by Saudi Arabian filmmaker Haifaa Al Mansour and based on the novel by Trisha Thomas), the enlightened and empowered trajectory of the main character is marked by the evolution of her hair: processed and straightened to natural. In films and series directed or written by Black women, we see natural hair celebrated as empowerment, strength, and grit. But look at programming created by whites and Black, women are largely portrayed with "white-like" hair: smooth, flowing weaves, and wigs. Five years ago, it would have been unthinkable for a Black anchorwoman, newscaster, or news personality to sport natural hair. Only recently have mainstream film actresses in Hollywood been portrayed with natural hair styles (*Moonlight* 2018, *Dolemite* 2019, *Black Panther* 2019, *Sylvie's Love* 2020). Viola Davis rocked a natural Afro at the 2019 Golden Globes and magazines and websites were all a twitter. It was a statement. Since leaving the White House, Michelle Obama has been photographed with long, natural curls, a stark contrast to the straightened and smooth styles when she was First Lady. As a result of Black women owning their natural hairstyles, we are, for the first time since the 1970s, once again equating natural hair to pride, empowerment, and strength. In the 1970s, natural was considered powerful and beautiful, courtesy of Black Panthers, specifically Angela Davis and her righteously big Afro. The tagline "Black Is Beautiful" manifested most readily in natural black hair, a marker of pride and self-esteem (Mercer 2005). "The Black Power movements of the 1960s and 1970s reified that hair was both important and political. The Afro would challenge hegemonic beauty norms that devalue natural Black features" (Lemi and Brown 2019, 265). Saro-Wiwa (2012) argued that racial consciousness was typically part of a woman's process when transitioning to natural hair. If she was woke, she rocked the curls and kinks.

As with any cultural movement, when a subculture rises up to seize power, the WSCP dominant culture works overtime to slap back. The WSCP's backlash against the Black Power movement lasted from the 1980s through the 2010s. And this push back affected Black hair: tame your hair; straighten it; process and smooth it. In 2008, the magazine *New African Woman* published an article on hair stating the Afro/natural hair was passé; "The days of the natural afro are truly over. Sad but true, these days the natural afro is considered unattractive by many Black women (and men)" (Jere-Melanda 2008). Cultural theorist bell hooks countered the flowing mane obsession with an argument for natural hair, but hers was a bleat into the wind (hooks 1988). In the WSCP, there were real consequences, psychically and financially, for women with natural hair (Tate 2007). Natural hair was out; processed hair was in. From the 1980s through the 1990s, permed/straightened hair and sew-ins that modeled white beauty aesthetics were championed by such celebrities as Janet Jackson who immortalized the silky, sexy, flowing mane as the desired "norm" for Black women.

NATURAL'S BACK

By the turn of the twenty-first century, the tide was beginning to change. *Ebony* magazine declared natural hair was gaining a renaissance (Miller 2014). "Within the past decade, a natural hair movement has arisen that rejects the dominant beauty standard and pushes back against Eurocentric norms of Black women's beauty. In choosing to redefine the norms of Black women's beauty, 'naturalists' have begun to wear their natural hair and challenge conventional norms of what is acceptable, attractive, appropriate, and professional" (Lemi and Brown 2019, 270). Kinky was/is back. Today, curly, natural hair is gaining champions and is once again celebrated as beautiful, powerful, and a statement of Black pride, even if "nappy" is still considered an insult. Unsurprisingly, this resurgence of natural Black hair in part corresponded to a Black family—and Black female hair—being in the limelight with the Obama First Family. Much in mainstream press and in academic scholarship discussed Michelle Obama's physical body and hair (Desmond-Harris 2009, Reliable Source 2013, Brown 2016, French 2017, Roundtree 2017, Cruz-Gutierrez 2020). Both Michelle Obama's and her girls' hair were topics of critique. Black women's hair became part of the mainstream conversation.

By 2015, more Black female characters were portrayed with natural hair and scenes of hair intimacy were portrayed, especially in media directed by Black women. Cultural theorist Rowe (2019), in analyzing scenes where characters contemplate their natural hair in *How to Get Away with Murder*, *BMJ*, and *Beyond the Lights*, writes that these moments communicate specifically to Black viewers. Rowe (2019) stated, "Black women's un-styled hair serves as a space of authenticity and of intimacy . . . each of them offers a nuanced take on hair as a space of agency, negotiation, and embodied experiences of beauty" (33). These moments of Black female protagonists' relationship with their hair says something about them. Inversely, female characters with badly kept hair (nappiness or Gerry Curls) are often portrayed as grifters or emotional messes. The con artist CeCe on *BMJ* (Season 3) sports messy Gerry Curls topped with a cheap fedora. Rob, the wreck of a young woman on *High Fidelity* (2020), has messy braids with frayed ends because her life is, well, quite a mess. The raggedy dreds of Nova in *Queen Sugar* make as much of a statement about who she is as her tattoos, wardrobe, and jewelry. Whether strong, sure, insecure, emotionally fragile, unloved, poor, abused these Black female characters' status, or lack of status, is reflected in their hair.

For characters such as CeCe and Rob, their hair reflects their moral and emotional state. These biases against certain hairstyles are not limited to unkempt or outdated dos. In the dominant culture, Blacks choosing to wear their hair natural or in Afrocentric styles have been discriminated against for decades. But perhaps the tide is turning and this type of discrimination is seen as wrong. In 2019 and 2020, several state legislators (California, New York, New Jersey, Michigan, Wisconsin, Illinois, Kentucky, and Nebraska) passed laws that stated discriminating against someone's hair was a type of racial discrimination (Jones and Nicquel 2019). These laws and proposed bills were a long time coming. Between 1976 and 2016, it was perfectly lawful to demand that a Black woman change her hair as part of her employment as several state and federal court cases determined hair was not protected under EEOC regulations (Bias employment 2018). As a result—but only since 2019—activists and legislators approached the problem of Black hair discrimination with new laws. Such anti-hair bias laws were initiated after several national news stories covered Black students and workers being told their natural hairstyles were inappropriate. In 2013, a little girl named Tiana Parker was sent home from her Oklahoma school because of her locs. At a Banana Republic in New York City, a Black worker was told her box braids were too "urban." She told *The New York Amsterdam News*, "[The manager at the store where she worked] told me that my braids were not Banana Republic appropriate . . . if I didn't take them out then he couldn't schedule me for shifts" (Barker 2017). The responses to such incidents were immediate: natural hair had a community of new champions. Instead of succumbing to white cultural pressure to conform, Black women took to social media and created organizations and legislation to not only celebrate but protect natural hair (Brown 2018). These cultural shifts to championing natural hair were/are reflected in films and series featuring Black women.

Particularly within the Black community, natural hair is often seen as a positive choice, one that indicates someone with strong moral character who will fight for their community. Research in 2017 and 2019 confirmed these beliefs in regard to political candidates. Black female candidates with natural hair were seen as fighters and advocates for the Black community (Lemi and Brown 2019, Orey and Zhang 2019). Natural hair was seen as a political choice, one that was tied to fighting for Black issues. If natural hair is seen as a marker of critical consciousness and political activism, processed and straightened hair is sometimes seen as reflecting a lack of critical consciousness; this belief is reflected in the female characters of contemporary films and series.

NATURAL HAIR AS A JOURNEY

Natural hair is seen as a marker of identity, of Black pride, of resistance. For female characters, hair is often part of the storyline where natural hair cues viewers to read the character as empowered, aware, and politically engaged. In speaking about natural hair, both female actors who play these characters and participants in my research speak of moving from straightened to natural hair as an intentional and lengthy process: a journey. Black female characters are now sporting natural styles: several characters on Lena Waithe's *Twenties*; Issa Dee on *Insecure*; most females on *Grow*-ish, *Mixed-ish*, and *Black-ish*; Nova on *Queen Sugar*; Rob on *High Fidelity*; the college students on *Dear White People* to name a few. Many women in the audience are on their own journey to natural styles. Most of the women I interviewed couldn't remember a time when they were allowed, as a girl, to have natural hair, but as adults many are choosing to go natural, or at least experimenting with it. As children their hair was permed, hot combed, braided, twisted and anchored with barrettes. It was something to be controlled and tamed, perhaps a metaphor for Black womanhood in a racist culture. Black feminist academic Norwood (2018) described her move to natural hair as a "journey" from being shackled/enslaved by white standards and oppression to liberation/freedom. Recently there has been more discussion and concerted efforts to "go natural," a journey, a path, a process of not only changing one's hair but also changing one's identity. Women tended to describe their hair styles when they were girls—processed, barretted, pig-tailed, or braided—as being imposed upon them. As adults, many moved from the processed hair of their childhood to claiming their natural hair. Often this process of identity reclamation takes years.

Drayah, a college senior about to graduate with a degree in film production at Midwest university, tells me about transitioning to natural hair, proudly sporting a fabulous Afro left to fall loose around her face. "Hair, for me, it has been a journey. My senior year I started going natural. These past five years I have grown into my womanhood," she said as a way of articulating why the way Black women's hair is portrayed in the films and shows she watches is so important to her. She recalls the moments of her younger self, sitting in the kitchen, having her hair styled:

> Easter: you are sitting next to the stove. You are sitting next to the hot comb and with the blue goop [Blue Magic]. Your hair gets burned off, you wear the piggy tails. Then you get older and get braids. I started finding all these different products. Instead of taming, I was able to embrace the curl. My curl pattern got better. For me it represents how I am feeling today. These past two weeks [the business of mid-semester at college], I wasn't taking much care of my hair. It's looking coarse; I need to get to it. Wash, detangle and it is good. (Drayah)

Drayah is one of the many women who today are embracing natural hairstyles. Actors are also doing this and talking about why. Echoing the idea that moving to natural hair is a journey, one of the actors who starred in Justin Siemen's *Bad Hair* (2020), a mock thriller set in 1990s Los Angeles amid the straightening craze, articulated her relationship to her natural Black hair as a vexed path of personal growth and self-acceptance. *Bad Hair* is a tongue-in-cheek "thriller" where the pursuit of natural, long, and flowing hair is the demise of the women who seek it. The hair, haunted, comes alive and possesses the women on whose heads it is woven, seeking blood and killing everyone in its path. In promotional materials for the film, there was an attempt to connect the actors' journey with their own hair to the film's message. In the official *Bad Hair* trailer (2020), one actor, Yaani King, said she had locs since she was sixteen years old and before that it was permed. The decision to go with locs was one that impacted her not only personally but also professionally. "I just woke up one day and said, 'my hair feels dead. I'm done with this [permed hair].' And I started locking it. And that was its own journey of hair. Especially being an actor with locs. No one knew what I was doing . . . I almost lost a job because the hair stylist told the director, 'I can't do anything with that' " (Donnelly and Lang 2020). In this interview with the director and actors, the women all spoke to the politics of going natural as well as the feelings of liberation and empowerment when they did. They also cited the negative reaction they received from white directors or hair stylists. Going natural is a journey of personal affirmation, but one that also involves cultural resistance and consequences.

Dawson, Karl, and Peluchette (2019) also found that women they interviewed described the process of changing to natural hairstyles as a journey. One of their respondents said, "My hair story has in part shaped who I am today. I went from short 'fro, to natural two strand twists, to locs and now back to a 'coiled' 'fro—but while I've been on this journey—I was forced to look at myself in the mirror . . . and I appreciate the physical beauty that I found. . . . Now, I love me and I love my natural hair and it [is] as free as I am" (397). Other scholars documenting "going natural" have also used "journey" as a way to describe the decision and process that often takes years and answering identity questions (Ndichu and Upadhyaya 2019). Cheryl Thompson (2008), a professor of Gender Studies, wrote, "Since I was a teenager, I have chemically altered the natural state of my hair. At the time, I never really thought about why I did it, or the extent to which that chemical would rule over me. But my *hair*story is not unique. For the vast majority of Black women, hair is not just hair; it contains emotive qualities that are linked to one's lived experience" (831). Women confront the politics of hair both in their personal and professional lives. Protecting one's hair is akin to protecting one's self. In the promotional materials for the psycho-thrilled spoof *Bad Hair*, actor Ashley Blaine Featherson said, "I'm protective of my sew-in because it is a form of protection in an industry where I am constantly getting my hair done and no one knows how to protect my own hair. . . . I am grateful for my sew-in because it is how I maintain the integrity of my natural hair. And I think that is something that a lot of people don't know about Black women and what we are dealing with in the industry" (Donnelly and Lang 2020).

Hair choices form an identity and changing one's hair to natural is a decision borne of questioning that goes far beyond a hairstyle. *Bad Hair* actor Yaani King put it this way, "How many women outside of the Black community have to go through that, take a year to decide about a hair style? This [*Bad Hair*] was definitely a validating moment" (Donnelly and Lang 2020). The binary of "bad v. good hair" is entrenched in racism. Robinson (2011) defines the distinctions this way, "'Good hair' is hair that minimizes African ancestry, more reflective of a European, Native, or Asian ancestral mix within the Black individual. It is more wavy or straight in texture, and more likely to be long. 'Bad hair' is the extreme opposite of good hair—tightly coiled, thicker, and more likely to be short, clearly reflecting African ancestry" (358). Within the context of a film spoofing the trials and tribulations of Black women and what is at stake with their hair choices (judgment, shame, pride, respect), the Black women acting the roles in *Bad Hair* revealed how moving it was for them personally to have permission to interrogate and change their beliefs about hair. The Black male director Justin Simien wanted to question "the system that marginalizes and oppresses black women" (*Bad Hair* 2020). Another actor from *Bad Hair* talked about not having natural hair since she was seven years old and when deciding to go natural had no idea what to do. She said,

> There weren't as many YouTube tutorials as there are now. I was putting honey in my hair, eggs, anything. I don't know. I was just following nonsense that I found online. And constantly trying to stretch it and twist it and manipulate it to still be acceptable in some way. . . . I had a moment when I thought, "I am done with twisting my hair out. I am going to wash it and walk out the door and this is what it is going to be." It took a while to really own that, but I was tired. I was just tired. (Yaani King, Donnelly and Lang 2020)

These women are expressing the relief they found when they embraced natural hairstyles. They feel validated when they see characters in their favorite shows also going natural. In series such as *Twenties*, *Queen Sugar*, *Dear White People*, and *Black-ish/Mixed-ish/Grown-ish*, the characters have various versions of natural hair and their styles change almost episode to episode and sometimes multiple times within an episode. Films such as *Nappily Ever After*, *Bad Hair*, *Good Hair*, and *Hair Wolf* center the films' arcs on cultural beauty aesthetics and Black women's value as reflected in hair choices. The Afrocentric themes of these productions include hair that is unprocessed, braided, twisted, and locked. The details are noted by viewers. Michelle, an EMT and college pre-med major, pointed to two female characters on *Grown-ish* (2019) that she felt reflected a positive representation of Black womanhood. "The twins on *Grown-ish*, I really like them. One is thicker; she has hips, she has curves. The other twin is skinny and delicate and very soft spoken. They have natural hair. . . . That is how I look, that is how I am. I can relate to that."

The trend toward natural is codified in these contemporary productions featuring Black women. As with most features of Black culture, from music to dance to food to clothing, natural hairstyles are not only gaining popularity with Black women, but whites are attempting to appropriate them. In the brilliant short spoof on white appropriation of Black hair beauty, *Hair Wolf* (2019), the writer/director Mariama Diallo doesn't waste a second articulating issues regarding Black hair, when Black hair is appropriated as a white girl's commodity. From iconic hair products (Blue Magic and Afro Sheen) to hair texture ("You know I'm a 3B," one character snaps when she is called "nappy"), the film articulates the details of Black hair culture and white people's obscene violations of Blackness: "She was knuckle deep . . . I think she pulled out some of my hair!" The thirteen minutes of *Hair Wolf*'s sharp narrative is packed with Black culture violated by whites in the name of embodying "hip." Even as the hair artist is rattling off mantras of powerful Black women to keep her safe from the white wolves ("You wanna talk Black pride? Black

Don't Crack. Tina Fucking Turner. Janet Jackson. Angela Bassett Bitch. Gabriel Union Wade."), in the end, no one is safe from the white female Hair Wolves who consume Black culture and possess Black people.

GET YOUR HANDS OUT OF MY HAIR

Although *Hair Wolf* is satire, as with all good satire, the truth cuts close to the farcical elements. The women I interviewed spoke often of white hands, uninvited, in their hair. This bodily invasion, a white privilege that goes unchecked, happens in grocery aisles, at their workplace, and at their schools. In the Hollywood film *Little* (2019), a high powered, tyrannical boss is taken down a peg by a magical Black girl. The boss, Jordan (Regina Hall), becomes herself at a younger age (Marsai Martin), geeky and at the mercy, once again, of school bullies. Her hair transitions from expensive wigs and processed cuts to a large Afro that is the target of bullies in school. Jordan learns lessons in how to be a better grown-up, a more effective boss, and a bigger advocate for the less-empowered through her "little" experience. In a middle school lunchroom scene—the epitome of school hierarchies, cliques, and bullying—random peers shove colored plastic straws in her hair, creating a visual of raggedy social status manifested on the top of Jordan's head.

Subtle references to whites disrespecting hair are noted in the quick moments when white characters touch the girl's hair. The demeaning habit of whites who mess, meddle, and treat Black hair as a public touch-and-feel sensory experience is communicated in two moments during the film. Both moments are inflicted on little Jordan by low status white men, one a valet and one a server in a high-end restaurant. Both men pat the outer reaches of her Afro with a sort of tentative, patronizing tap. Jordan responds with an impatient eye roll, shrugging off the invasion, largely ignoring the white hands invading her personal space, but this white obsession with the right to touch and meddle with a Black female's hair is real and reoccurring in the WSCP. The moments on screen that nod to or discuss this issue of white obsession and "right to touch" Black hair offer the Black female audience affirmation: yes, Black girls/women deal with this white presumed right to touch our hair; no, it is *not* OK, but most women endure these invasions. And those invasions are captured on screens large and small as affirmations regarding the ridiculousness of white fixation on black hair. In one episode of *Black-ish*, a white neighbor simultaneously reaches out as she says, not waiting for the answer, "Can I touch your hair?" Ruby, the grandmother, rears back with slow surprise. Raising a wagging finger and looking down her nose at the offender. Ruby, eyes wide, says, "Ooh. Don't do that," as the puzzled white woman is left to contemplate her faux pas (Season 3, Episode 5: "The Purge"). These moments of white people violating Black female space may seem minor, but they are not unnoticed by Black women in the audience. To see a white character violate a Black female's space articulates the indignity Black women experience daily in white culture. Whereas the touch of another Black female in one's hair is love, when whites touch Black hair, it is an assault. "Can I touch your hair?" Before even asking, whites assume the answer is yes. The white fingers are already in the locs, even before the woman has a chance to answer. On one hand, the white person realizes it may be impolite—a violation of personal space at the very least—to touch someone without asking; however, the consent is assumed and not waited for. As Black women's bodies have historically not belonged to them but to whites, the fondling of their hair by white people is yet another example of how daily violations to their autonomy occur, remnants of slavery where a body was property.

When films/television acknowledge these maddening moments of white encroachment on their body via their hair, there is a righteous affirmation that many Black women feel: this is not OK; it is wrong; white folks should *not* be touching our hair. Drayah brought up the moment in *Good Girls* where the mother is braiding her daughter's hair (an act of care and affection) and followed it with this story:

> When a Black woman touches another Black woman's hair, it is love. But when a white person touches a Black woman's hair, it is anything but love. I was in the store and this lady just *touched* my friend's hair. We were in Hobby Lobby and an old white lady *ran her fingers* through my friend's crocheted locs. She didn't even ask. (Drayah)

These extremely invasive violations were echoed by many interviewees. It may not even be touching, but just the language of inquiry feels like a violation because of how frequently these questions by whites posed to Black women happen. Janae, a full-time student who also works at a nursing home, articulated the connection between moments of affirmation in a film and her reality of dealing with whites' comments about her hair. She said:

> So many [white] outsiders will make comments about our hair and not realize how dangerous it is. When I clock into my job, I hear it all the time, "Your hair is so beautiful. It isn't all yours, is it?" We don't ask that of white women. I have made a decision to stop answering people's questions on that.

A woman with long, rope-y locs told me how a small moment in Spike Lee's movie *Crooklyn* (1994) affected her. "I love *Crooklyn* . . . . It was a childhood movie for me and I still watch it. . . . It was the hair thing. Nappy hair and being told it was difficult. That was very accurate for me" (Ruby).

These on-screen hair moments may seem fleeting and unimportant, but they are significant in that they affirm and celebrate the beauty, the fraught cultural messages, the connection to self and love that Black women feel.

Hair is love; self-love is hair. This theme recurred over and over again in interviews with Black women and in quiet moments easily missed on screens large and small. Aliya, a nineteen-year-old graphic design major, articulated that one of the main reasons she loved *Black-ish* was because of how the women's hair was portrayed. "I really like *Black-ish* . . . . The main characters have natural hair" (Aliya). For Aliya and many others, how female characters' hair is represented creates an affinity, an affirmation with the audience. For those audience members, the authentic portrayal of a Black family, a Black girl, and a Black woman is reflected in the show's treatment of her natural hair.

Chapter 2

#TeamLightSkin versus #TeamDarkSkin

High Yellow. The Tragic Mulatto. The Paper Bag Test. The Blacker the Berry, the Sweeter the Juice. Blue-Black. Bright Light. And most recently, #TeamLightSkin and #TeamDarkSkin. The rhetoric of skin tone places value. The white supremacist culture values light skin. Being able to pass as white means having light skin and "good" hair. Darker skin not only means one has more difficulty accessing white cultural power but also means one is a target for police brutality, harassment, racial slurs, and sometimes even discrimination in one's own family. Advertising, television, and film created for and by the white culture reinforce these ideologies; light-skinned Black women are the acceptable/desirable version of Black. As with the cultural shift to address the politics of natural hair, the politics of skin tone are also openly discussed and debated among viewers and often within films/shows. In white-produced and -directed films, ads, and series, darker skin often implies bad intent: the criminal, the tragic slave, the poor hustler, the abused, and the neglected. However, in Black-woman-produced and -directed films and series, those stereotypes of skin tone can be flipped: the darker women are those with drive, grit, and determination, the characters we are rooting for. Although perhaps not privileging darker skin for *beauty*, women directors/producers often feature darker-skinned actors and include commentary on dark skin being preferable to lighter skin, at least in relation to success. The darker-skinned women of these narratives produced by women are often the underdogs we want to succeed. In *Bessie* (HBO, 2015), the biopic about Blues singer Bessie Smith, and in *Self Made* (Netflix, 2020), the biopic about Madam C. J. Walker and her beauty empire, skin tone is the topic of several exchanges between characters and both films imply that darker is better, a trend worth examining.

Lighter may be more desirable to men and the white supremacy, but in productions by Black women, darker women get things done. They are powerful; they are resilient; they are the ones we want to see succeed; they drive the narratives of triumph over oppressions. The darker women prevail as the lighter-skinned women fall away, weak, and trifling. *Self Made* (directed by DeMane Davis and Kasi Lemmons) and *Bessie*, (directed by Dee Rees) are just two examples where skin tone is an open conversation, flipping the script that "light is all right" and "Black needs to get back." Both are directed by Black women. Although Queen Latifah, who plays the title character in *Bessie* is not exactly dark-skinned, the woman she is portraying, Bessie Smith, was a darker woman and the theme of how she struggled against biases is regularly addressed in the film. Other series that feature darker actors in female roles include *The Last O.G.*, *The Chi*, *She's Gotta Have It*, *Twenties*, *Pose*, *Chewing Gum*, and *Atlanta*. In series such as *Black-ish*, *Grown-ish*, and *Insecure*, scenes and episodes are devoted to the politics of skin color among Black females. Stars such as Issa Rae, Viola Davis, Octavia Spencer, Tasha Smith, Rutina Wesley, Raven Goodwin, Danielle Brooks, Florence Kasumba, Leticia Wright, and Lupita Nyong'o are popular darker-skinned stars who defy the preference for light-skinned actors. Perhaps it is no coincidence that most of these women got their start either by producing their own shows or being cast by Black female producers. Similar to how a Black female character's hair is addressed, the color and tone of her skin is noted and discussed by attuned viewers. Although we can see there is progress being made regarding casting of darker-skinned actors with open discussions about the politics of skin tone, respondents in my research were quick to point out that darker-skinned actors still seem the exception to the preference for lighter skin tones. Although there have been some strides in #TeamDarkSkin when it comes to entertainment media produced or directed by Black women, there is still room for improvement, especially in regards to female leads. In media produced by Black women, however, we see a shift in the traditional preference for Team Light Skin. The darker-skinned women are the ones with power and fortitude; their lighter-skinned counterparts often are the nefarious nemesis, an attempt to defy or rewrite the white supremacist notion that lighter is better.

COLORISM DEFINED AND MANIFESTED

It should go without saying that in a white supremacist culture, the lighter one's skin the more cultural capital one has. The very definition of what it means to be Black or African American largely rests on skin tone, although hair texture also may factor in. Research in life expectancy, mate selection (Hughes and Hertel 1990, Hunter 1998), socioeconomic opportunities (Collins 2000), prison sentencing (Hochschild and Weaver 2007), and political candidate success (Lerman, McCabe, and Sadin 2015; Terkildsen 1993; Weaver 2012) shows having darker skin decreases economic, social, and political opportunities. Having darker skin is a definite disadvantage in the dominant culture. "Dark skin evokes fears of criminality . . . light-skinned people generally are advantaged" (Hoschild and Weaver 647). According to Hunter (2007), the existing body of research indicates that despite the progress realized by Black people in more recent U.S. history, colorism still remains an issue of debate and significance. Skin tone continues to play a role in opportunities and experiences (Hannon and DeFina 2014, Hall, 2017). These messages regarding skin tones are internalized in the Black community. Not all Black skin is equal; and we are beginning to talk about these biases of skin tone within the identity of Blackness. Within the past five years, there have been films, series, and television shows produced that openly address the issue of skin tone discrimination (colorism) within the context of the Black community; all of these offerings are by Black directors, producers, and writers. Opening the conversation is essential; making sure all tones are cast and portrayed is the next step.

In her book *In Search of Our Mothers' Gardens*, Alice Walker (1983) coined the term "colorism," defining it as prejudices based strictly on skin tone, with lighter-skinned Blacks typically seen as the top of the skin tone hierarchy. This hierarchy exists not only in the dominant culture—as one would expect—but also in parts of the Black community. These hierarchies of tone were first defined during the system of slavery, lighter-skinned people being the result of white-on-Black rape and thereby the offspring of those rapes being of higher value to the slave holder. Tate (2007) uses the term "pigmentocracy," writing "status, life chances and very often freedom were based on skin colour and that skin colour itself was also a matter of official record and Surveillance" (318). Light-skinned enslaved women who were the offspring of rapes were seen as "better" and therefore often treated with more regard by their white owners. Lighter-skinned Black women were often "house slaves," placing them in a position to be raped more easily than the enslaved women working outside the master's living space, thereby creating lighter-skinned offspring. Black femininity became fused with these light skin traits. Even today Black femininity is caught up in skin color, body type, hair texture, and facial features that mimic the dominant white culture (Collins 2004, 194). These traits of Black femininity are replicated in advertisement, films, television, and other media created by whites. But these markers of Black femininity can often change when the text is created by Blacks, particularly Black women. More research is needed on the connection between femininity and colorism in the Black community (Travino, Harris, and Wallace 2008). This chapter offers a small contribution to this needed research, arguing that colorism in entertainment media is minimized when Black women produce and direct.

The relationship between a female's worth and skin tone is a fraught one with no clear conclusion. "Today, [Blacks] are taught to be proud of their skin color, but remain 'color struck' in noticeable ways by attending and responding to different shades of Black skin," wrote Lemi and Brown (2019, 268). The term "color struck" indicates a sort of smitten desire toward light-skinned Blacks in the Black community (Russell, Wilson, and Hall, 1992). Lemi and Brown (2019) found that darker-skinned female political candidates with natural hair were more likely to get the support of Black voters, but at the same time those voters felt the candidates would be less successful within the context of the dominant culture's political machine. In other words, the Black respondents valued an Afrocentric aesthetic in female candidates, but questioned whether these candidates would be able to get as much done within the context of a culture of white supremacy. In a similar study, Orey and Zhang (2019) found that Black Millennials in their study thought light-skinned candidates would be less supportive of Black policies and HBCU. In both these studies, the results seem to point to the idea that darker skin, at least today, is seen as a marker of a person more invested in politics, resistance, and activism. This connection between darker skin and the embodiment of grit, resilience, social justice work, and expressing Black pride is reflected in films such as *Hidden Figures* (2016), *Bessie* (2015), *Self Made* (2020), *Harriet* (2020, and *Black Panther* (2018). Whereas the dominant culture may send the message through ads, television, and film that lighter skin is "better," within the context of the Black community, lighter skin may be seen as suspect. The outcomes of current studies and entertainment analysis seem to contradict previous scholarship that indicated people are more likely to describe dark-skinned Black women to be more aggressive, less intelligent, and less educated compared to lighter-skinned Blackss (Maddox and Gray 2002). However, it is important to note that Maddox and Gray did not specifically limit their study to Black participants whereas both Lemi and Brown, as well as Orey and Zhang did. The difference in responses may indicate non-Blacks have a bias against darker skin whereas Black respondents may be aware of the dominant culture's mandate that "light is better" and resist that by seeing darker skin as an asset, particularly in political arenas.

This phenomena of "dark skin is more trustworthy/better character" seems to be reflected in some recent entertainment sources created by Black females. Assumptions regarding skin tone, both within the Black community and in the dominant culture, are a complex construct involving cognitive, affective, and behavioral components (Brown et al. 1989). Within and outside the Black community, skin tone is not seen the same for men and women. Black women are judged more harshly for darker skin than Black men. Hall (2017) found, "In every focus group, women with darker skin tones were typically described as loud, suspicious, unattractive, and less intelligent" (75). Keith et al.'s (2010) research found that "girls as young as six are twice as likely as boys to be sensitive to the social importance of skin color" (51). The vexed relationships between gender, skin color, and hair create standards of Black female identity or beauty that may still reinforce preferences for light skin and "good" hair (Arogundade 2000, Badillo 2001, Robinson 2011, Wolf 2010, White 1991). Contemporary entertainment produced and directed by Black women (and sometimes Black men) disrupt this typical stereotype.

THE BLACKER THE BERRY

To further muddle the complexities of skin tone stereotypes and preferences, generational and educational divides impact how the dark skin/natural hair combination in women is perceived. Orey and Zhang (2019) focus on younger Black students at a HBCU because they anticipated younger people would have less skin tone bias than older Blacks. They write, "As is indicated by our title [Melanated Millennials], many younger African Americans have adopted such words as 'melanated' to describe their love for their dark-colored skin. Such phrases as 'loving the skin I'm in' have gained popularity" (2460). Yet this celebration of darker skin color is not universal. In the early 2000s, there was a number of studies that suggested anti-African American bias among Black respondents (Nosek, Banaji, and Greenwald 2002; Ashburn-Nardo, Knowles, and Monteith 2003; Jost, Banaji, and Nosek 2004; Craemer 2007). Rudman and McLean (2016) reported their African American participants identified whites as aesthetically more appealing. Moreover, Rudman and McLean reported that their participants expressed strong biases against Afrocentric features and hair and less bias against Eurocentric features and hair. Within families or communities, light-skinned Black women often reported feeling a bias against them. A participant in a 2013 study is quoted as saying, "I am always having to answer the 'what are you' question and being accused of thinking I'm better than other black women because of my [light] skin color. Recently I got in a heated discussion with a brother who told me that all light-skinned black women are stuck-up" (Russell-Cole, Wilson, and Hall 2013, 87–88). The issue of skin color is fraught with conflicts and contradictions. In some contexts, it is better to be a female with lighter skin; in other contexts, being a dark-skinned female is seen as preferable. Young female respondents in Tate's (2007) research attempted to look *more* Black within their community because what they felt was a bias against looking/acting light. Tate writes, "Faced with the denial [of her Blackness because of her lighter skin and less-curly hair] Teresa in her youth plaited her hair and wore an African head-wrap to hide the straight-ness of her hair" (307). Tate argues that adopting an aesthetic that is more Afrocentric is a performance in the same way that Judith Butler argues gender is an adopted performance. Tate writes, "If black beauty is performative then it can be performed differently and disrupt the normalized racializing black beauty of black anti-racist aesthetics" (307). Depending on context, therefore, a woman will perform, put on, her race in different ways in order to access acceptance similar to the way she engages with gender tropes that are put on/taken off depending on context and purpose. In the context of a social group, an activist group, or a campus/work community that emphasizes Black pride, for example, Black women will attempt to appear darker/more Afrocentric; in a context in which lighter skin is celebrated (perhaps even in her own fam-ily), the woman/girl will change her behavior or dress to appear "lighter/less Black." Code-switching, the ability to swap in and out of language practices depending on context, is not limited to linguistics; it can also relate to hair, clothing, and body language.

The erroneous idea that dark skin equates to a more Afrocentric worldview or is somehow the "correct" way to be Black may be an over-correction to the historical bias toward lighter skin. One example of this dynamic where darker seems to represent a more authentic, Afrocentric Black identity is in the popular Hulu series *Queen Sugar* (2016–2019). This family drama of the genre that generated the *Dallas* and *Dynasty* series wildly popular in the 1980s, features two Bordelone sisters, Nova and Charley. Nova is dark-skinned and Charley is light. Nova is invested in politics of social justice, a practitioner of traditional medicine, and highly involved in Black culture and community; in contrast, Charley is light-skinned, assimilated to the dominant white culture in appearance and lifestyle, and often resides/moves outside of Black culture/community.

In the opening episode of *Queen Sugar* (2016, written and directed by Ava DuVernay, Oprah Winfrey Productions), there is a slow pan and a close-up of Nova's dark-skinned naked body. The camera's frame luxuriates over her arm, shoulder, and cheek as a ballad plays in the background. Nova (Rutina Wesley) is rough around the edges, tattooed, sporting messy dreds and bohe-mian clothing. In sharp contrast, the light-skinned Charley is controlled and smooth, ironed and assimilated. Whereas Charley is a defender of the domi-nant culture (she initially defends the basketball players who are accused of gang raping a woman until she is presented evidence that her husband—also on the team—was one of them), Nova is organizing marches and protests, selling weed, and making her living through alternative/folk medicine. One could interpret these two polar representations as alluding to the idea that darker-skinned women are more "authentic" and Afrocentric than their light-skinned sisters.

Some viewers, however, see these messages as a way to correct the light-skinned bias of the past. One young woman told me:

[Lighter] skin tone did matter at one point. I feel like we are in a time period where we are shifting. In *Black Panther*, [Nyong'o] is dark-skinned; she is rocking all different types of hair styles. . . . Darker people have it worse; they get criticized more. There are already the stereotypes placed on us, and colorism was a big thing, but now it is getting to the point we are all facing the same struggle. We are risking the same things, you get pulled over, I get pulled over. Now there is more of a sense of community than there was. (Tania, in her twenties, single lesbian, mother of two "fur babies," stylist, St. Louis)

Tania sees the way dark-skinned women are portrayed as the heroines, the protagonists we root for, as progress in correcting the dominant culture's bias for light-skinned women. In my interviews with women Nyong'o (*Twelve Years a Slave*, 2013; *Black Panther*, 2018; *Us*, 2019; *Star Wars*, 2015, 2019), Viola Davis (*How to Get Away with Murder*, 2014–2020; *Fences* 2016), and Octavia Spencer (*Hidden Figures*, 2016; *The Shape of Water*, 2017; *Self Made*, 2020) were noted specifically because of their skin tone (darker). Spencer and Davis also were mentioned by my participants because of their larger body types. One woman told me, "I love Viola Davis because she is dark-skinned. I never see her with weave. And I love her body type: she is not super skinny. Her character in *Fences* was wonderful" (Marta, in her thirties, partnered with a man/no children, insurance agent in Nebraska). Many times, darker skin tone is associated with natural hair and evokes positive comments about these actors. Both Marta and Tania are expressing the connection between the dark-skinned representations on their screens and more cultural and community acceptance of dark-skinned people within the Black community. The biases exist, but the complex conversations have started and entertainment media is beginning to open up to a broader range of darker skin.

Jordan Peele, a Black man who was raised by a white woman, is noted for creating films that feature dark-skinned actors. The movie *Us* (2019) features a darker-skinned mother played by Nyong'o. The twist at the end of the movie is that the mother is really one of the evil characters, which could be read as reinforcing the stereotype that darker-skinned women are less trustworthy. However, since Peele makes a point of casting darker-skinned actors to ensure he isn't falling into the light-skin preference cycle, this may be an unfair critique of Nyong'o's character in that film. Critically conscious consumers are talking about these sorts of nuances, asking themselves questions such as "What is the ratio of dark to light?", "Are the darker-skinned characters seen as the 'bad' people? Are lighter-skinned characters—especially when female—seen as the 'good' people?" When looking at these

representations, the analysis is complex. Yes, there are some of these ten-
dencies, but there are also enough examples to argue that these biases and
representations are changing, largely due to enlightened Black directors, both
male and female. Stereotypically and historically, in the white supremacist
dominant culture, darker-skinned females would be considered sexually
available in a negative way, even if that availability is portrayed through rape.
When contemporary roles of dark-skinned women include any sort of sexual
openness, critically conscious viewers note it. As Janae, a poet who publishes
a Black-centric zine by/about/for women, pointed out:

> [In *Awkward Black Girl*], Issa's dark-skinned friend is overly sexual. IRL she is
> a virgin, but in the show, her character is sexualized. I didn't have an issue with
> that because Issa isn't light-skinned. [Issa Rae's series] did Black culture justice
> because maybe you are corny, you don't have rhythm, or you have corny things
> that you were picked on for, but that is OK. [Issa Rae's character] isn't "woe is
> me," but "I am different and artistic."

Janae, a critically conscious consumer, is looking for and finding the nuances
in the shows she watches. She is considering the critique she has heard or
read, but evaluates the representation for herself and sees it as more complex
than simply a dark-skinned woman being cast as the stereotypical "hoe."
    Regardless of the complex representations—some of it progress—in Black
entertainment, there is still real discrimination against dark-skinned people
not only within the WSCP, but within the context of the Black community.
As an act of resistance and to push back against the WSCP beauty aesthetic,
many women are turning with pride to Afrocentric markers such as darker
skin, natural hair, and Afrocentric clothing. Skin tone, however, is decidedly different from hair and clothing: it can't be swapped out or easily cast
off. Although skin tone is a fact, not a choice or option, that doesn't seem to
prevent people from judging someone's character, strength, and power based
on darker skin. There is evidence in recent films that darker-skinned females
are seen as strong leaders, strong activists, and of higher moral character than
their lighter-skinned counterparts. In films such as *Bessie, Harriet,* and *Self
Made* the female protagonists, played by darker-skinned actors, carry positive traits, whereas their lighter-skinned counterparts are portrayed as weak,
superficial, and in some instances corrupt.
    The HBO biopic *Bessie* (2015) stars Queen Latifah as blues singer Bessie
Smith, a dark-skinned woman who makes a name for herself. The film, written
and directed by Dee Rees, portrays Smith as a savvy, rough-around-the-edges
character with a fierce determination. Ma Rainey is played by Mon'ique and
both defy the paper bag test, celebrating their darker skin and larger-than-life
personalities. In one early scene, a young Bessie Smith is rejected for a part

in a Vaudeville troupe because her skin is too dark; later, in control of casting her own dancers, Smith categorically rejects light-skinned dancers, stating, "Give her the bag test." (Smith's brother holds a bag against the dancer's face; she is lighter than the bag, so the dancer grins, relieved that she will "pass the paper bag test.") Bessie scolds, "What are you smiling for? You gotta be DARKER than the bag. NEXT! No yellow bitches!" The film indicates that Smith's bias against light-skinned Blacks is justified, a wrong that needs to be corrected by casting dark. She does not want to perpetuate the stereotype of "light women are better/more attractive" within the context of her own Vaudeville troupe. Later in the film, Smith is attempting to get a record deal with the first Black-owned label. When Smith enters the room to meet the executives, they are all very light-skinned Black men. We can see Smith chuckle, assumingly about how assimilated they are in speech, dress, and mannerisms. Their lighter skin tone is part of this. The unspoken argument is that they are light-skinned and successful because the WSCP allowed them to be successful, whereas the darker Blacks would be shut out of systems of power. The men, oblivious to their light-skinned privilege and how they got it, are gatekeepers who continue to reinforce the "light is all right" idea.

Smith sings for them, only after hawking a viscous loogy into her teacup in defiance of their refined behaviors. They tell her they are going with Ethel Waters, a very light-skinned woman, who they believe better "uplifts the race." Smith exits, defeated in this context due to skin tone, but not deterred. In this film, the darker-skinned women are the ones who stand up to bullies, fight for the Black cause, uplift others, and rise above racism and sexism despite the systems of power that are determined to beat them back.

This theme of an invincible protagonist who is a dark-skinned underdog appears in *Harriet* (2019), the Hollywood film about Harriet Tubman, and *Self Made* (2020), the Netflix film about Madam C. J. Walker, who built her empire on beauty products for Black women. *Harriet*, directed by Kasi Lemmons with Cynthia Erivo playing Tubman, does not overtly address the dark versus light skin dynamic, but Erivo is a dark-skinned actor playing an invincible protagonist who is determined and survives and succeeds against all odds. Tubman has a light-skinned sister who is a "house slave." When Tubman comes back to save her sister, her sister declines; she wants to stay on the plantation instead of attempt escape to freedom. The unstated nuance in this scene is that the "house slave" sister does not have the fortitude, courage, or strength to do what Tubman wants her to do. This scene hints that the lighter-skinned enslaved women who toiled in the masters' houses were more aligned with their masters than with a desire to be free or live outside the reach of whites. In both *Bessie* and *Harriet*, a subtext exists suggesting light-skinned Blacks are somehow "less Black" both in appearance and alignment with the white oppressors. Lighter-skinned characters are portrayed as having sold out their Afrocentric communities to align with and assimilate to the white-dominant culture.

In *Self Made* the predominant messages are: light skin equates to betrayal of Blackness, light skin indicates assimilation to white culture at the expense of Black community, and light skin signals lower morality. The main character, Sarah Breedlove, a.k.a. Madam C. J. Walker, is consistently betrayed and attacked by light-skinned women. Breedlove, played by dark-skinned Octavia Spencer, overcomes all of these attacks, but these dark-skinned versus light-skinned dynamics are the driving tension in every major conflict portrayed in the film.

Self Made opens with Breedlove being thrown over by the light-skinned, elegant, well-heeled Addie, the epitome of a Victorian lady who sells a hair growth pomade among other products to Black women. Breedlove wants to sell Addie's product, but Addie turns her down. Breedlove's skin is too dark. Breedlove says, "Hiring a bunch of mulattos to hawk your product ain't gonna work. . . . When a customer looks at my hair, they know it works." Addie retorts, "Colored women want to look like me," further driving home the point that white assimilation is the key to Black beauty. Later in the scene, Addie tells Breedlove, "These are my products and I won't have the likes of you associated with them. . . . you look like you just stepped off the plantation." Breedlove refuses to accept her lot as laundry woman and the film is built around the repeated attempts of Addie to take down stalwart Breedlove through conniving and backhanded ways, solidifying a stereotype that light-skinned Blacks cannot be trusted and are ready to betray their own, whereas darker-skinned Black women will persevere with vim and vigor.

Later in that same episode, Addie follows Breedlove and her daughter, Leila, from St. Louis to Indianapolis with the purpose of opening a shop that would compete with Breedlove's blossoming business. When Breedlove and Leila run into her, Addie is attempting to cover a black eye. Breedlove and Leila speculate that Addie is on the run from a no-good husband. Leila laughs, "I guess light-skinned don't mean you have a good marriage." Breedlove retorts, "Please. She ain't set but a toe in our boat. Always going to be easier for folks like Addie." Breedlove's comment denies the audience any opportunity to sympathize with Addie. Breedlove is saying, "We don't need to be sorry for her; she will always have it better and easier because of her light skin." The first episode ends with a voice-over of Addie saying, "Colored women will do anything to look like me, even if, deep down, they know they can't," putting a finalizing punctuation mark on the portrayal of Addie as someone who is not a sister, but taking full advantage of her light-skinned privilege and attempting to grind dark-skinned women under her well-turned, satin-slippered heel in the process.

Addie emphasizes her shallow and crooked personality when she engages John, Leila's feckless husband, to spy on Breedlove (Episode 2). We also see

Addie take to drink, more evidence of her low character. The only empathy afforded to Addie is a short conversation she has with her mother on the phone (Episode 3). Her mother, clearly not as refined as Addie, replies to Addie's confession that things are not going well, "Not a high yellow gal like you! Massa may have cursed me with a daughter, but you have good hair and nice bright skin. You'll be fine!" In these three short sentences, complex dynamics of race, color, and gender are articulated. We understand that Addie is the product of a rape and that her mother felt a son would bring her more benefit than a daughter, which seems incorrect since Addie's success as a business woman is evident. Addie's mother also believes that Addie's light skin will save her and her mother from poverty. In Addie's mother's eyes, Addie has nothing to complain or worry about because her light privilege will save both of them.

The point that light-skinned women have a cultural advantage that they exploit is one that Breedlove continually battles. Added to this dynamic is also a narrative that argues light-skinned women push down their darker sisters; light-skinned women are not to be trusted. There is a phantom Gibson Girl character who rides her bike through Breedlove's imagination, taunting her menacingly. The Gibson Girl is a doppelganger for the assimilated "Bright Lights" who are out to destroy Breedlove. As the Gibson Girl mockingly laughs in Breedlove's imagination, there is another light-skinned Black woman—other than Addie—out to take down Breedlove. Dora is Breedlove's top sales representative, a light-skinned woman who seduces Breedlove's husband, C. J. C. J.'s infidelities with Dora tear Breedlove's family apart. "That high yella heifer is out here trying to destroy me!" she yells at C. J. (Episode 3). Later in that episode, plagued by Addie, Dora, and the Gibson Girl, Breedlove mutters an old childhood rhyme, "If you are white, you are alright. If you are brown, stick around. If you are Black, get back." She tells Leila that everyone loves Addie because she is light-skinned. "No one looks at me that way. Not your daddy, not anyone. Everybody want a nice, bright gal with silky hair. You and me we gotta work harder. Be smarter." And they are. The resounding message of this short series is that #TeamDarkSkin is smarter, better, harder-working, and more trustworthy.

The series ends with Addie and Breedlove reconciling. Overcoming skin tone bias is central to their reconciliation. Addie tells Breedlove, "I am more than a Light Bright." Breedlove responds, "I would have done anything to be in business with you. Anything . . . we could have done it together. White folks out here killing us. We have got to stop fighting over things that don't matter" (Episode 4). The olive branch is extended and it hinges on both business women getting beyond their bias regarding skin tone: Addie needs to accept Breedlove despite her biases against Breedlove's dark skin; Breedlove needs to accept Addie despite her biases against light skin. However, if the entire series was spent reinforcing these differences, is the audience to believe that they are so easily overcome?

This theme of acknowledging one's own bias and working against it to be better together was also brought up in my interviews. EJ, a nineteen-year-old college student who described herself to me as "always wanting to dig deeper and look more closely," said, "[For Black women actors] lighter-skinned, skinny, nice hair is more of the forefront. Not just in Hollywood, but even in the Black community. Even within the Black community with Black women and Black men you can hear them talk about light skin versus dark skin. #TeamDarkSkin and #TeamLightSkin. That's a real thing. I always tell people, 'Our president [Donald Trump] doesn't care whether you are light-skinned or dark-skinned.' [Racists] don't care. They see everyone as Black, so it doesn't matter" (EJ). EJ is articulating Breedlove's sentiments at the end of *Self Made*, but she is also echoing insights born out in research. Landor et al. (2013) found that skin tone did not determine the type or severity of racial oppression. They wrote, "Neither lightness nor darkness of skin protects African Americans from or exacerbates the experiences of racial discrimination" (822). However, Landor et al. also found that light-skinned daughters reported higher quality parenting than dark-skinned daughters. This research reinforces other findings regarding light skin bias in families (Wilder 2010).

For Janae, the colorism issue is personal. As a light-skinned woman with Afrocentric awareness, she has been the target for colorist comments within her family and within the Black community. She said she feels frustrated by the discrimination within the Black community based on her light skin. Janae told me,

> I have seen light skin is a privilege *outside* of race, but inside race you have to *prove* yourself if you are light-skinned. In the dominant culture I am seen as Black, but in my race I have had to prove my Blackness. The media tries to represent only light skin. [Skin tone preference is the] elephant in the room. In this season of *Grown-ish* (2020) there is finally a dark-skinned girl. So, I know they have heard the concern [that their cast is too light], but they aren't addressing it in the story line.

Janae and EJ both point to the phenomena of the colorism in the community being named and known, but that change is slow to happen.

TEAM LIGHT SKIN

These complex biases both in favor of and in judgment of skin tones are not easily separated. For Black females, the definition of beauty is often related to skin tone (Celious and Oyserman 2001, Hunter 2002/2007). Colorism affects Black women more than Black men (Hunter 2007). Colorism puts more value on light-skinned aesthetics (Yancey 2004) and Anglo instead of African features (Hunter 2005), but in the context of the Black community, colorism can manifest in an opposite way. As Janae pointed out, the Black community and families often place more value on Afrocentric features and darker skin tones. This issue was overtly discussed in the *Black-ish* episode "Bow-racial" (Season 3). This *Black-ish* episode is attempting to engage in these complex discussions of gender and skin tone, bias and bigotry, in ways similar to *Self Made* and *Bessie*. *Black-ish* puts the discussion of colorism into the context of a family who is exercising these skin tone biases against each other.

Girlfriends, *Black-ish*, *Grown-ish*, *Mixed-ish*, and *Black AF* are Afrocentric series all produced by Kenya Barris[1] but written and directed by a plethora of people—including many women. All of these shows regularly discuss issues of race as they manifest in individuals, families, work, school, and communities. However, Barris has been sharply critiqued because his shows primarily feature actors who are light-skinned. One might argue that *Mixed-ish* could be outside this critique since the family is biracial and so all three children are light. In *Mixed-ish*, the mother (Tika Sumpter) and her sister Dee Dee (Christina Anthony) are played by darker-skinned actors as are some of the oldest girls' school chums. Barris, or his writers, attempted to address this issue of colorism face-on with the *Black-ish* "Bow-racial" episode (Season 3, Episode 8).

The "Bow-racial" episode focused on the light/dark skin fissure in Black individuals, families, and communities. In that episode, each member of the family articulates the bias they see, feel, and have regarding dark and light skin tones. Diane, the youngest daughter and darkest member of the family, is barely visible in the school group photo because she is dark and in the back. What ensues is a complex and lively discussion on colorism in the dominant culture, in the Black community, and in their own family. There are two history lessons inserted within the episode. One is about the mythical Willie Lynch who purportedly created the skin tone hierarchy to separate Blacks; the other is about Thomas Jefferson, "house slaves v. field slaves," and anti-miscegenation laws. Dre delivers these mini-lessons to the audience. He says, "Black people come in many shades from Mariah Carey to Wesley Snipes. . . . Sometimes we even discriminate against each other. It's called Colorism. . . . People are color struck all over the world. (He offers the examples of Asia, India, Latin America)." These voice-over history lessons are narrated by the father with quirky, entertaining graphics and educate the audience, deeping the nuances of colorism.

The family starts to discuss colorism within their ranks. Junior declares that his family is colorist. "I am just saying the light-skinned people in this family don't get treated properly." Ruby, the grandmother, responds by saying, "Light-skinned people don't have problems." When Rainbow protests, Dre snipes, "Calm down, Team Light Skin." Rainbow asks whether it would be OK for her to make dark-skinned jabs. Ruby argues making jest of being light is not the same as making fun of being dark because of the colorist preference for light skin. "Light skin is the Black standard of beauty. . . . I would gladly trade some light-skinned jokes for light-skinned privilege," says Ruby. Rainbow fires back that the dominant culture still categorizes her as Black. "When I walk down the street, people don't see a light-skinned woman, they see a Black woman." Junior rings in by adding gender bias to the conversation, saying to his father, "You love light-skinned women, but you think light-skinned men are soft." Ruby exclaims, "What is everyone crying about? Are the light skins crying beige tears?" Her comment is cutting, implying that her light-skinned family members are whiney, emotionally fragile, and immature.

Just as things are getting heated, Diane, the darkest member of the family, interjects, "Since when did you (referring to Ruby and Dre) become dark-skinned. No one in the family is as a dark as me. That is the problem. It is everywhere I look (cut to a clip of her getting a light bandage placed on her knee), it is everywhere I go (cut to her admiring some red lipstick and the clerk steering her to a neutral shade); it is everyone I talk to (cut to a market scene where a woman comments on her tone)." Ruby retrieves a photo album.

> I was the darkest one in my family. They were Creoles . . . they were all light enough to pass the brown paper bag test . . . . They were evil to my father. And they were evil to me. I had to play by myself in the back so my dark skin and nappy hair didn't embarrass my family. I can still remember the nursery rhymes: "If you are light, you are right, if you're brown, get down; if you are Black, get back."

This "nursery rhyme" surfaces in several other films/programs, across genres, an imbedded part of Black culture, taught to children as a way of unwittingly embedding colorism in generation after generation. In *Self Made*, we hear Madame C. J. Walker muttering this same rhyme as she is betrayed by lighter-skinned women (Episode 3). One of my respondents, a sixty-five-year-old grandmother and accountant in Ohio, said, "We grew up saying the 'If you are light, you all right . . . if you Black, get back" as a jump rope chant. It was just something kids said. We didn't realize what we were saying, but there it was, over and over" (Ta'Nisha).

In *Black-ish*, Dre is a father of children who have a range of skin tones, so he attempts to shut down the discussion, even as he often makes comments about his wife's lighter skin that disparage her. In the episode that addresses colorism, he declares, "Willie Lynch may not be real, but he was real today and we will not allow that in the house anymore." The end of the episode includes Dre's voice-over, "Colorism is our secret shame and the pain it causes keeps growing because we rarely talk about it. . . if we talk about it our wounds will heal . . . nothing gets better in the shadows." Just as in *Self Made*, the lessons of color bias in "Bow-racial" are clear: the moral of the story is that Black people need to stop dividing each other according to skin tone. The irony, of course, is that throughout the *Black-ish* series, Dre regularly comments on the fragility of his wife, the un-Blackness of Bow, in asides that point to her light skin. These asides are supposed to be funny, but they codify the very colorism he speaks against so strongly in this episode. Further critique is that Barris, upon whom the character Dre is based, has been criticized for his proclivity to cast light-skinned actors in his productions. Perhaps Barris, in a way, alludes to this preference for light Blacks in the *Black-ish*, *Mixed-ish*, and *Grown-ish* titles: the "ish" implies the show/characters are "not very Black" due to the lighter shades of the leads' skin.

The color of the mother in Black-ish (Rainbow played by Tracyee Ellis Ross) is regularly the target of teasing comments by the darker-skinned father, Dre. He references her "light-skinned privilege" in their exchanges: "I'm sorry. Do they not talk that way in Light Skinsylvania?" (Season 1, Episode 22: "Please Don't Ask, Please Don't Tell"). This is one example of several different quips that Dre makes alluding to derision of Bow's light-skinned fragility and privilege. On one hand, these shows do an amazing job of parsing out the complexities of skin tone issues and other fraught issues regarding race, class, gender, sexuality, and color. However, Barris has been the target of much critique for what is seen to some as unapologetic colorism in his casting. One woman said, "[His show Black AF] is more 'Biracial AF' . . . with pretty, curly hair. But that fits the 'black people on t.v.' guidelines [of light skin] so . . ." (ShanTale). Another respondent, Eboni, echoed this critique. "Kenya only chooses one darker-skinned character per cast, literally one; except for Girlfriends there hasn't been much dark skin representation from him." Eboni and ShanTale are not alone in their views. When Barris promoted Black AF in December 2019, four months before the show premiered on video-on-demand platform Hulu, Barris was unceremoniously blasted on Twitter and other social media platforms. One Twitter post read, "Sir, we've supported these iterations of your paper bag test black families . . . the majority of black ppl are not represented on these 'black shows' " ("Unbought and Unbossed" 2019). Barris fired back on Twitter by saying the show reflects his Black family and he wasn't interested in "filling quotas." The unwillingness to see an issue with his "color struck" preferences, even as his characters talk in detail about such issues across many of his shows, was annoying to many. Barris further dug in his heels by tweeting, "to cast people like some kinda skin color Allstar game would actually do more harm than good" (Barris 2019).

Barris did not articulate how casting darker characters to star in his programs would do "more harm than good." The lack of deep chocolate skin in Barris's shows may indicate that his target audience is really more white than Black. However, even as some critique Barris for his light-skinned bias, his shows offer value in the overt conversations about issues such as race, colorism, sexism, homophobia, and class alongside the complexities of how these issues manifest in Black relationships, families, and communities.

Eboni, in her thirties and a single entrepreneur with a social media presence celebrating bigger female bodies, said:

> What I love about *Black-ish* is we get to see an all-Black family and they tackle different concepts. The one episode I really liked was the feminist one (Season 6, Episode 3: "Feminisn't"). Zoey was getting into feminism and they didn't really acknowledge that Black women used to be slaves. A white woman said, "Well, this is the most oppressed women have ever been." Then another episode with the youngest daughter [Diane] was about how she wanted to wear her hair: natural or not (Season 6, Episode 11: Hair Day). And then another [episode was about] recognizing her chocolate skin. And that was probably really helpful for young girls. The family is made up of multiple shades [of skin] so I thought that was really helpful for young girls who are going through that [having a skin tone darker than most in their family]. . . . I was glad they brought that to light. (Eboni)

Grown-ish, a spin-off of *Black-ish*, follows Zoey, the oldest daughter, to college at a predominantly white institution. The show features a mostly Black college friend group (with one white lesbian and one politically conservative Latinx from Cuba), but all of them are relatively light-skinned. Barris' light-skin dominance was noted by Janae. "On *Grown-ish*, Zoey's character has been bothering me this season (2020). She is not recognizing her light privilege. The producer [Barris] has this tendency with Black-orientated shows: for the women and girls it is paper bag or lighter. The cast is all light with a new idea" (Janae). Janae makes a good point, and she is enough of an astute viewer to understand having a male producer may have a hand in the preference for light-skinned female actors. Although the show is primarily written by women (there are more women than men listed under the writing credits between 2018 and 2020; there are an equal number of male and female directors), the producer would ultimately make the casting choices. The types of issues and conversations being addressed in the show would be the purview of the writers. How these scripts are staged and filmed would be largely the directors' choices. With *Grown-ish*, we see light-skinned privilege (casting choice) juxtaposed against storylines that focus on issues of sex, gender, race, size, economic, political, and skin tone discriminations (writing choices). Considering all of the perspectives in any one production, the issue of colorism is complex and multi-dimentional, impossible to escape.

Being "color struck." #SkinTeams. Pigmentocracies. The biases and hierarchies of colorism are playing out in varied ways in contemporary shows, often in surprising and unpredictable turns and flips. One could say although there is still a tendency to cast light-skinned women, particularly if the director is white or male, there is evidence in some storylines to addressing light-skinned bias in writing, or casting, or both (*Grown-ish, Black-ish, Bessie, Self Made*). We can also see movement in that darker-skinned female actors are getting more prominent roles both on smaller screens and in Hollywood films such as *Black Panther, Harriet, Fences,* and *Us*. One might argue that there is but a handful of darker-skinned female actors who are getting lots of play, but these popular stars are paving the way so that other directors become aware of the colorism issue. Issa Rae, a darker-skinned woman who is now starring in Hollywood films such as *The Photograph* (2020) and *Love Birds* (2020), made a place for herself through her self-produced YouTube series, offering one example of alternative avenues available to women traditionally locked out of the Hollywood's light-skinned preference. The conversations and critical awareness that will change the #TeamLightSkin versus #TeamDarkSkin divide have begun and are happening in spaces that are both outside and inclusive of major entertainment industries. Traditional stereotypes of the Tragic Mulatto have been replaced by complex characters of all skin tones. In her truest sense, the Tragic Mulatto, a female character who is bereft of love and community, rejected by both whites and Blacks, has been replaced by complex conversations about race, gender, and colorism. Certainly biases exist, but the conversations about these skin tone biases generate awareness that serves to change perceptions and critiques of those biases both within and outside of Black culture. Betina, in her forties and a director for a nonprofit, told me, "I am very aware of the colorism thing. I didn't realize until my late teens and early twenties how big of an issue colorism is in our community. We are living in this. We use hashtags: #TeamLightSkin, #TeamDarkSkin. . . . I saw it in my kids' middle school. We never realize how degrading that is for Black women. We are so beautiful. I wish we knew that." Perhaps these productions, their fans, and critics, by calling attention to skin tone biases, particularly in the way females are portrayed and treated, will help us realize that beauty.

NOTE

1. Although Kenya Barris is a light-skinned Black man and therefore outside of the focus of my media analysis, each episode is written and directed by different people, many of them Black women. Therefore, I include an analysis of the shows he produces here as it relates to colorism.

Chapter 3

All the Single Ladies

Sex and the Single Woman

Although iconic and catchy, seemingly impossible to resist singing along with, Beyoncé's song celebrating "All the single ladies" is anything but liberatory. She sings/raps, "If you liked it, you shoulda put a ring on it" implying if the unnamed man Beyoncé is singing to enjoyed being with her, he should have married her, claiming ownership. Otherwise, she is free to see whomever she wants. What is equally regressive is the use of "it"—referring to not only a woman, but her sexuality, or the relationship between two people. This idea that a man can own a woman if only he marries her speaks of patriarchal ownership of women. Considering the history of white ownership of Black bodies and lives, the idea of marriage creating ownership of Black women by Black men is even more troubling. Moultrie (2018) defines this sexual restriction of women through marriage as:

> coerced monogamy . . . does not just refer to the expectation of heterosexual black marriage but is concerned with all forms of compulsory coupling that restrict sex and sexuality within certain parameters in order for sexual behaviour to be considered moral. Coerced monogamy differs from compulsory coupling because the former highlights the reality of power structures rooted in hegemonic sex and gender ideologies, which reinforce cisgender heterosexual marriage as not only a cultural force but normative—and everything else as abnormal. (233)

Instead of coerced monogamy, Black women should be free to embrace their sexuality and resist regulating it to fit inside patriarchal constructs. Moltrie continues, "a more expansive womanist erotic relationality is necessary that celebrates sexual honesty and responsibility beyond monogamy or heterosexual marriage" (244). The model that Moltrie proposes is present in many shows and films created by Black women since 2015. These shows/films are those that are popular with the young Black women I interviewed. For women who I interviewed in their forties and beyond or those who are in their thirties and happily partnered/married, these shows may not be as appealing. But for the young, single female demographic shows such as *Insecure*[1] (HBO, 2017–2020), *She's Gotta Have It* (Netflix, 2017–2019), *BMJ* (BET, 2016–2019), *High Fidelity* (Hulu, 2020), *Twenties* (BET, 2020), and *Chewing Gum* (Channel 4, 2015–2017) are keenly interesting due to the open and honest ways Black female sexuality is portrayed and celebrated.

Through these women-directed/produced/written shows, viewers in their teens, twenties, and thirties will learn what it means to be Black, female, and sexual. One of my younger respondents told me:

> We are all battling insecurity. I had a friend who wanted to get surgery for her boobs. Society wants you to change to fit in: smaller waist, bigger butt, bigger boobs. When I was 16, I started watching the Kardashians. I started thinking, "Look at her. Her lips are full and mine are little. Look at her nose. It ain't flat like mine." Everyone has this expectation of what a Black woman is supposed to look like. But that is why I love *Insecure* and *She's Gotta Have It*. . . . I love characters like those. They are so lost, but also so intelligent and woke. [Nola and Issa] say "This is who I am; love me or leave me." I love everything about those shows. They are not scared to voice their opinions. They are not scared to step out the box and do what they want or need. (Michelle, 23, single, St. Louis)

Young Black women like Michelle have access to a plethora of shows and films that offer empowering versions of young women exploring their sexuality, openly discussing female pleasure (and frustration), and doing so in the context of supportive girlfriends. The ones that are written/directed/produced by Black women often offer healthier and progressive ways of being. Jones (1993) articulated the importance of media consumption in defining sexual mores:

> With well over half of moviegoers under the age of 18 (and African American youth disproportionately represented in that number), the motion picture industry is now arguably the chief socializing agent of this society, often preempting the power of schools, churches, even families, to prescribe behavior, establish values, and impart grave societal information. (248)

Jones' attention to "moviegoers" may be outdated as now streaming services have overtaken the way people access films, but the statement is clear: young people are learning from screens more than from families, churches, and schools. Programming that features independent young Black women openly exploring and owning their sexuality can change young people's views of sexuality and compulsory heterosexuality. Whereas, in the past, young Black women were burdened with "respectability politics" regarding their sexuality and shackled to damaging stereotypes such as Jezebels, Sapphires, and Hoe, defining Black female sexuality as voracious, dangerous, aggressive, and destructive, particularly for white men, today Black women are offered something different. Many of today's Black female characters are defining and exploring their own sexuality, talking about sexual pleasure, and parsing out the complicated relationships they choose with a tight cadre of girlfriends in ways that deviate sharply from past stereotypes of what it means to be a sexually active Black woman looking for romance.

Some of the characters are looking for love; others just want some hot sex. But either way, these shows portray women as seeking relationships, sexual and romantic, on their terms. Drayah, a college film production major, told me that she immediately related to Nola Darling in *She's Gotta Have It* because of the dual struggles with relationships and making her way as an artist. Drayah said, "*She's Gotta Have It* allowed you to go deeper in everything. She gave me a sense of what the questions are that I have now. . . . I AM a struggling artist. Nola Darling is someone who is trying to make it in the career I am in. I see how being a young female artist affects her social life. The theme is 'dudes really frustrate you.' They try to take away your power and put in a box. Naw, I have something for that." Drayah theorized that hip-hop culture had paved the way for shows like *She's Gotta Have It*. "Now you have women talking about this stuff (sex, relationships, being Black and female). We have moved into a different era. I am doing it [having sex] because I want to do it."

Through these programs, young women like Drayah and Michelle feel empowered. That is not to say there aren't flaws with these shows, such as predominantly heteronormative story lines. Yet there is much to celebrate. The availability of several different Black female character-driven series created by young Black women themselves is reason to believe there has been a sea change. To be clear, just because it is produced by a Black woman and featuring a Black female protagonist is not always cause for celebration or empowering perspectives. But these programs set a standard that is positive and empowering regarding young women and sexual liberation. In Lena Waithe's *Twenties* (BET, 2020), one of the featured female characters says, it is important to watch and support Black women's programming. "I'm just glad it exists. . . . We need to support Black shit," Marie says. Another friend, Nia, agrees, "I just want to see Black love." Hattie is the lone dissenter (she doesn't like the *BMJ*-esque show called *My Bae*). "No. We need to support good shit that just happens to be Black." Yes, Hattie, but most of this *is* "good shit" including complex female characters who are experimenting with their sexuality and talking about it openly with their girlfriends who act as sounding boards and support systems. More than one of the young women I interviewed remarked upon the power of seeing these characters with a community of friends who supported her. Trinity, a young woman attending school in the Washington, D.C., area, said, "They all have these friend groups that keep them real. They have lots of fun together, but they also speak the truth to each other." From the young women I interviewed I heard again and again how much they loved these shows featuring strong, smart women who were taking control of their lives and their romances, typically with the help of close and long-term female friendships, creating a model of feminist sister-hood, Black-on-Black love, and sexual exploration.

OWNING HER SEXUALITY MEANS SHE COMES FIRST

A scene in the fourth season of *Insecure* opens with Issa on a bed having vig-orous sex with Calvin, a nice man who she occasionally fucks. She orgasms first and he instructs her to "push my booty button" (anus) so he can come. She complies, a good partner, even as she is a bit unnerved. When they have finished sex, she casually looks for something to wipe her hand on. It's then he tells her he can't find the condom. She thinks it is still inside her and goes into the bathroom to fish it out. She catches her own eye in a hand mirror. "I'm not mad, just disappointed. Yeah, me too, bitch." The condom splots out on the mirror (Season 4, Episode 1: Lowkey Pause). The scene ends in classic Issa: she is addressing herself in the mirror, stating her truth and her inner, more sensible Issa talks back. But more than that, the scene is signifi-cant that Issa orgasms first. She chooses lovers who are certain to make sure she experiences pleasure and she, herself, is determined to seek pleasure and to give pleasure. The level of trust between these two partners (she coming first; he telling her what pleases him and her reaching to meet that desire without judgment) is pro-woman, feminist, and sex-positive, a direct contrast to stereotypes of Black female sexuality in the WSCP.

What would Black female sexuality look like outside the context of the white supremacist patriarchy? Can we even imagine it? Perhaps not, but we can work against the definitions of Black female sexuality as defined by the WSCP. Women can seek pleasure; women can achieve orgasms first; women can openly discuss what pleases them because they know: they masturbate without shame or guilt. Women seek pleasure and connection on their own terms. Black women seek Black partners. In this new, pro-feminist version of Black female sexuality, desire and sex are not couched in notions of "respect-ability politics" where women's desires and orgasms come second (if at all) and men—within the context of a committed relationships/marriage—reap the benefits. Nor are they couched in Black women as wanton seductresses of white men. By rejecting respectability politics of Jezebel/Sapphire/Hoe stereotypes, Black women reject the myth that Black women have to depend on men to define their sexuality. Instead of reinscribing these harsh and bitter stereotypes of fickle women who use their sex to entrap men, characters such as Nola Darling, Mary Jane Paul, Issa Dee, Tracey Gordon, and all their friends own their sexual desire, their erotic, and their right to both refuse and engage with partners. Their freedom is a model for young Black female audience members to reflect on and consider, even as these characters are often fumbling about and making wild, cringe-worthy connections. Regardless, their sexual forays are their own, forging new ways of considering Black female sexual liberation, fraught with humanness, and social dynamics that can't be ignored. In addition, what is important to note about these characters is that they are relying on a strong group of girlfriends, sisterhoods that act as counsels and cheerleaders, to their sexual exploration. This strong dependence and connection with women rang true for my respondents. One young woman told me, "When I am called out by a man, I question his motives. But when it is a woman, like my momma, I know she don't want anything from me. When they (girlfriends, sisters, mother) tell you something it holds more weight. I became more conscious of how I come off to people when a woman calls me out. It makes me want to be better" (Drayah).

This connection, trust, dependence, and love between women adds to the intimacy of their lives and acts as a safe place, a sounding board, a coterie of sisterhood that offers refuge and often hard truths to anchor them. This love between Black women (sisterly, friendly, maternal, or romantic) is important to defining the Black female erotic. Dillard (2016) writes these places of sisterhood and female-to-female connection act as a way to affirm Black women's identity and worth: "Even as we are disregarded by others, we can also be and think . . . . We form these spaces and places of recognition and love and hope that declare that our lives matter" (Dillard 2016, 203). In an episode of *Insecure*, Issa and her best friend, Molly, are talking about failed romance. Issa tentatively speculates that perhaps Molly's vagina is broken. Later in the episode, drunk at a bar, Issa begins an impromptu rap about her "broken pussy." "Maybe it's dry as hell; maybe it really smells. Broken Pussy. Maybe it's really rough. Maybe it's had enough. Broken Pussy." Although the moment initially angers Molly, the rap—which goes viral and causes Issa much embarrassment—serves to show both women that the problem is not with them and their sexuality, but the men they have been with. When Molly goes on a date with a white man she hooked up with through a dating app, Molly asks if he wants to go to coffee and he says what he really wants to do is fuck. She says, "You think because you know some fancy wine I'm gonna fuck you? I didn't break my pussy. Niggas like you broke my pussy" (Season 1, Episode 2). Molly and Issa quickly discover the problem is not with their sexuality or their vaginas; the problem is with men who only want to fuck with little concern for their pleasure. The series shows how they attempt to change that patriarchal and misogynist dynamic and explore the female erotic. The female erotic, empowered and bold and seeking female pleasure, is in direct contrast to the real restrictions of respectability politics.

"Respectability politics" was a term coined by Evelyn Brooks Higginbotham (1993) in her book *Righteous Discontent: The Women's Movement in the Black Baptist Church, 1880–1920*. Respectability politics refers to a Black woman who assimilates to the dominant WSCP as a way of gaining privilege. It is often related to acting in ways that the WSCP defines as "good manners" or "appropriate behavior" and sexual discretion. Behavior associated with respectability politics reinforces white, patriarchal cultural mores, including the mores of a prim and proper "lady" who is submissive and quiet in the bedroom, only engaging in sex as an act of committed or marital engagement, and is a proud member of a Black church. The church, a stealth agent for the WSCP, often provides a regulatory function for Black women's sexuality. In the Black church, sex, for women at least, is a marital act and does not include asserting one's desires. This regulatory function of the church on Black female sexuality was noted in an episode of *Insecure* where the girlfriend group was talking about fellatio.

The girlfriends go to a sex toy party and they are listening to someone pitch a workshop on how to fellate a man. Kelli says, "Who gives a blow job with a condom on? Like licking candy in the rapper?"

Issa: "I never fellate without a condom. Keep dicks safe." Kelli admits she hasn't given a blow job since high school. Issa says, "Yeah, honestly, I'm not into it either. I got big teeth. Plus the whole eye contact thing. It is just too intimate. Like I have to really fuck with you to put you in my mouth."

Tiffany: "I really don't understand black women and their hang ups about oral sex."

Issa: "I used to think that guys see Black women as disposable after you give them head. Like you are forever a hoe if you do it."

Kelli: "I blame the church. The Black church."

Issa: "Kelli, you can't do that for everything."

Tiffany: "Why do you think Black men are out here chasing after white women? There is so much power in blow jobs. I am the one fully in control. Every man is into his dick. The closer you get to it, the more control you have. And if you are good at it, the sky's the limit."

Kelli: I'd rather go down on a woman. At least our shit cleans itself." (Season 2, Episode 6)

In this scene of rapid-fire exchanges, there is a lot going on. We understand that some of the women are concerned about using condoms (safe sex), while others aren't. Some believe they will be judged by the men as dispensable for performing oral sex; others believe it can leverage a woman with power, but is not something the woman necessarily enjoys or feels comfortable with ("It's too intimate"). Kelli is quick to attribute some men's baggage about fellatio to the Black church (chaste/good women don't give head). The women allude to the contradiction of wanting to make their own decisions in this complex issue, but they also realize the larger constructs that are telling them to do it; don't do it; if they do it, they are a whore. They want to take control of this sex act so it isn't used against them and they call out white women for being submissive: white women are more deferential to men and give more head and therefore Black men desire them. Kelli categorically rejects that she would give a man head in order to obtain faux power, saying she would rather engage in cunnilingus. It is not the act of oral sex that bothers Kelli but having a man's dick in her mouth feels too close to a subservient, disempowered position to appeal to her. Dicks are "dirty." To put one in her mouth would be an act of self-deprecation. Cunnilingus, however, is devoid of the vexing patriarchal dynamic of men controlling women and therefore is perfectly acceptable to her. This scene stands out because in one short ninety-second exchange all these complex issues are discussed. They may not be fully addressed, but they provide fodder for the audience to continue thinking and talking about the layers of these issues.

Later in the episode, Issa decides she is going to try out this theory of being able to control a man through fellatio by giving Daniel a blow job. When he comes on her face, she is furious. Instead of being in control, she was degraded; her very intent was subverted with his actions and she was put in a subjugated position. In the next episode, Daniel apologizes for ejaculating on Issa's face. But then he says, "We have both done some bad shit." She interprets this as meaning he intentionally ejaculated on her face as some sort of payback for a time when she hurt him. Issa tells him to never call her again, shutting him out immediately and without hesitation (Season 2, Episode 7: Hella Disrespectful). It is obvious to her that he used the sex act as a power play, a way to intentionally degrade her. In fact, we understand that the title of the episode, "Hella Disrespectful" is referring to Daniel's actions. Blow jobs, to be sure, are complicated. And they are not part of respectability politics. Ladies don't do that. But Issa learns that even as she engaged in fellatio with Daniel, he had the upper hand and was the one to demonstrate power over her.

Frank scenes and open conversations about female sexuality such as these serve to open conversations and change attitudes. These scenes are a direct result of women writing, directing, and producing the narratives. Mashell, a

Christian mother of six children, with daughters ranging in age of seven to twenty-two, told me she is glad there is programming that talks so openly and honestly about female sexuality. "They are showing now that it is OK for women to say 'I want it' or 'I need it. I am not married, but I am going to sleep with this person even if it is only for sex because that is what I want right now.' " Mashell, as a woman in her forties, feels this openness about female sexuality is a very new and positive change. When she thought of sex scenes in movies of the past, the women didn't seem to be having any pleasure or it looked fake. She said:

> I always think about men watching [programs where it is only about men's pleasure] and it makes me think we don't matter. [These older movies] show that it is more important for the man to be satisfied and the woman is just there to make sure he is satisfied. Her satisfaction doesn't matter. One of the positive changes I have seen in the way sex and relationships are portrayed is when mistakes happen. Maybe a condom wasn't used or maybe a condom broke, but the woman has enough sense to fix the situation. They take the morning after pill or the panic sets in and you see it. But now it doesn't always end with a pregnancy or being a single mom. I think that is positive. Especially for people Janae's age (college-aged daughter). It shows women going to the pharmacy to purchase the morning after pill. It isn't all shame and dark glasses. It is just matter of fact: I need this.

Mashell is celebrating this new version of empowered female sexuality, defined by women for female pleasure, especially as it relates to her daughters. Although she identifies strongly as a Christian, she is not letting respectability politics shape her attitudes on this topic. The sexual desires and antics of these characters and plots she admires defy the norms of what the church has historically defined as a respectable Black woman. These characters are revising the norm to include sexual freedom. These female characters may be seeking acceptance, approval, and success, but it may not be from men. Their circle of girlfriends, or a single best friend, is often the person or people they are using for counsel. And their counsel is often nonjudgmental in ways that the patriarchy in the form of church, medical establishment, or family is not. When Nola Darling (*She's Gotta Have It*), Issa Dee (*Insecure*), Mary Jane Paul (*BMJ*), and Tracey Gordon (*Chewing Gum*) explore multiple partners and multiple kinds of relationships, they may be casting respectability politics to the wind, but they are doing so with the strong support and advice from their best female friends, thereby subverting the patriarchal order and seeking female spaces to define who they are or what they want to become.

CRINGEY SEX

On *Chewing Gum* (Channel 4, 2015–2017) not only are there no respectability politics in play (other than manifested in Tracey's mother, a good Jehovah's Witness), Tracey openly and wildly engages in both fantasy sex and in-person sex that are explicitly awkward and cringe-worthy. Tracey breaks every rule of what would be considered acceptable female sexuality in the patriarchal structure. But she is no Jezebel in that she is seeking *her* desire, not looking to seduce a man for personal gain or to take him down. She is desperate to learn about and experience sex. She is determined to seduce her Christian boyfriend, but he freaks out and asks her why she is acting so crazy. She says, "I don't know. I'm scared. We haven't done anything. I haven't kissed you. I haven't held you. I haven't sat on your face." He is aghast. "Why would you sit on my face?" She pleads, "I'm, I'm, I'm not sure." Because he is unwilling to satisfy her sexually, she breaks up with him. She knows what she wants and she intends to find someone who will deliver.

Even before she engages in any sexual activity, she wants to present herself as if she knows about sex. In the process, she says horrifically nonsensical and hilarious things. In one episode, she is telling a friend that she has had sex and that Connor (the man she is currently crushing on) has an immense penis. She says, "It's big (she spreads her hands as wide as a five-gallon bucket). It's hard. If he put it up me, it could have come through, out my mouth, yeah, and then I would just have to knot it around itself and then strangle it dead. That's how big it is." Her friend looks on in horror.

Later her friend tries to teach her how to take a "blow job selfie." She demonstrates for Tracey by positioning the phone above her and opening her mouth to a large "O" and looking up into the camera. When Tracey tries it, she makes a pained face and doesn't know what to do with her tongue which fishes in and out of her mouth in odd ways. Her friend says, "Do you want to suck his dick or smile at it?" "Neither." "Tracy, he wants you to push your pussy in his face like you are about to take a shit in it. He wants to get his nose way up in there." Tracey looks a bit disgusted and unsure, "Yeah, I don't think that is normal."

In her pursuit of sexual knowledge, she consistently gets really horrible advice about sex from her girlfriends. One tells her, "If he tries to put it in your bum, just breathe through it. Don't tell him it hurts or he'll dump you." A gay male friend says, "My mother always says, 'Those who love their coffee black, love the taste of semen.' " Tracey takes notes. She is hungry for any and all information she can get, eager to try it all. In another episode, her friends and her friend's mother are addressing a perceived problem with her breasts. The mother says, regarding Tracey's breasts, "I told you to tell her about underwire a long time ago." Tracey's friend furthers the commentary, adding, "They droop . . . earrings dangle; her tits droop; cuz you're always running for the bus." The mother confirms this opinion by exclaiming, "You do! And I worry. I say to myself, 'They are going to be straight on the floor in half a decade.' " The friend, in an attempt to explain these judgements further, tells Tracey, "They are like kiwi . . . all any man wants is two good boobs and a good meal." The second friend chimes in, "Yeah, and if not two good boobs, then four of them," implying that if a woman's breasts are unacceptable, a threesome with another woman is always an option. Tracey takes it all in, for the first time considering that perhaps her breasts won't be appealing. On threesomes, this same friend group tells her, "They all want a threesome, but not with John or Mark." Tracey interjects, "Because they are biblical names." "No! Because their guys!" "If I ever said to a guy, 'look, I'll wiggle my clit while you two do each other,' he would die instantly." Tracey soaks it all up, even as the information from her friends is consistently useless. However, similar to *Insecure*, these women are sharing information and supporting each other, no judgment. The advice may be sound, may be righteously incorrect, or may be simply *bad.* But the community of women is encouraging and supporting, cheering on Tracey to explore her sexuality in any way she wants.

Because Tracey is in hot pursuit of sex, when she learns that her Jehovah's Witness sister, Candice, has had sex with a man before she has, Tracey is incredulous. Candice, like Tracey, is very matter of fact about owning her sexuality. When she is ready to throw off the mantel of her heteronormative, church-defined virginity, she picks up a man off the street. The man Candice randomly selects is a geeky white guy who has no idea why she invites him to her place. After some awkward sips of wine, she says, "OK. I'm ready." "Ready for what?" he asks. "Ready to fuck," she says. He lowers his jaw in surprise and swallows slowly. "You're just going to give it to me?" She says, "I'm not *giving* it to you. We are sharing it." This line indicates Candice's awareness that she owns her sexuality. She has not bought into the Christian/ patriarchal ideology that virginity is "given" to a man. She presents the shocked man with a condom as if it is a communion wafer. She tells him, "I broke my hymen in preparation, so I'll lie down . . . now put it around my knicker area. Now enter the dome. [She clarifies after a pause:] With your penis." He penetrates her and she keeps nattering on; this deflowering is as perfunctory as a pap test. She tells him that it is scientifically proven that intercourse does not stretch the vagina. He tells her to talk less. He facilitates her terrific orgasm and Candice seems pleased with the encounter. She has initiated and driven the sexual experience even though she has never had sex with a man before. Candice is exclusively concerned with her own experience, leaving him to take care of what he desires in the exchange, an important message for the show's female viewers.

When Tracey eventually does have sex, it is with similar gumption and determination, enjoying the experience of finally casting off her virginity. The scene portrays her as expressing giddy delight as she is being fucked from behind by a ripped hottie. The man seems slightly perplexed at her effusive enjoyment, as her thrill is not of the sex per se, but of finally no longer being a virgin. Tracey sings as he thrusts, a wide smile of absolute delight (but not sexual pleasure) on her face, "It's the world of adventure . . . will I smile, will I mourn, now that my hymen has been torn. . . . wet like rain, what will you do to my membrane . . . I don't want this moment to be over." As with Candice, Issa, Molly, and their friends, Tracey embodies a woman in control of how/when/whether she engages in sex, the epitome of female-empowered sexual autonomy.

However, there is one problem with Tracey's choice of male for her intercourse initiation: she chooses a schoolboy who is sixteen. Does this constitute statutory rape? In most places in the United States, it certainly would, giving the finale of Season 2 a rather sinister and dark edge. Why does Tracey choose someone so young? The scene seems to reinforce the stereotype that men are always ready, always willing, and there is no problem when a twenty-five-year-old is fucking a sixteen-year-old, as long as the older partner is female and the younger partner is male. For a show that is billed as a Cringe Comedy, this particular cringe goes too far and is never interrogated, a decidedly un-feminist, #MeToo/#MenToo moment.

This is not the only ick factor in Season 2, however. Later in the season, Candice sleeps with her boyfriend's father. When her boyfriend, Aaron, finds out, he confronts his dad (not Candice). The father informs him he wasn't being disrespectful to Aaron by having sex with Candice because he used a condom. The implication is that just penetration is not really sex or intimate sex. By not ejaculating inside of Candice, the father is informing his son that there is nothing to worry about. The underlying message implies that Candice is up for grabs, sexually, for both father and son and as long as the father wears a condom, no need to get upset.

Similar to the autonomy Candice and Tracey exercise in deciding when, if, or whether to have intercourse with men is a topic of conversation in Lena Waithe's *Twenties*. In the show's first episode, Nia, one of the protagonist's (Hattie's) besties, announces that she is a virgin. When Marie (the other woman in this trio of friends) and Hattie protest, Nia insists that she is going back to being a virgin, not engaging in sex (and by "sex" she means heterosexual intercourse, since she has plenty of sex that includes everything from masturbation to all acts short of penis/vagina penetration). Nia says she is going to remain celibate (re: abstain from heterosexual intercourse) until she finds the right man. Nia sticks to her pledge, at least in Season 1.

Of the three girlfriends, Nia seems to be the one most in control of expressing and demanding what she desires. Marie, although with a long-term male partner, can't seem to ask for what she wants or have open conversations with her partner regarding her dissatisfaction in their sexual relationship. This becomes a point of tension during the first season as Marie suspects her fiancé is secretly gay or at least bisexual. Hattie, similar to characters like Nola Darling (*She's Gotta Have It*), Mary Jane Paul (*BMJ*), Rob (*High Fidelity*), and Issa Dee (*Insecure*), can't seem to get relationships right, struggling through fits and starts, missing out on the decent partner because she is chasing after the beau (Lorraine) who treats her with indifference or ambivalence.

As with the other series, one of the functions of these female friends is to vociferously butt in to each other's sex lives, offering unsolicited and frank advice. However, Marie and Hattie's critiques of Nia often seem unjustified or just wrong. An example is when both Marie and Hattie call Nia crazy because she asks men to bring her their STD tests before she will have sex with them. Why is that crazy? That's smart, safe, self-preserving, and showing that Nia is in control. Marie and Hattie tell Nia that men will be turned off and she will end up crazy and alone. Which men? Loser men who don't respect and care for her? Why would she want to be involved with men like that?

Marie and Hattie also gently mock Nia for her celibacy pledge, telling her it is outdated and dumb. By Season 1, Episode 2: "I've Got the World on a String," Nia is rethinking her commitment to eschewing intercourse. Nia finds herself attracted to a sensitive, dredded, "I don't define myself by the way I make money," new-age guy. When he walks her home, he asks if he can kiss her (consent first). They kiss and he turns away. Nia says, "If you had a phone, I would text you all the freaky things I planned to do the next time I see you." He says, "I thought you were celibate." She says, "There are plenty of freaky things I can do to you that have nothing to do with intercourse." He says, "Don't text about it. Be about it." In this scene, we witness a respectful exchange between the two sweethearts. The man asks before kissing, allowing the woman to express desire, not assuming or taking. We see Nia articulating her desires, negotiating with her partner regarding how to fulfill her needs. We watch as he clarifies her position, showing that not only did at some point Nia tell him she was celibate, but he respected that, and is now asking for further clarification. This scene models the best type of sexual communication between a couple that respects each other. In the era of #MeToo and more awareness of issues regarding consent in the context of romantic connections, these sorts of deliberate and open conversations are tremendously essential. Nia is modeling a woman who is honest, forthright, and able to communicate what she wants; her sweetheart is modeling a respectful partner who listens, asks for clarification when he doesn't understand, and does not assume access, even to a kiss.

CAN'T KEEP A MAN OR DON'T
WANT TO KEEP A MAN?

One of the stereotypes that emerged in many of my interviews was regarding single Black women. The stereotype is that these women are single because they are too demanding of Black men. In shows such as *High Fidelity, BMJ, Insecure*, and *She's Gotta Have It*, one could argue that these women manifest that stereotype, but if one takes a closer look, the nuances powerfully negate this claim. These characters are not "hard on men"; they are sexually liberated and redefining the version of Black female sexuality on their own terms. They are not manifesting the stereotype of fickle, hard-to-please Black woman; they are stating what they want from a relationship and making sure they get what they want. However, not all viewers would agree with this analysis. One of my respondents, who describes herself "a Black feminist theologian whose emphasis is on philosophical constructions of god in the Black church" did not like how Mary Jane Paul was portrayed. She said,

> I did not like *Being Mary Jane*. It was poorly written and predictable. I'm tired of the cliché that strong Black women can't find a man, that you have to choose between a career and a relationship. You can't have both. I didn't enjoy the between sexy and classy that the main character was trying to portray. There were a lot of respectability issues with that show. It was hard for me to watch. For me, it represented Black Boogie. You can't be hood and be Black excellence. (Veronica)

Although I would agree with Veronica that Mary Jane Paul engages in some respectability politics in the way she assimilates to dominant ideas of success, I also see Mary Jane as a character who is owning her sexuality, engaging with various lovers to explore her personal erotic, and making sure relationships are on her own terms. Yes, she is upper class ("boogie"), but she also has an Afrocentric streak that runs through her identity, from the feminist/ Black activist quotes on post-its that paper her living space, to ongoing discussions about race, class, gender, sexuality, and sexual orientation that permeate the story lines, to an involved Black family that is dealing with tough issues of teen pregnancy and motherhood, infidelities, addiction cycles, and unemployment. We see Mary Jane code switch from her work persona to her friend/family persona in language, dress, and affect, a reality that exists for most Black women who make their careers in the corporate culture.

The other theme Veronica points to ("black women can't find a man") was a comment many of my respondents made when examining shows such as *Insecure, High Fidelity*, and *BMJ*. Many women I interviewed described a discomfort or a cringe when they felt a film or series depicted a Black woman as not knowing how to love or be loved, not being able to keep or know a "good man" when she has one. Most of this discomfort was expressed as a cringe against a stereotype, imagining an audience whose beliefs of Black women would be reinforced. *BMJ*, *High Fidelity*, *Scandal*, and *Insecure* were the predominant shows that were cited as examples of Black women who didn't know how to love/be loved by Black men. All four of these series fall into the category of "Black-Black" productions. Drake (2019) coins the term "Black-Black film" to refer to:

> the film's plot, casting, and directorship are *not* marketed around selling a stereotypical or familiar narrative of blackness to a white audience. Films fall into the category of black-black films not simply because the cast is all or predominately black and the director is black; they fall into this category because the themes, language, and ways of being are not concerned about white accessibility and instead are invested in portraying a black interiority that is complex, intimate, and unapologetically black. (165–166, emphasis added)

The distinction for Drake—and for many of the women I interviewed—is this question of audience and Afrocentricity. If the audience is conceived of or perceived of as Black women, the viewing experience and message drawn may differ radically from a film where the perceived or conceived audience is white or Black men. The women I talked to were most concerned with who *else* was watching and what *they* might take away from these shows, worried that the resonating message would be one of "Black women are too demanding to keep a good Black man."

Like most stereotypes, this one was not generated by the targeted group, Black women. Black *men* have often been the people who have defined Black women as hard to please. Writers/Personalities such as Tim Alexander, Steve Harvey, Jimi Izreal, and Hill Harper are Black men who have been very vocal in perpetuating the myth that heterosexual Black women are difficult to please and this is why they are more often single or why some Black men seek out white women. Black women have been denied the opportunity to speak to these issues or if they have spoken, they are largely ignored. In reality there are real reasons that, demographically, there are fewer Black men for heterosexual Black women with whom to partner. School to prison pipelines in poor school districts, a criminal justice system bent on imprisoning Black men, and a Black masculinity that is primarily defined outside the character traits of caring, nurturing, and attentive all create a dearth of Black male partners. The white supremacist patriarchy is powerful. By defining Black masculinity with traits that turn boys away from education and subsequently "white collar" professions the WSCP socializes Black boys against traits that would make them appealing partners to Black women. In addition to this dynamic, the patriarchy gives more credence to male voices and therefore Black male voices (even when speculating on why Black women can't find suitable Black mates) will be given privilege over the voices and experiences of Black women. As Wanzo (2011) writes, "The regulatory narrative that emerges [from Black men] is one that privileges black men's reading of black relationships, and faults black women for their unmarried status" (10). Programs such as *Insecure, BMJ, Twenties, High Fidelity,* and even *She's Gotta Have It* speak against that stereotype. These programs show the complexities of what heterosexual Black women face when attempting to engage with potential mates. These shows speak against myth by writing, directing, and producing their *own* stories about Black women and relationships. The results of Black women behind the camera yield a different narrative. Black women are not "difficult to please"; rather, they are honoring their own needs, their own lives, and refusing to subjugate themselves to the patriarchal narratives that insist they must "settle for less" rather than seek what they desire. The stereotype of Black women as fickle, perpetuated by some Black men, relates to what Collins points to as the weak man/ strong woman binary. Collins (2004) argues that the stereotype of weak Black man who needs a strong Black woman to care for him is a directive from white supremacy where, in white culture, the stereotype is flipped (a weak white woman needs a strong white man to care for her). By flipping the script, so to speak, the white supremacist patriarchy further "others" Black people by suggesting Black men are weak and Black women need to take care of them. This dynamic of weak man/strong woman is the hidden assumption behind the critique that some Black men make when the myth that "Black women are difficult to please or won't accept Black men" is trotted out; the underlying belief is that it is the strong Black woman's role to care for/accept the Black man regardless of whether he is an equal partner or not. Hidden within the misogynist weeds of "Black women are difficult to please and too picky" is the belief that Black men are owed a Black woman to take care of them. Collins writes, Black men and women need to "see one another in honest and loving ways, reversing the process of dehumanization associated with oppression" (2004, 306). Morgan (1999), in her book, writes about the curse of the social conditioning of the "STRONGBLACKWOMAN" and how it manifests in the stereotype that Black women must caretake Black men. Morgan writes that she felt socially conditioned:

> to live my life as BLACKSUPERWOMAN Emeritus. That by the sole virtues of my race and gender I was supposed to be the consummate professional, handle any life crisis, be the dependable rock for every soul who needed me, and, yes . . . require less from my lovers than they did from me because after all, I was a STRONGBLACKWOMAN and they were just ENDANGEREDBLACKMEN. (87)

Wyatt (2008) does an excellent job pairing Collins' theories with autobiographic texts by Black women who articulate the lived dangers of internalizing these white supremacist patriarchal stereotypes of Black gender politics.

In the shows and films analyzed in this chapter, we examine how sexuality and relationships between Black men, Black women, and white men are told. When Black women are writing and directing these stories, they have the opportunity to shift the perspective and begin to unpack and retell the narrative of Black romance, sex, and love from a womanist point of view.

Even as characters such as Issa, Molly (*Insecure*); Tracey, Candice (*Chewing Gum*); Marie, Nia, Hattie (*Twenties*), Rob (*High Fidelity*), and Mary Jane (*BMJ*) move through several fleeting romantic and sexual relationships, they are revising the narrative of Black female sexuality. By engaging in respectful ways (even if fleeting) with partners who similarly seem to respect them, these representations of Black love are complicated and caring, something that could be seen as revolutionary in the context of the WSCP. Wanzo (2011) writes of Black love as always seen in the context of the long history of Black representation that is "so overrun with negative stereotypes it can be difficult to produce a narrative that does not gesture to some racist history—particularly when fit into the conventional generic narratives that dominate the mass media . . . challenges of fitting black people into generic fantasies" (2011, 4). The writers, directors, and producers of these shows are attempting to do just that: create something other than generic racist, sexist, and homophobic narratives.

In looking at the complex lives of the characters (friends, family, lovers, work), the female characters portrayed in these shows refuse to be seen as generic or conventional. Instead they feel real, if flawed and messy. A single, heterosexual thirty-something respondent told me:

> I just love *Insecure*. For me it is about finding herself. I had a relationship very similar to hers. What happens a lot with Black women is we excel a lot more than our male counterparts. We struggle in our love for our Black men. It reminded me so much of past relationships I and my friends have had with men. We try really hard to motivate them, but they don't know quite how to motivate themselves. I went through a situation and my best friend was going through a similar situation [with Black partners who were unmotivated]. We both were in our relationship for five years. Now we have come out of it, we are single, and we realize that is time we won't get back. We invest all this energy in trying to uplift someone but in the process, we end up losing ourselves. (Eboni)

Eboni is articulating the ways in which the Issa Dee character was important to her because she identified as a Black woman who feels she is struggling to find a mate her equal in drive and direction. In addition to relationship dynamics, Eboni is very aware of the tension borne of the stereotype that "Black women don't know how to be loved." As a single woman in her thirties, Eboni is frustrated by this conundrum. Does she manifest a stereotype or just want to honor her criteria for a mate? Eboni is a strong, outspoken, business entrepreneur who is direct and open in her communication. She lamented that it was difficult to find a relationship and that the dance leading to a relationship often flummoxed her and her friends, particularly because of the toxic stereotype that Black women are difficult to be with.

As with the Angry Black Woman stereotype, there is no way out of the Fickle Black Woman stereotype. If she accepts the lesser male, she will find herself unfulfilled, taking care of an adult instead of having a partner. If she rejects this role, she is told she is too hard to please, fickle, and difficult. Take the character Robyn Brooks (Rob) from *High Fidelity* (2020) for example. Rob could be a character many young women might relate to in that she is trying to figure out love and relationships. She has a man she loves (Mac), but she is too young to commit. When he proposes, she panics and disappears for the night. He leaves for London without her and she is left both kicking herself and saying, "Fuck it; I'll get on with it" and ends up with several unsatisfying relationships. To characterize this as being fickle would be to refuse the nuances and self-critique that Rob engages in, to neglect the reality of what it is like to be a woman in her twenties or thirties who wants what she wants but is penned in by racist, patriarchal, misogynistic versions of womanhood and relationship expectations. In the first episode of the series, Rob chronicles her five "great loves" with much critical self-reflection:

> Justin Kitt (number 4). He loved Jay-ze, Eminem and the Dave Mathews band. So . . . he was kind of an asshole. He was also a standup comedian . . . . In retrospect, we were both kinda assholes . . . [Number 5 on the Top 5 Heartbreak list is Mac] We stayed in and made love. We went out and had fun. We just *got* each other. We built a life together. . . [Cut to Mac telling Rob he is "completely in love" with her. She tells him she loves him.] What went wrong? He moved to London after all. Without me. To tell the truth, I was totally out of my depth and I didn't want to do that again. So for the past year I have been paddling around in the shallow end . . . . The ugly truth of the matter is this. We suddenly heard that the world was going to end in 24 hours. The people I would call were my parents, Simon [employee/friend], Charise [employee/friend], I guess. But I would be calling them all to confess that I was spending the next 23 hours with Mac. (Season 1, Episode 1: Top 5 Heartaches)

Thus begins the series, a tale focused on Rob and her reflections, growth, back-slides, and fumbles regarding matters of the heart. Through it all, though, the audience doesn't see Rob as fickle or hard to please; rather she is a young woman attempting to find her way, unsure of what she can offer to a partner or what she wants from a partner. It isn't as simple as saying Rob can't keep a man (or woman). Like so many of these characters created by women/for women, she is working through her twenties, growing and maturing, and figuring out what she wants/needs in a mate. In order to do this, most of us try out a few models before we decide. And we learn how to be better partners along the way.

This stereotype of the fickle young Black woman is addressed in more than one *Insecure* episode. In one situation Issa tells Molly she wonders whether Molly really wants to be with a man because she is always finding issue with something he does or is. Molly's current complaint about her beau is that he doesn't talk enough or "open up" to her. Issa says, "Aren't you tired? Cuz I'm tired for you." Issa is telling Molly she needs to take a different approach and work on a relationship. When Molly seeks the counsel of her girlfriends, they encourage her to slow down on the sex and get to know him emotionally. Tiffany says, "You gonna put that pussy on pause?" and laughs. Molly says she is and is irked when her friends are skeptical. Issa says, "OK, girl. Mute that monkey" (Season 4, Episode 1: Lowkey Pause). Molly hears what her friends are saying and attempts to work on the relationship instead of simply hooking up; unfortunately, the beau ends up breaking up with her because he doesn't want something serious. Ergo, disruption of the fickle woman stereotype: Molly decides to work on the relationship and approach it more maturely, but it is the man who wants something superficial.

In another *Insecure* episode, a woman named Tasha invites her new beau, Lawrence (Issa's ex), to a family BBQ. Instead of engaging with the family, Lawrence leaves, ghosting her. When Tasha catches up with him, she doesn't mince words, "You a fuck nigga. No, you worse than a fuck nigga. You a fuck nigga who thinks he's a good dude" (Season 2, Episode 3). Tasha is not playing at sex; she wants a relationship and she is letting Lawrence know she won't settle for less. She will not tolerate disrespect.

Women in these shows seek and demand what they want and need. In *Twenties* (HBO 2020), Hattie, the lesbian protagonist, treats Idina, a barista who is sweet on her, callously. Idina shyly makes overtures to an oblivious Hattie. While Hattie and Idina are talking at the coffee shop, Lorraine—Hattie's trifling crush—unexpectedly shows up with a white guy on her arm. Lorraine embraces Hattie knowingly, asking "Who's that?" nodding toward Idina. Hattie says, "We don't know each other that way." Idina walks off in a huff. Hattie seems stumped. Later she apologizes to Idina. Hattie earnestly explains to Idina that she would like a close friend who isn't straight. Idina makes her annoyance known, saying, "I get it. I'm not your type." Hattie says, "We are both soft studs." Idina corrects her saying *she* isn't soft.

I am a lesbian. That means I like all women. Soft women, masculine women, trans women, Black women, Asian women, Cameroon women . . . so if you want to limit yourself to the type of women you date, that's cool. But I think you should reconsider. Because I know you see me out in the world with my locs and baggy clothes, but you have no idea what I am like behind closed doors, if I like it rough or if I like to take it slow. We got the same anatomy. And I am pretty good at taking care of myself. What makes you think I can't take care of you? Why should you be afraid to try new things? You just might like it. When I take my clothes off, when I take my hair down, you don't know whether I am dominant or submissive.

Hattie repeats that she wants them to be friends, but Idina is having none of it: "I already have enough friends" (Season 1, Episode 8). Idina isn't willing to compromise what she wants, stating clearly and directly to Hattie her position, willing to walk if Hattie can't deliver.

These examples show that these women aren't fickle or hard to please, they simply want good partners who treat them well. In the fourth season of *Insecure*, Issa, after lots of wild escapades, decides she is ready to commit to commitment. She chooses to get back together with Lawrence, the man who—at the beginning of the series—she broke up with because he was directionless and boring. Since then, Lawrence has started on a career. The scene opens with time lapse sequences of Issa and Lawrence on the living room couch over a period of several days or weeks. They are watching television, making love in various places in the room, cuddling, working, talking, and eating. When the sequence breaks, Issa is telling Lawrence that Nathan (former lover, now a friend) contacted her and asks Lawrence if it is OK for her to spend time with Nathan. "I just want to be honest. I don't want to mess this up. Whatever this is. What is it again?" Lawrence turns it back to her, indicating that Issa is in control of defining the relationship. "What do you want it to be?" "I don't know. Are you still wrapped up? Loose ends dangling? Any loose vaginas flappin about?" He assures her there are not.

Later, when she meets up with Nathan at his apartment, it is clear he is annoyed when she tells Nathan she is back with Lawrence. "The one you cheated on?" he jabs. Issa says, "Yeah. We're figuring it out." Nathan chuckles. "I just thought you were over that shit. He seemed one-timey." Issa says, a bit annoyed, "He's not." Nathan snipes, "I hope he keeps his shit together this time." Issa retorts, "Yeah. At least he knows how to use his words and doesn't disappear." Nathan: "I just didn't disappear. I found out I'm bipolar." He tells her he is trying to take care of himself and he wants her in his life. Issa faces a choice: stick with Lawrence or fall back with Nathan. The episode ends with her putting Nathan in the friend zone and recommitting to Lawrence (Season 4, Episode 9: Lowkey Trying). In these two scenes, we see that Issa is defining both relationships in ways that benefit her, not how the men want the relationships defined. She recommits to Lawrence because she wants to, but not before getting his assurance that he is done with his previous girlfriend; she puts Nathan in the friend zone rather than let him guilt her into being with him. She is empathetic regarding his mental health issues, but she has made her choice: Lawrence.

Similar to Issa, Rob is also weighing options and her wants/needs regarding with whom she engages. Clive (a temporary love interest who is white) stops by her apartment. He brings her French toast. She doesn't want to let him in. She addresses her audience: "OK. So, he's a nice guy. An actual nice guy. So why did I just act like such a dick?" These rhetorical questions ("What went wrong? Why did I act like such a dick?") function to both draw in the audience (we attempt to answer the questions for Rob) and cue the audience that Rob is trying to figure it out, she is trying to do better, she is attempting to reflect on her lack of success in the relationship department and figure out what *she* is doing wrong. Unlike the stereotype of women who blame the men they get involved with for not being better mates, Rob doesn't push off the blame onto the men. She wants to know what *she* is doing to create these failed relationships or her lack of sustained desire for men who appear to treat her well, engage with her emotionally and physically, and have direction and purpose. She wants to be smart and choose wisely. In both these examples of Issa and Rob, the women are engaging with men who treat them well, who care for them, who are not seeking them out just for a self-satisfying fuck. They are "good guys." The writers/directors are showing the audience that the women are aware of this, being honest, and attempting to engage in mature ways that satisfy their needs.

In addition, most of these characters are perfectly happy with being single. They aren't, as Issa regularly says of others, "thirsty." Even if they are engaging with good men, they are not going to jump into something just because he is a nice guy. They are resisting the patriarchal order that mandates coupling, unless that is what they want. Rob asks, "Why is there such a stigma to being single. You are born alone, you die alone . . . as a single person, this is actually pretty great . . . Clyde (famous musician boy-friend potential; he seems like he really likes her) is great. He's like riding a bicycle. Sure, he is good for you. Sure, he is fun" (Season 1, Episode 7). Rob may seem as if she is beginning to fall into the category that many of the women I interviewed critique: Black female characters who can't seem to accept a good man, a good romance; they always fuck it up or say "meh!" when a *good* (smart, caring, employed, serious, hot, attentive) man expresses interest in a serious relationship. But perhaps characters like Rob aren't fickle. They are just resisting the patriarchal mandate to couple with a man. They want to maintain their autonomy and independence. They are resisting marriage. That isn't being fickle, that is pushing back against a strong culture force that is attempting to coerce them into matrimony simply because a good man wants it.

The men, however, get annoyed. They are used to having their way. They don't understand a woman who wouldn't choose them, who would choose being single. Outside the bar, Clyde exclaims to Rob:

> Well, this [learning that Rob was once engaged to Mac; she didn't tell Clyde] is fucking chaos. This isn't on you, but I have worked so hard to cut this fucking shit out of my life. This fucking chaos out. It's fucking messy. I think about you all the time, Rob. I don't really know what to do with it. I just want you to know that I would do this. I would do this with you . . . if you would want to do it. But I don't want to do this thing where I am your fake boyfriend . . . so I am asking you if this is a thing. Yes or no.

To Clyde's outburst, Rob responds honestly: "I don't know." Rob isn't ready to commit to Clyde, no matter how good, nice, interesting, and kind he is. *She* gets to decide when/how to commit and with whom. And, yes, she makes mistakes. She breaks some hearts. She treats Clyde poorly (in the next episode she tells him she will meet him and then ghosts him as he waits all night for her to show). She is flawed, but she is honest with herself and she knows she is not ready for a capital R "Relationship" right now. She wasn't ready with Mac and she isn't ready with Clyde. But this is important, too: women deciding for themselves and not allowing the mandate for coupling to force them into something they don't want.

Eventually Rob explains to Mac that she knows she is the one who pushed him away. She was stung when he left for London without her and to learn he was engaged. But she knows she wasn't ready for that kind of relationship with Mac or anyone. She says, "It [the reason the relationship ended] wasn't your fault. I slept with someone else while we were together . . . The night we got engaged" (a miscellaneous man she met in the bar). He tells her, "You are the most selfish fucking human being in this world. You are the most fucking selfish human being. It was you."

Rob can't win. Even in her honesty, Mac lashes out and insults her. Rob attempts to explain her callous behavior to the audience, even as she is—once again—being heartbreakingly callous to another good man who cares for her: "Did I cheat on Mac? Did I crawl in bed with him afterward? Yes. Did I get engaged thinking it would erase everything? Yes. Did I push him away, push him away, push him away until he had no fucking choice? I am such a fucking asshole." Perhaps Rob is too hard on herself. Instead of seeing her as an asshole, I see her as a young woman who doesn't yet feel she can commit to a forever relationship. Why should she have to commit simply to spare Mac's feelings? Women, in the context of the patriarchy, have to fight for the autonomy to remain single and free. The centrifugal force of compulsory coupling is almost irresistible. We need to admire and celebrate those who resist, no matter how messily.

SCRATCHING THAT ITCH

In *High Fidelity, Chewing Gum, Insecure, She's Gotta Have It*, as well as other programs, these women engage in sexual relationships on their own terms. They may or may not end up in a partnership, but they will seek out casual sex or masturbate until they decide. There is no judgment. Most of these characters seem ambivalent about long-term partnership (Rob, Nola, Issa, Molly, Hattie). They are in their twenties or thirties. They want to *play* with their sexuality. In more than one context, the sexual desire without strings attached is described as "scratching that itch." In a bar, Mary Jane and her friends talk about engaging with men "just to get that itch scratched." With her best friend, she says, "He is not my boo; he just someone I do." More often than not, the audiences see Nola and Issa and Hattie and Tracey strike out deliberately, even if awkwardly, in their pursuit of scratching the itch. But they are also willing to scratch that itch themselves. Masturbation and the use of sex toys are also part of these sexual liberation narratives. When Issa attempts (and fails) several times at a crowded dance club, she goes home and gets out her vibrator. The battery dies, so she rummages through the apartment trying to find batteries (phone, smoke detector) and gives up. Defeated, she sinks back, ironically wearing a t-shirt emblazoned with "HUMP: Make American Gyrate Again" (Season 2, Episode 3). Tracey delights in wiggling dildos and questioning whether they will work for her. Mary Jane's sex toys are discovered by her niece, followed by a disinterested shrug. Part of being a woman in control of her sexuality means being able to pleasure herself. In these shows, masturbation and auto-arousal are themes treated as part of a healthy and empowered female sexuality.

   In 1993, Spike Lee wrote, directed, and produced the feature film *She's Gotta Have It*. The protagonist, Nola Darling, was engaging in sex with three men, each of them differently inferior in personality, but serving her sexual needs. The film was heralded as groundbreaking by some (a woman in control of her sexuality) and tone deaf by others (Lee had no idea how to write female sexuality). Jones (1993), writing about Lee's original version of *She's Gotta Have It*, said that although Nola Darling was heralded as a "liberated, post-modern Black woman, she was only allowed to be viewed through the attitudes of three clearly deficient men – a narcissist, a dullard, and a social retard [*sic*]—who ultimately defined her existence" (254). In 2019, Lee recast Nola Darling, creating a series for Netflix by the same name. Lee directed all the episodes, but the writing was by various people, mostly Black women. The Black female writers created more depth and authenticity in Nola Darling who is a character making her place in the art world, creating political statements through her art about misogyny and racism, and fucking, but always on her own terms. Added to the series is a lesbian relationship, one that is deeper and more intimate than how Nola engages with her men.

Nola originally engages with Opal as a way of purging herself from the toxic masculinity that she has sworn off. The moment the relationship between Opal and Nola starts to get more complicated and intimate, Nola bails. Season 1, Episode 5: #ForMaNigusAndMyBishes opens with Nola in front of a blank canvas in overalls, readying to paint. She speaks directly to her audience, establishing an intimacy:

> Can I be honest? When Opal cut me off it hurt like a motherfucker. I thought we had a connection. Well, I lit up a joint, finished some work for the dystopian show, and decided to end my man-cleanse. Admittedly I am still learning the meaning of commitment and learning how to trust someone, even if that someone is me, and learning how to trust my intuition, not just my impulses. I'm a work in progress. But your girl is back in the saddle, though! I know. I'm buggin'. But I wouldn't say it like that. I would say it in a way that empowers me. Instead of saying I'm buggin' I'd say I'm multi-tasking.

After Opal breaks up with her, Nola takes her place once again as a player among men. She is hopping from man to man instead of committing to a woman. In the end, are we to understand Nola as an independent woman who is choosing a path that deviates from the confines of serial monogamy, whether she is with men or women, or are we to see her as immature and cavalier? At the end of Season 2, Jamie (male lover) questions Nola's actions; his ego will not believe that Nola would walk away without walking away *to* another man. At the end of the episode, she addresses the camera and says, "You were right (Jamie). There is someone else. Me." With this statement, the audience is to believe that Nola is tearing off the yoke of patriarchal coupling and focusing on her own liberation, freedom, and growth. Nola wants the sex, but not the baggage of relationships, regardless of whether they are heterosexual or queer.

One of my interviewees, Veronica, offered up the series *She's Gotta Have It* as one of the few representations of Black female queerness in mainstream media.

> (Nola Darling) is a black queer woman, so I like that. But there are complications with how I feel about her lesbian relationship and what that meant for all these other men. It was weird how (Spike Lee) portrayed that: when you are with a woman, you can only have one woman; if you are with men, you can have as many men as you want. It felt like bi-erasure. She became incapable of focusing on who she was when she was with men; she could do that with a woman. So, what is (Lee) saying?

This rhetorical question hung in the ether between us. I didn't know how to answer it and Veronica did not answer it either. What *was* Lee trying to do? In looking back on the episodes that focused on the lesbian relationship (or relationship with another woman; the character Nola Darling defines herself as "sex-positive, polyamorous pansexual"), Nola Darling does seem more respectful of an intimate/emotional relationship with her female lover Opal than with any of the men she beds. With Opal, Nola is part of her personal life, interacting with Opal's young daughter. This sort of intimacy is never broached with Nola's male lovers. Nola seems to genuinely enjoy mentoring the child, further entwining her into a life with Opal, a distinct departure from her "fuck buddy" treatment of the men. Perhaps Lee is attempting to set a lesbian stereotype on its head: the stereotype of young women having a lesbian relationship as an "experimentation" part of an immature sexual lark and nothing more. Perhaps, by showing Nola is more emotionally and domestically involved with Opal, Lee is saying *this* is the more mature and evolved relationship in juxtaposition to the "sex only" agreements Nola has with the men.

The credits for episodes that include the lesbian (or pansexual) storyline indicate that Lee is the director, but the episodes are written by Eisa Davis and Jocelyn Bioh among others. The episode with the steamiest sex scene between the two women is written/directed by Lee himself (Season 2, Episode 1: #I'mFeelingMyFeelings). The sex scene between these two women lasts 2.5 minutes, a rare occurrence for lesbian lovemaking in film and television. Typically, lesbian sex scenes, particularly when involving Black women, include a non-Black female partner, so Black-on-Black lesbian sex is not common. Lena Waithe also adds to this new inclusion of Black-on-Black lesbian sex in that Hattie only engages with Black women. However, the sex scenes in *Twenties*, unlike those in *She's Gotta Have It*, are fleeting and from a distance.

When Nola is exploring her female partner's body and we watch her hold back her braids to perform cunnilingus, it seems revolutionary for its tender realness. However, others have argued that the scene written, directed, and produced by Lee, offers a porn-like male gaze. What would the scene look like if a queer Black woman had directed it? We can only speculate. Zoe Samudzi (2019), a writer for the feminist magazine *Bitch*, calls the faux lesbian relationship "queer bait," a trope used to attract LGBTQ viewers, but then following the sidebar queer moment with a conventional realignment to heterosexual relationships. These "sidebar lesbian relationships" have appeared in other series and films as well (*Grown-ish, Bessie, Self Made, Dear White People*) but in 2020 Lena Waithe offered us Hattie, who is the center of the story in the series *Twenties*. However, when Hattie—who works for a Black female television producer—pitches the idea for a lesbian relationship in her boss', Ida B.'s, new series, *Cocoa Butter*, Ida B. says they already had a lesbian story line. Hattie points out that it was so minor she had forgotten about it: the characters never even kiss, other than on the cheek. Hattie is expressing a frustration (and Waithe answers that frustration with the show *Twenties*) that lesbian sex and relationships are either not accurately portrayed or are relegated to minor moments. Lesbian relationships are never as big and interesting as the heterosexual relationship stories. In each of these Black-on-Black relationship series featuring Black females, there tends to be some sort of sidebar romance that is either gay or lesbian. However, only *Twenties* takes lesbians and builds the show's narrative around them, thus establishing a mainstream acceptance of lesbian identity and giving Black lesbian viewers a representation that they have previously not had: a protagonist, perhaps flawed and looking for love in the wrong people, but one who is forging her own path with support of family and friends.

Unlike the decidedly lesbian representation that Hattie embodies, Nola Darling seems to use her lesbian relationship as an escape from toxic masculinity in her heteronormative relationships. What may be equally problematic about Nola's foray into a lesbian relationships is that she turns to lesbianism only as a rejection of toxic heterosexuality. In Season 1, Episode 4: we see Nola seated on her bed, legs crossed at the knee, in a black lace bra and panties. She droley declares to the camera:

> Enough is enough. There are some mad toxins in my life. I need a break and some radical self-care. And when I say radical, boy, do I mean radical. Treating myself to an internal cleanse that really gets the stink out, ya know? That means no weed, no social media, no alcohol and no men in my loving bed. Ya heard? That's right, fellas. There will be no penis between us. No men. Nada. None. Zero. Not even virtual. Oh, you don't believe I can do it? You wanna bet? But that mean I can still smash, though.

The scene then switches to voice-over and direct address of woman who is talking about how she met Nola and why she is attracted to her, introducing us to her lover Opal. And how, shortly after Opal began intertwining their lives, Nola "benched her," throwing her over for no discernable reason. Yes, this is a callous move on Nola's part, but she treats the men in the same way. So what is the take away? Regardless of whether Nola is engaging with a man or a woman, she simply is not ready for a partnership. And that should be OK.

Nola and Hattie and other lesbian romances in these shows/films are reason to celebrate. No longer are queer love affairs seen as tragic or the center of a cautionary tale. When directors included the bisexual side of iconic blues singer Bessie Smith in *Bessie*, the lesbian daughter of Madam J. C. Walker in *Self Made*, Lena Waithe's protagonist Hattie in *Twenties*, and Nola Darling's sexual fluidity, the directors allowed contemporary viewers to access lesbian romance normalized as a female sexuality continuum. Each of these female characters engages in lesbian relationships in different ways, but all of them do so without judgment or dire consequences. They are making the choices of loving women in ways that feel refreshingly new. The relationships are generally portrayed in the same way as heterosexual relationships: messy, healthy, respectful, and if there is dysfunction, it is a point of tension that leads to growth and acceptance. And they all choose other Black women with whom to couple. This is significant: Black-on-Black love must be portrayed as healthy and desirable not just for heterosexual unions but lesbian unions as well. In her scholarship, Brooks (2017) interviewed Black lesbians. She found:

> Choosing Black women as dating and/or marriage partners is a symbol of racial pride within the larger Black community. This is an example of symbolic interactionism because Black lesbians view marriage as recognizing Black women as marriage partners, and acknowledge the strength of Black women in the face of racism and sexism. In this context, while reinforcing aspects of Black respectability politics critiqued by some Black queer studies scholars, Black lesbian marriage serves as a symbol of racial pride and family connection, especially among middle-class Black lesbians. Thus, the symbol of two Black women married communicates meaning to the larger Black community of Black lesbians' investment in Blackness, which can trump their experiences of homophobia in their own families. (40–41)

The acceptance of their daughter's lesbian relationships is prominent in *She's Gotta Have It*, *Self Made*, and *Twenties*. Hattie's mother, Leila's mother (Madam C.J. Walker), and Nola Darling's parents don't seem to care that their daughters' partners are women. In each show/film, the parents are supportive of their daughters' lesbian relationships and in all cases, the women are partnering with other Black women. Just as important as these Black-on-Black lesbian relationships are, it is refreshing to note that these characters rarely experience homophobia in the form of family unacceptance, workplace bias, or intolerant friends. Hattie, Leila, and Nola are typical protagonists, young women, who happen to be in lesbian relationships.

JUST ONE OF THE (BUTCH DYKE) GIRLS

In the show *Twenties,* although Nola and Leila are two feminine characters, Hattie is not. Not only is Hattie part of a small club for being a Black female character engaging in lesbian relationships with other Black women, she is unique for being butch. It wasn't easy for Waithe, Hattie's creator, to find funding to produce a butch lesbian show. Once again (as with Issa Rae's work) self-producing and posting on YouTube generated a following for the program when mainstream producers turned away.

Waithe originally pitched the idea for the series *Twenties* to mainstream network producers in 2015 without success. She pitched it several times and the trite response was, "We aren't ready for this" ("Lena Waithe Discusses the Premier Season of *Twenties*," 2020, #TwentiesonBET). Not to be deterred, she and a friend produced an episode and put it online. It got lots of attention and so it was picked up for production. Waithe said the show is based on her life and her two straight girlfriends. "We are definitely living through a wonderful Renaissance right now and a lot of Black folks are working, but behind the scenes, if you are not at BET, you will only have like one Black exec on your project. Usually there is always one Black woman and one Black guy" ("Lena Waithe Discusses the Premier Season of *Twenties*," 2020, #TwentiesonBET). Waithe's series is the first series to feature a Black lesbian lead. Hattie (Jonica Gibbs) is a scrappy and charmingly masculine butch lesbian who seems to falls for straight women and works as a writer's personal assistant on a Black drama called *My Bae*.

Hattie is confident in her identity, but she also is portrayed as having to deal with ongoing annoyances because of her butch lesbian identity. Because of her masculine gender performance, she is regularly misgendered. On the campus of the television show, there is a tour going on and the tour guide points out Hattie and says, "She . . . I mean he . . . or they?" Two episodes later, Hattie is picking up tampons at the quickie mart for her friend, Nia. A man in the same aisle says, "Excuse me, sir . . . Oh, my bad for misgendering you. My brother's trans, so I should know better . . . You on hormones?" Hattie tells him she is not trans. He says, "Non-binary." It is a statement. He is telling her. She says, "I still don't know what that means." "Genderqueer?" This time it is a question. Hattie just says, "This is a lot. I am going to check out." Although Hattie is mildly annoyed at being misgendered, it doesn't upset her terribly. The man is not being aggressively, intentionally homophobic; he is only inappropriate in a nonthreatening way. She rolls her eyes at the well-intentioned Black man who is determined to prove to this stranger in a grocery store aisle how accepting he is.

In addition to well-intentioned strangers going out of their way to express eager acceptance, everyone in Hattie's world embraces her lesbian identity, from her close friends to her coworkers to her mother. Even as they may not fully approve of her choice in mate (Hattie seems to repeatedly fall for non-lesbian women who seduce her and leave her, for example Lorraine and Ida B.), they fully approve of her identity as a lesbian. Not even two minutes into the pilot episode, Hattie and Lorraine engage in tender, passionate kisses. The following scene cuts to Hattie's mother (they are talking on the phone). Her mother chastises her: "You still messin' with that straight bitch?" Hattie tells her mother that Lorraine is not straight. The mother says, "What is she . . . bi- sex- you-AL?" Hattie says, "Mom! She doesn't believe in labels." The mother dramatically rolls her eyes and says, "What is she, like that Janelle Monae girl?" Although the mother is expressing an anti-bisexual bias, she has Hattie's best interest at heart: her daughter deserves more. In another episode, Hattie's mother calls her and asks if she is scissoring anyone. Hattie says, "You know that is not a thing." The mother insists it is, "I saw it on a lesbian porno." Hattie laughs and tells her mother, "If you have questions, just ask." Their relationship is open and honest, even if her mother regularly blurts out homophobic asides. The point of including this relationship is that the mother offers her lesbian daughter unconditional love, even if she is misinformed about lesbian identity or bisexuality.

Similar to the mother, both Marie and Nia, Hattie's best friends, have her best interests at heart and therefore also do *not* like her current bae, Lorraine. In the pilot episode, Marie establishes her stance on Lorraine, "I just want you to stop dating these basic bitches who treat you like a pit stop on their way to dating some whack-ass dude with a wave cap and ashy ankles." Hattie patiently responds by saying sexuality is fluid, a similarly vague comment akin to "she doesn't believe in labels." Both responses by Hattie are attempts to explain away Lorraine's clear lack of interest in commitment. We get the sense that Lorraine's primary attraction to Hattie is the novelty of having sex with another woman while maintaining her heterosexual privilege. Marie tells Hattie to stop dating women who are straight but going through a lesbian phase. We don't see Lorraine again until Episode 3 when Hattie tells Lorraine, "I love you." Lorraine chuckles and says, "I know." It is a stinging moment, but Hattie waits around for Lorraine regardless, much to the chagrin of her friends and mother. They want something more for her, a full and actualized relationship with a woman who loves and respects Hattie in reciprocal ways. But what does Hattie want? We are unsure.

Marie is the most vocal about Hattie's attraction to Lorraine, regularly telling Hattie she needs to stop waiting for Lorraine. "You are tripping over yourself to get to her when she facetimes you." Marie tells Hattie she wants more for her, "more" meaning a partner who is as smitten with Hattie as Hattie is with her. Instead, Hattie keeps pursuing the women who seem ambivalent toward her.

Even as Marie is a champion of Hattie's pursuit of lesbian love, she is facing homophobic suspicions about her own partner, Chuck. She begins to mentally checklist cues that Chuck might be gay: they haven't had sexual intercourse for three months because Chuck prefers anal sex; Chuck wants to watch "threesome porn" as foreplay and the threesomes feature two men fellating each other; Chuck accepts a business card from a server at a party and says he threw the card away, but then Marie finds it in his wallet months later. When Chuck proposes to Marie at the end of Season 1, Hattie shakes her head in wonder, but the audience is not sure why she is perplexed when Marie says yes to the proposal. Is it because Hattie also suspects Chuck to be gay? Is it because she believes Marie can do better? Is it that she finds marriage at this stage in their lives (the twenties) to be a mistake? Her reason for the head shake goes unarticulated, but what the viewer does understand is that there are doubts, some by Hattie, some by Marie, about this relationship. The audience is not cued to seeing Marie as fickle. Rather she is careful; she has doubts.

AM I A HOE? IS THAT A BAD THING?

These young female characters are all engaging in sex on their own terms in ways that, in the past, would be seen as unacceptable—at least for women. At different times in many of these series, the women ask of themselves and their friends, "Am I a hoe?" Who decides? And who cares? Mary Jane tells her girlfriend she hasn't had sex with the man they are discussing because she has already had sex with another man that week and two different men in one week would make her a hoe. Her friend replies, "Absolutely not! You're grown. You do what you want to do." Mary Jane then enquires about the hoe threshold. "How much sex, and blow jobs, and feel-me-ups am I allowed before I am officially a hoe?" Her friend tells her that if her partner count is in the single digits, there is no problem and "three sucks equals one smash." But, she continues, "The longer we stay single and keep having sex, somebody is going to call us a hoe." Mary Jane decides that a woman can reset her "hoe button" if she gets to thirty-five men and she has never been married. The friend says she knows too many women who "get to reset their hoe button once they get married" meaning once she assumes her appropriate patriarchal role as a monogamous married woman, the hoe label magically disappears. Her friend celebrates how many men she has bedded (off her fingers and toes; off Mary Jane's fingers and toes): "Yes, completely," she smiles. "I'm a hoe." Mary Jane responds gleefully, singing back to her, "You's a hoe!" In this exchange, the women are embracing their sexual freedom, and even if at first Mary Jane seems afraid to act in any way that might cause someone to apply the hoe label. In the end, she throws that fear aside is, embracing the label, and resisting any respectability politics that might imply her sexual liaisons should be regulated by outdated patriarchal standards for women.

Issa Dee takes a similar approach to defying respectability politics and delightfully claiming the label of hoe as a way of exercising sexual freedom on her own terms. In one episode, Issa and Molly, her best friend, are talking and Issa says, "Girl, you know I always wanted a hoe phase. But then I got with Lawrence (former partner). You know what? Fuck love. Fuck getting to know these niggas. Fuck feeling feelings. I just want to get on my Halle Berry shit, you know? . . . Can you teach me how to hoe?" Molly rolls her eyes, "Bitch, that's rude! And, yes" (Season 2; Episode 3: Hella Open). Casual sex is what Issa is after, sowing her wild oats, and making no apologies. At the end of the first season, her ex, Lawrence, surprises Issa by showing up at a fundraiser: "I wanted to look you in the eye and ask you why you are treating me like some random ass nigga." Issa is flippant, "You were just an itch I needed to scratch" (Season 1, Episode 7). Issa wants to explore sex for the sake of sex, but she also misses the emotional connection. Later, she talks to herself: "Dick on E[mpty]. Bank on E. Life on E. I gotta be cute and careful and charming . . . . And I compare every dude to Lawrence." Issa articulates that she is still thinking of Lawrence even as she knows she doesn't want to be in a relationship with him right now. She cut Lawrence out of her life because he seemed directionless and too boring, but she doesn't like the anonymity of casual sex. She finds dating apps demeaning. We see Issa contemplating the app profiles on her phone, featuring photos of topless men displaying hypermasculine bodies and beefcake outdoor poses. She grimaces and swipes them away (Season 2, Episode 1: Hella Great). Even as Issa is off to the races regarding her sexual exploits, she will not engage in what she perceives as degrading and shallow interactions.

All these characters (Hattie and her friends, Issa and Molly, Mary Jane, Tracey and her chums, Nola, and Rob) eagerly engage in lots of sex with various partners, and they often refer to themselves and others as "hoes." Perhaps the updated vernacular for Jezebel is "Hoe" or "Ho." There is some nuanced distinction between a Jezebel, who primarily seduces white men and is sexually voracious, and a hoe, who typically is simply a woman who likes to have sex with more than one partner, presumably male. However, as with the word "promiscuous," the underlying misogyny of "hoe" implies that any woman who is having sex—or even presumed to be having sex—with the "wrong" (culturally defined in many different ways) man, even if it is just *one* man, runs the risk of being called a hoe. Sometimes the word doesn't even relate to actual sexual activity. It could be how a woman dresses or walks or talks that will earn her the degrading and disparaging title of hoe. Hoes are dirty, low, unintelligent, and often ugly (as defined by the WSCP). It is always a bad thing to be called a hoe. Unless it isn't.

The female characters who embrace the title "hoe" are doing so to reclaim the word, reclaiming their sexuality from the patriarchy. Some films and series include conversations between close girlfriends about whether being a hoe is a desirable label. These girlfriends also talk about how to be a hoe, as in how to engage in experienced and *interesting* sexual moves that will increase a woman's value in the bedroom, especially with a particular man. In both *BMJ* and *Insecure*, there are scenes where the protagonists contemplate the desire to be seen as a hoe and what that means. Mary Jane asks her best friend, "What is the hoe threshold?" The friend puts her mind at rest: Mary Jane gets to decide (Season 3, Episode 6: Don't Call It a Comeback). *She* can engage with anyone and with any frequency she wants. No one is going to judge her. Or if there are people who would judge her, who cares?

Issa fully embraces the belief that she gets to decide how often and with whom she engages. She explains to her friend Molly, "We (Daniel and Issa) are friends who fuck. Daniel knows what it is . . . I am all about putting niggas in my hotation. I got Daniel, I got Lawrence, and I am about to add one tonight . . . Latino" (Season 2, Episode 5: Hella Shook). Later in the same episode, Issa hooks up with a Latino at the bar. She says to herself, "I want the hochata: easy on the chata, heavy on the hoe . . . . Are you good with your hands? Or are you better with your dick?" Issa is fully embracing the title of hoe, aggressively pursuing various partners and relishing in the adventure. She tells Molly,

> "This is MY hotation! I make the rules. So, when I call you to come over, bring over the dick. Why do these niggas even need to fuck anybody else? Like, granted, I know I am not Rihanna. You know, sex with me isn't amazing. But it is like 'Huh. OK, yeah. I'm satisfied. I'd do that again. With her.' You know who I fucked up with? Nico. I shoulda told him, get in my line up." Molly quips, "Girl, that's the hoe spirit." (Season 2, Episode 6: Hella Blows)

Issa needs these pep talks. She gives them to herself in her mirror and she depends on Molly to cheer her on as well. She is bold, but she needs to be reminded that she is bold, that she can do what she wants, no one is going to judge her and if they do, she doesn't care.

Issa decides she is going to go over to the neighbor's for some sex. She talks to herself in the mirror: "You look great . . . who's gonna get that dick? You are. You are gonna walk in there and say, 'pull down your motherfuckin pants, nigga. You ready to like this pussy? There is fire in this pussy . . . Now come and get this African pussy.' " She knocks on the door of Eddie, the neighbor, but he is with another woman. She goes back to the bathroom and has another conversation with the mirror, this time imagining she is speaking to Eddie. "You sloppy-ass nigga. You gonna treat me like that? I'm over here serving you my finest and you gonna send my shit back? I could cry right now I am so embarrassed and mad. I hope you can't get it up and her pussy is trash." What she actually says to him is, "No, that's cool. I mean, that's what's up, right?" These self-pep talks and bold actions by Issa demonstrate that she is willing to take a chance with sexual experiences. Some work out for her; most of the time they end awkwardly. But the character doesn't take the mediocre experiences as reasons to rein in her sexual exploration. They are all part of what she wants: the ability to make her own decisions, to put her sexuality out into the world, to orchestrate experiences so that she can better know what she wants.

Seeing these female characters embracing sex with various partners and not apologizing for it was noted as remarkable by one of my respondents. She said, "[Shows like *Insecure* and *BMJ*] are different from when I watched *Waiting to Exhale* (1998). It was a show about women, but the woman who slept with all the guys, she was judged. It wasn't like it was said. But it made you think like she was a hoe" (Mashell). In portraying women's sexuality as full, complex, and deserving of exploration, in these shows we see the female characters cast off the negative perception and judgment of a Jezebel or hoe. No judgment; she gets what she wants. She learns about herself; She goes on. And she processes all of it with her girlfriends.

THE POLITICS OF DATING WHITE

In their sexual explorations most of the female characters are involved with—and actively seeking—Black men. There are the exceptions: Issa putting a Latino in her "hotation" and Rob regularly engaging with white or mix-raced, light-skinned men. The politics of interracial dating are pertinent to viewers: Black women note when a Black man dates a white woman or when a Black woman dates a white man. In each of the series *Insecure*, *BMJ*, and *Twenties*, there are moments when one of the main characters deliberately chooses to engage romantically or sexually with a white man and it is noted and discussed both in the context of the show and by viewers. However, the predominant relationships featured on these shows are Black-on-Black love. These series show Black men respectfully engaging with Black women, providing a model of Black men who love and care about Black women. In *Insecure*, regardless of which beau Issa chooses to commit to, she is in a position of self-determination and making the choice in healthy contexts. This is also true of Mary Jane, Nia, Tracey, Candice, and Molly. By Season 4, Issa has two men (Daniel and Lawrence) who are both seriously interested in committing to her; both have had past problems, but are trying—as Issa is—to learn, grow, and change to be better partners. With either choice, the viewer understands that Issa will be with an attentive and caring partner who admires and respects her. This scenario of Black men loving Black women and working hard to be good partners is an important narrative. Eboni told me:

> We have to uplift. People fall in love with whoever they fall in love with. I have a lot of friends who are white girls who are in relationships with Black men. It

is what it is. But there needs to be more of a spotlight on Black men who love Black women so it can be equal . . . with Black men it is different because they feel so empowered to say "I don't date Black women." They need to show Black men who love Black women . . . . The narrative that I continue to see pushed the most that I can't freakin' stand is Black men who are so emboldened to say they don't date Black women and they don't think that that is fucked up. We all have our dating preferences, but when you can't . . . . It is a form of self-hatred. There are Black men who think white women are status. They think, "If I date a white woman, it will elevate me." And I see that a lot, like in Hollywood. They think, "I have more status if I am with a white woman than I would if I were with a Black woman." And there are so many stereotypes. White women are submissive and Black women aren't; if you get with a Black woman, she will run your life. That is a big narrative that I see all the time.

One of the many reasons Eboni is drawn to shows such as *She's Gotta Have It*, *Insecure*, *Twenties*, and *BMJ* is the representation of Black-on-Black love. In each of these shows, the female protagonists seek out Black men. If they—or one of their girlfriends—happen to engage with a white man, it is noted and discussed. Likewise, the phenomena of Black men who engage with white women is noted and discussed.

In *Twenties*, Marie is talking to her male partner, Chuck, about books. He tells her there is a book in the bag that is for him. He excitedly explains to her:

[The book is] all about how Black men are carrying the trauma of slavery in our epigenetic DNA, like PTSD. We have intimacy issues because our brains won't let us love ourselves, which means we don't' know how to love anyone else, especially not a woman. Cause we want to be strong like the warriors we know we can be. But how can we be warriors if we can't even protect ourselves out in these streets? (Marie looks surprised and puzzled). So, we need to heal the warrior within so we don't end up in jail or with a white woman. (Season 1, Episode 3)

The parallel Chuck is suggesting between "in jail or with a white woman" is a false parallel: one is systemic racism in the form of a corrupt criminal justice system and the other would be a personal choice to gain social status in the WSCP. The humor is in the attempt by the Black man to turn the tables on that choice or preference for a white woman and say, "It isn't my fault! I'm the victim!" But the women are not taking any excuses. Issa and her friends speculate that Black men turn to white women because Black women will not subjugate themselves in the same way white women will. These characters understand the politics of interracial dating and openly discuss "dating white," both for Black men and themselves.

In *BMJ* and *Insecure*, there are episodes that feature the protagonists engaging with a white man for the first time. The act of dating or having sex with a white man is talked about as if it is a taboo that is also a rite of passage. Neither Mary Jane nor Issa has any desire to have a relationship with a man who isn't Black, but they feel compelled to engage briefly in the taboo of sleeping with a white man. When Mary Jane picks up a white man in the club, she confesses to her girlfriend that having sex with a white man is a unique experience for her. She asks her friend, "Have you ever been with a white boy?" "Girl, yeah! It was during my experimental phase. . . . I never felt a reason to venture back to the baloney pony either" (Season 3, Episode 6). Likewise, when Molly (*Insecure*) dates a white man, the two friends discuss whether they have ever done that before. In *Twenties*, when Marie discloses that she has slept with white men, her two friends are aghast. "Why didn't you tell us before now?" When Hattie, in *Twenties*, waits too patiently for a bisexual paramour to pay her attention, one of her friends quips that she needs to stop waiting for her bisexual girlfriend to throw her over for a white boy; in one of the following episodes, Hattie is at a coffee shop and encounters the woman with a white man who she is presumed to be sleeping with. The message is clear across these shows: Black women who date outside their race are players; they don't *seriously* engage with white men. These programs establish that anything other than Black-on-Black love is considered immature and undesirable. White men are OK for a romp, but never as a partner.

A WEDDING AT THE END OF THE AISLE

As shown in this chapter, there are many ways in which these female characters, their friends, and these shows feel revolutionary regarding sexuality and relationships. Although *BMJ* and *Scandal* both end with the women marrying (respectability politics, for sure), the other series seem to, so far, avoid that trite "ending" to the romance. Perhaps Issa will marry Lawrence in the end (she sometimes has fantasies that they are married and parenting a baby), or Hattie will find her true love and exchange vows, or Nola Darling will decide her lesbian lover is the only person who truly gets her, but for now the viewing audience is spared those neat and tidy patriarchal conclusions. In an episode of *Twenties*, the Black woman producer, Ida B., tells Hattie, "I know what Black women want. Black women want nothing more than to see a Black man sweep a Black woman off her feet. They want a fantasy, so that is what I try to give them" (Season 1, Episode 6). Ida B's breakthrough production is called *My Bae*, which could be a spoof of either *Scandal* or *BMJ*. The audience of *Twenties* is expected to see through Ida B.'s statement: certainly, marriage isn't what *all* women want. Hattie openly tells Ida B. as much, stating how much she dislikes the show *My Bae* (although her friends do say they like it or feel they need to support it because a Black woman created and produced it). Ida B. is implying that the Black-on-Black relationship dramas need to follow the heterosexual, patriarchal fairy tale/myth because that is what Black woman want. She implies that Black women are waiting for a prince to rescue them from their lives, make them their wives, and live happily ever after. However, for women within the context of the patriarchy, marriage often leads to a very different conclusion. Single women are more likely to describe themselves as happy than married women, leading one to believe that the hype about marriage is a patriarchal construct designed to convince women to desire it instead of reject it (Dolan 2019). Ida B. suggests that the narrative, even if damaging, is lucrative. It is "what Black women want."

As a feminist, I see the marriage ceremony and legal coupling as a convention of the patriarchy by the patriarchy serving men but not women, yet the institution of marriage becomes even more complicated when addressing groups of people traditionally locked out of marriage legitimacy such as Blacks and LGBTQ people. There is little question as to why we socialize girls to play with bride dolls and shows such as *Say Yes to the Dress* and *Bridezilla* take hold: girls/women are conditioned to believe that they are not fully an adult until there is a wedding. Within the WSCP, the analysis and reality of what marriage is/does for or to women is particularly complex when thinking about Black women. Drake (2019) writes:

> Like marriage, the notion of "black love" is both complicated and celebrated. The notion is ultimately steeped in a history of bondage and chattel slavery. How love is expressed, represented, and analyzed among African Americans as an ethnic group in the heteropatriarchal context of the United States is rooted in a philosophical history in which African-descended people were deemed objects who were not fully human or sentient. (162)

On one hand, Black marriage is an institution that has been historically denied Blacks by the white supremacist culture; on the other hand, to choose not to marry for feminist or other reasons feeds into WSCP stereotypes of Black "broken family" narratives where anything but patriarchal matrimony is seen as unacceptable. In order to resist or revise this history steeped in slavery and misogyny, many Black shows and films feature weddings as the legitimizing happy ending.

Drake (2019) states that a large number of Black-directed films at the end of the twentieth century featured a "happy ever after" marriage plot. This phenomenon continues today (e.g., *Deliver Us from Eva* [2003], *Just Wright* [2010], *Jumping the Broom* [2011], *Baggage Claim* [2013], the *Think Like a Man* franchise [2012, 2014], and the *Why Did I Get Married?* franchise [2007, 2010]) (163). Drake speculates that these films emerged as a way to talk back to political and cultural stereotypes perpetuated about Black women, for example, the single mother welfare queen. This theory is intriguing in that it suggests Black art/media will "talk back" to racist stereotypes perpetuated in the culture of politics. Similarly, then, it would make sense that during one of the most openly racist and misogynistic administrations in recent U.S. history, Black art would speak back by creating woman-centered, Black-centered entertainment. And in these narratives, the women—for the most part—are rejecting the institution of marriage as central to their story.

Because most of the wedding films Drake references are written and directed by men (with the exception of *Just Wright*, directed by Shanaa Hamri and *Jumping the Broom*, written by Elizabeth Hunter and Arlene Gibbs), who are the audience for these films? Is the narrative attempting to convince men that marriage to a Black woman is the coming-of-age narrative they should aspire to? Or is the intended audience Black women to convince them that marriage is the ideal? Drake's argument is that by ending the film at the wedding, audiences do not have to imagine a marriage. They can focus on a wedding, thereby leaving intact racist stereotypes regarding Black men and women that marriage is for white people. Regardless, the current shows that feature young Black women seem to resist this narrative, offering instead one of sexual exploration and awakening, curiosity in engaging with various partners, and a period of life where a wedding is definitely not the focus of the story. Instead, the focus is young women claiming and exploring sexual relationships on their own terms.

#METOO AND CONSENT

The harsh and hard reality regarding Black women and sexual assault is that the majority of Black women will be assaulted in their lifetime. Nearly 22 percent of Black women reported being raped; 41 percent of Black women experienced sexual coercion or unwanted sexual contact (West and Johnson 2013, 3). As we know, these statistics are woefully under representative because most women *don't* formally report their assaults and rapes. In light of this sobering reality, it would be remiss to engage in an analysis of representations of Black women's sexuality without addressing the walking wounded, the fact that most Black women are survivors of one, and more often many, assaults on their bodies. These assaults have ripple effects in a woman's life, whether they are the result of a date or acquaintance rape, a consensual moment that suddenly becomes non-consensual, or a trusted male who crosses personal boundaries. She may no longer trust herself or she may feel her body is no longer her own. She may no longer trust men. She may deal with the violation by engaging in random and anonymous sex by way of taking control of her own body. She may no longer find pleasure in sex or sex with a partner may cause such severe anxiety as to be a barrier to any sort of physical or emotional intimacy. These effects change and run throughout a survivor's life, affecting every relationship. Some women seek and find healing in therapy. Most bury the assault, tell themselves they are "over it" and attempt to move on. But it will always be there. It would be a lie of great omission if contemporary representations of Black womanhood did not address the real and complicated effects of assault in the lives of females. And there are some films and series that attempt to do that, but not very well.

In *Twenties*, there is a through line of a woman boss who preys upon and then ditches younger female assistants. Before Hattie goes to work for Ida B., the TV producer, Marie warns her that Ida B. will seduce Hattie and then fire her. The boss, Ida B., is a light-skinned Black woman who looks the part of conventional feminine beauty and is presumably heterosexual except for her predilection for young female assistants. This set up is the quintessential example of a #MeToo moment: a young assistant who is smitten by her older, more experienced mentor who holds the younger woman's career in the palm of their hand. The only difference is, instead of it being Harvey Weinstein or Bill Cosby, the serial perpetrator is a Black woman, one of the only success-ful Black women in the television industry.

Even as Hattie has been warned, she is still surprised when Ida B. starts to come on to her. Yet, Hattie is intrigued and not exactly unwilling. Ida B. makes her moves slowly, like a carefully executed game of chess. In the beginning of the series, Ida B. is scolding and dismissive of Hattie. Hattie apologizes and nearly begs for a job that is granted: a lowly personal assistant to a group of writers. Hattie ingratiates herself to Ida B. by jumping in antici-pation of what would please her boss. Eventually, Ida B. starts to lob more tasks Hattie's direction, trusting her with keys to her house and scanning per-sonal documents. At the end of the first season, Ida B. isolates Hattie to make her move. In one scene, we watch as Ida B. tells all the other workers to go home (Season 1, Episode 8). She has been drinking and is vaping weed in her office when she begins her seduction of Hattie; her pose and the camera angle harken back to the famous scene in *The Graduate*: the camera is behind Ida B.; her leg is up and bent seductively; Hattie stands across the room looking small and shocked. Hattie paces, saying "no no no no no no no." The camera frames the shot through Ida B.'s bent knee, her leg featuring sheer, black lace-top nylons. Hattie, framed behind the bent knee identically to the iconic scene in *The Graduate* over fifty years ago nearly recites the same lines as Dustin Hoffman's character: "Ida B. You are trying to seduce me." Instead of asking the question ("Mrs. Robinson, you trying to seduce me. Aren't you?") Hattie is making a statement. Hattie knows how this is going. Cue soaring violin music; the frame closes in on four lips about to touch in a slow kiss when Ida B. snaps awake in her bed. It has all been a clichéd dream of the older female seductress. The original film, telling the story of an older woman seducing a young man (1967) was in a context of a culture where women were just beginning to be entitled to their own sexual power and was therefore considered provocative, shocking, and, yes, liberating. Yet now, in the context of a culture where sexual assault, especially of younger people by older, more powerful people, is considered an obvious wrong, the call back feels decidedly anti-feminist. The fact that Hattie is insistent in her protests ("no, no, no, no, no, no, no") adds an even ickier element to this sexual fantasy: resistance as a turn on is the oldest rape horror around; and Black women know it well because they have been victims of it since they arrived on this continent as enslaved people.

Worse is the actual scene of seduction that ends the first season. In super-creepy, stalker fashion, Ida B. fires Hattie in a fit of rage and then later shows up, unannounced and waiting for Hattie, on Hattie's doorstep. Hattie, surprised, approaches Ida B., and asks her what she is doing. Without words—or consent—Ida B. pulls Hattie in for a passionate kiss and the cameras swirl up and over the two women. The tone of the scene is set up to evoke romance and passion, desire and longing. Yet isn't this assault? Isn't this creepy, rape-y behavior? We have seen this narrative, ad-nauseam, featuring the disempowered ingénue and the suited-up rich man who *always* gets what he wants and he wants women and runs through them as quickly as he pleases, tossing their bruised bodies aside when the next pretty thing comes along. Yet in Waithe's version, it seems she would like to revise that narrative and see this scene as a romantic kiss instead of a wildly inappropriate power move. This sort of scene may have been framed as romantic a few years ago, but can we see it that way now?

Other series, however, get it right, showing consent even in awkward and comedic moments. In *Insecure*, typically there is an exchange to indicate consent before any sexual contact. When Issa goes to Eddie's apartment, a man in her complex who she vaguely knows from a party, she is looking for a hook up. She makes a couple of small overtures, but he seems to be missing the cues; he is engrossed in watching television. Issa excuses herself to the bathroom and gives herself a pep talk in the bathroom mirror: "You got to go for it; go for it, hoe!" Back on the couch with him, she moves in for a kiss and they awkwardly undress. He says, "Would you mind if I titty fucked you?" Issa pulls back, "I'd like to respectfully decline" (Season 2, Episode 3: Hella Open). The man seems unoffended by her rebuff and the scene ends. He knew to ask and not assume; he is not assured a yes, nor is he offended. It isn't a problem, he asked; she said, no; moving on.

In *Insecure, Chewing Gum, She's Gotta Have It, High Fidelity,* and *Twenties,* we see young women taking control of their desires, their bodies, and their sexual needs. They express what they want and most of the time they get it with few mishaps or hard situations. None of these women is date raped; none of them seem to engage in activity that is painful or uncomfortable simply because their partner wants to. They speak openly with their female friends (and often their romantic partners) about their sexual desires, habits, pleasures, and what they *won't* do.

Michaela Coel, creator, writer, and star of *Chewing Gum,* moved away from the empowered and sex-positive thrust of her first series when writing, producing and starring in her dramatic series, *I May Destroy You* (2020). Unlike her light-hearted comedy series *Chewing Gum* that shows quirky, funny, sexual escapades driven by female characters, *I May Destroy You* offers up the dark side of rape and the ripple effects of sexual assault. The rape, not exactly acquaintance rape, but drugged rape from a bar encounter, is only alluded to in murky flashbacks. The series (seven episodes) focuses on Arabella, a well-known U.K. author who writes about race, sexuality, gender, and other cultural issues from a critical thinking, Black female Millennial's perspective. In the first episode, she comes back from Italy, leaving a male lover there, and has a twenty-four-hour turnaround time for an article deadline. Instead of chaining herself to her screen and writing, she goes out, does some drugs, dances at a club, and wakes up disorientated with a gash on her head. She stumbles to a meeting with her agents and they hint that the copy she has submitted reads incomprehensible. In the befuddled, hazy state she is in, she has a difficult time finding her way home and flashes to an odd image of a pasty, scrawny white man thrusting as if in front of her.

The series is built upon her realization that she was drugged and raped; the odd image a vague, hazy memory. Who the man is, she does not know. The identity of her rapist is really beside the point. The narrative is about the effects of rape: to the body, to the mind, to the psyche. We watch as her life spirals out of control even as she tries to grab hold.

Coel revealed that she, herself, was drugged and assaulted in 2018 (St. Felix 2020, 66). As with *Chewing Gum,* this series is more than a bit autobiographical. Unlike *Chewing Gum, Insecure,* and *Twenties,* it is anything but a quirky comedy about being Black and female and sexually curious and empowered. Instead, *I May Destroy You,* as the title suggests, is about the way a rape destroys a woman's life in various directions, permeating every fiber of her body and brain—even if she can't fully remember it. The "Who raped me?" is a secondary question to the primary question of "How can I heal from this; how can I prevent this from destroying me?" The tragic and maddening fact of rape is that typically the man walks away, only five minutes of his time spent in fevered sex to orgasm. He is untouched by the act in any permanent way. A rapist will rape again. And walk away again. And never think about it again. A woman, a girl, a human who is raped, will carry that with her for the rest of her life, dealing with the consequences of his five-minute act, the horror of which is relived over and over again whether in conscious memory or not. In this sense, *I May Destroy You* offers a realistic version of what rape is. For Arabella, it is not about naming her rapist or finding her rapist to seek justice. It is about surviving, trying to move beyond the rape she can't consciously remember but her body does. It is the story that every woman who has been sexually assaulted knows too well. As Inga Musico wrote in her manifesta *cunt* (1998), "Because of the action of two completely unknown males in the year 1948, I was slapped across the face and grounded to my room for a week in 1974 . . . . A man could, feasibly, sacrifice his coffee break raping a woman. The woman would then spend her entire life dealing with it. So would her daughters. So would theirs. The distribution of power is not acceptable" (154–155). The reverberations of rape infiltrate and permeate every corner of a woman's life. And for years. What *I May Destroy You* shows us is the first few months of that lifetime. The title alludes to a hope, perhaps: the rape/the rapist *may* destroy her; but perhaps it/he won't.

FAUX BLACK FEMALE SEXUALITY CAST AS SEX WORK

Rape for pay. That is what those who do the long and difficult work treating sex workers who want to escape "the business" call it. During the 1990s, I volunteered at a transitional living center for sex workers in Omaha, Nebraska. During training and orientation, there were two statistics that struck me, that I carry with me, that I repeat to students and friends regarding sex work. One of the center's directors told me that 98 percent of the women who sought assistance at the center were survivors of childhood sexual assault. "And," she added, "The other two percent are probably blocking the memory." She told me that in her work she came to believe that no woman would engage in sex work unless they had learned early to separate themselves from their body; that they had learned their body had no worth unless to be used by men for sex; that they had learned that they had no autonomy, no right, to their body. The other thing she told me that seared into my memory was that sex workers, be they trans women, cis women, gay men, or teen runaways, used drugs and alcohol to numb themselves from the reality of sex work. They took drugs to engage in sex with strangers, "rape for pay," she said. They needed more drugs to do more sex work. They became addicted. Then they had to turn more tricks to pay for more drugs. The cycle became even more tragic when pimps exploited the addicted and vulnerable women to keep them poor, desperate, and unable to escape. What she told me and what I learned in that stint as a volunteer run in direct and violent contrast to the narratives the WSCP tells us about sex work: it is easy money; the women do it willingly; it is lucrative for women; the women have control over the men they serve, not the other way around; it is not exploitative; women *choose* sex work like they would *choose* any other kind of work.

This harsh reality of sex work is never—or rarely—depicted accurately in entertainment media. Happy hookers in the form of *Pretty Woman*, smart-assed trans men in stilettos and patent leather mini-skirts, fresh-faced escorts in limos, and now "phone and video sex stars" who pay for their college through virtual sex work airbrush the degrading nature of sex for money. And disproportionately, Black women are depicted as these dispensable sex workers. If they are killed, who cares? If they are raped, that is part of the job description. If their pimp or John beats them up, what do they expect? Because Black women represent a disproportionate number of poor people and because Black women represent a disproportionate number of rape victims, it makes sense that they would then represent a disproportionate number of sex workers in WSCP. Series and films featuring Black women are no different, pointing to the false narratives of empowerment and financial stability through selling one's body. Within the context of the white supremacist patriarchy's use of Black women's bodies for white male sexual pleasure, an unarticulated but understood birthright given to every white male born in the United States, the revisionist narrative of Black women empowered by sex work deserves attention.

In the Netflix movie *Jezebel*[2] (2019), written and directed by Numa Pierre, an older sister, Sabrina, who engages in phone sex for a living grooms her younger sister to engage in video sex. The younger sister Tiffany (played by Tiffany Tanille) chooses *Jezebel* for her work name, a too-obvious reference to the stereotype of Black women whose hypersexuality seduces and exploits the unwitting white man, who is, in turn, seen as a victim of her wanton wiles. In the movie, the mother of Sabrina and Tiffany dies, leaving her three adult children without a matriarch or any parental guide. The two sisters engage in sex work; the brother lays around and judges them for turning tricks. Sabrina's white boyfriend comes and goes as he pleases, providing an apartment for everyone, happy to allow his girlfriend to turn tricks through phones and screens to support them.

Pierre references the complicated and fraught dynamics of race and sex throughout without ever getting her audience to feel too uncomfortable with Black women performing sex acts for white men's money. In the opening scene, Sabrina is twisting a phone cord around her finger, cooing into a receiver, an erect nipple pushing through a pink teddy. "Do you want to touch my hair? My long, blonde hair? You want to touch my pussy, don't you . . . you like my pink pussy don't you?" She feigns a breathy orgasm and then hangs up and pushes a button. "Next call." Tiffany, attempting to sleep nearby, rolls her eyes. The opening scene portrays the myth that women dress in sexy lingerie, lie on their backs, and writhe seductively while engaging in phone sex as if they are performing for a camera instead of a miscellaneous voice on the other end of the phone. This scene establishes for the viewer that the work is easy and comfortable; nothing to it. Next call. Also imbedded in this opening scene is the performance of whiteness: the sexual fantasy is white, blonde, with long hair and a pink pussy.

Instead of encouraging her sister to do something else (find other ways to make money; get an education), Sabrina grooms Tiffany for sex work, encouraging her to apply to a video sex ad and giving her a wig for her sex work personae. Sabrina coaches Tiffany and gives her bikinis and lingerie and Tiffany looks excited and happy to share this bond with her sister. Tiffany seems giddy about getting the lingerie and listening to her sister's advice about sex toys. After Sabrina helps Tiffany put on the wig, Tiffany looks at herself and cries. "I can't believe she's gone." The audience is to understand that Tiffany is talking about her recently dead mother, but we can also see that Tiffany is gone. In her place is Jezebel; she has been reduced to a white man's sexual siren, a seductress borne of white supremacy and the rape of Black women by white men.

Unlike her sister Sabrina's sex work where she can pretend to be white, Tiffany as Jezebel is exotic and erotic because of her Blackness. She is hired and trained by a white man and woman. (Husband and wife? Sister and brother? The relationship is defined in both ways in the film.) Tiffany's Blackness is a topic of interest among the men who call in. One says, "I want to drink your chocolate milk." Tiffany doesn't react to these comments, but a few weeks later an even worse racist comment is made by a white customer. Tiffany is posing for the video with two white women and someone named Dylan types "WHO'S THE N____ BITCH" in all caps. Tiffany immediately reacts saying, "Hey did you see that?" The white women ignore her and continue their simpering poses. "Did you see that?" she repeats. "That's not ok." "They can say whatever they want," one of the white women tells her, not breaking her gaze from the camera lens. "No! No! He cannot call me that." "We get called names, too." The white women then go through the litany of insults they have endured: Ugly Bitch, Fucking Cow, Cum Bucket. Tiffany is not satisfied. She complains to the boss who tells her to go home and that she will be paid for the day. Although Tiffany tries to stand up for herself, the boss refuses to ban Dylan from the website. Tiffany takes a stand and quits, eventually being lured back with a promise of $20 per hour and a no-tolerance policy regarding racist comments. "And no more guys using *that* word," she tells her boss. He offers a compromise: "If they say it once they get a warning; if they say it again, we ban them." She agrees to these terms.

The film ends with Tiffany going off to meet a John she has fallen for. Sabrina is once again coaching her on how to act and what to say. "Don't be scared," she tells Tiffany. "I'm proud of you." Tiffany thanks her, and Sabrina says, "I didn't do nothing . . . It's a date. And you are Jezebel." The film ends. What are we to understand from this narrative? Tiffany is grateful to her sister for coaching her and grooming her into the role of sex worker? That both Sabrina and Tiffany have bought into the myth that a John will fall in love with Jezebel and rescue her from her $20/hour life? That sex work is an empowering and fulfilling career even as these women's lives seem humorless and bleak? If the women have to deal with misogynist and racist bullshit, isn't that true of *any* workplace? The narratives of sex work as a way out of poverty, as a way to empowerment, as a model of Black women taking charge of their destiny are dangerous myths to perpetuate. In reality, sex work, particularly for Black women, often ends tragically, pushing them further into racist subjugation and robbing them of agency, often ending in death (Sankofa 2015).

There are some scholars who have argued that Black women engaging in sex work are not victims of desperate situations but actors in an economic system that offered them a way to financial security. In Blair's book *I've Got to Make My Livin'* (2010), Blair uses first-person accounts of Black women in the sex industry to argue against seeing Black sex workers as victims. Blair states she wanted to:

> challenge the static, timeless image of the prostitute-as-victim and the invisibility of her activity on her own behalf, by examining sex work as precisely that, as labor—work that has a history and work that undergoes profound economic, social, and geographic change over the fifty-year period of the study. Moreover, I focus on how black women *used* the local sex trade and how they engaged in and helped to transform the racially shifting sex economies in Chicago before and after the Great Migration. (6)

What is missing in Blair's and other academics' analysis of sex work as economic empowerment is the equation of rape and assault to "labor." Simply because the patriarchy makes sexual exploitation/rape/assault of women lucrative for some women (although for most women it is not a lucrative or sustainable "career") does not mean the economics of the trade are empowering. The patriarchy wins if it can convince women that rape for money, sex-on-demand, is somehow an empowering subject position for the sex worker. This false narrative, this patriarchal myth, not only removes guilt from the man who pays to rape a woman, but it removes any social/cultural/governmental obligation that would work to change this system of exploitation.

P-Valley, a Starz dramatic series (2020), follows a similar air-brushed fantasy of sex workers and their day-to-day realities. The show, created by Katori Hall with women heading the creative team, features Black sex workers in the Mississippi Delta at a dancer bar that is inexplicably called Pynk. Most of the dancers at Pynk are *not* pink but brown and Black. Hall said she wanted to create a sex work drama that "pulsed with the female gaze." Hall defines the female gaze as "presenting these women and shooting them through the lens of their experience" (Soloski 2020, 11). However, Hall seems to have missed the mark. The grinding and twerking that permeate the show represent male heterosexual fantasies of titillation, right down to the thigh-high stilettos and long, flowing hair. The women, rather than acting like autonomous agents, are performing tropes that disempower them, positioned as mere props for male sexual gratification and getting paid horribly for the honor.

Does Hall consider it a "female gaze" because the protagonists and storyline are about the sex workers and not about the Johns? Or because the sex workers' stories are the plot as opposed to the sex workers being props or murder victims? To shift the gaze from male to female more nuance is required. A female gaze would address the complex issues of race, sexuality, misogyny, class, and the fact that sex work dooms a woman to years of poverty until her body is too old to be considered valuable to the men watching. Unfortunately, *P-Valley* dodges most of these complex issues just as *Jezebel* does. There may be occasional references to racism or poverty, but, overall, these real and damning systems of power that position Black women sex workers at the very bottom of the social caste system in the WSCP go unchallenged by Hall and her cohort of female writers and directors. She speaks of her show as representing "Black female sexuality," conflating sex *work* with sexuality; this conflation is excruciatingly false. People who do sex work are not exercising or expressing their sexuality. They are performing a male version of female sexuality that focuses on male titillation, not female gratification and pleasure. There is no female sexual *pleasure* in sex work, yet Hall states Black female sexuality is the focus of the dancers' performance in interviews and promotional materials for the series (Solinski 2020, Inside the world 2020).

Perhaps we can celebrate that both *P-Valley* and *Jezebel* put the woman as sex worker as the protagonist and we see her as a full human. She is not *just* a sex worker. She is a sister, a mother, a woman attempting to keep her head above water and her family together; a woman pining for love and wanting to believe in the fantasy that a prince charming will come carry her away from all this, even as all around her there is evidence to the contrary. Part of her job description is putting up with degrading racist, misogynist comments and behavior, including assault and abuse. Addiction is a given: alcohol and drugs are needed to get through the shift. The promise of being able to "stack a G in one night" or earn \$20 per hour for writhing in front of leering men is not as lucrative as it sounds. At what cost to the psyche? For how many years before the body is no longer an object of male desire? And then what? All of these real and important realities of sex work are swatted away, if they are brought up at all.

CONCLUSION

In contrast to Beyoncé's pop hit, the female characters analyzed here attempt to offer a different model of female sexuality, one that is not dependent on male approval or ownership for validation. Through series such as *Twenties*, *Insecure*, *BMJ*, *She's Gotta Have It*, and *Chewing Gum*, the audience is served "model[s] of womanist erotic relationality . . . [featuring] non-marital or non-monogamous relationships that are nurturing, mutually respectful and beneficial" (Moultrie 2018, 245). These characters do not "covet the ring over their own best interests" (Moultrie 2018, 245). Instead, they offer empowered, woman-centered sexuality. It may get messy, and these characters may not have their lives, romantic or otherwise, in the best order, but they are celebrating their right to choose for themselves, to reject the pressure to marry without first exploring options. They are preserving and exercising their right to explore the erotic that is within in every way that is healthy, empowering, and affirming. Their bodies, their choices. The choices they make might have us screaming at the screen, but in the end, these are *their* choices that allow them to take charge of their sexuality and define their own way of exploring and experiencing the erotic.

Mary Jane, Issa, Nola, Rob, Hattie, and all of their friends struggle with their romantic lives but learn along the way. We need to see and celebrate these representations of women struggling through relationship after relationship if, in the end, they grow, and delay partnering until they are ready (or resist coupling altogether). At the end of the series, Mary Jane Paul is walking down the aisle. Issa Dee seems to have settled in with Lawrence. Nola Darling never purported to desire a mate. Hattie and Marie and Nia are doing it all their own way. Rob Brooks is still a mess, but she might have had a few episodes to figure it out, but Netflix cancelled the series. These women, like most young women, are on a journey. And isn't that mostly what growing up and maturing and finding who we are and what we want as women is like? Don't most of us, in fits and starts, fail and succeed in increments with various people, learning along the way before we commit to a mate or chose to go solo? Don't many of us even fail after we chose the grand commitment? Life and love are messy and full of mistakes and heartaches and lessons that we learn—or are doomed to repeat. Perhaps these characters, although criticized for exemplifying women who "don't know the love of a good man" or "demand too much from their Black men partners," are closer to the flawed reality than we care to admit.

As a queer woman long in the tooth, as they say, I can affirm and attest that I cringe to remember my younger self and who I was (and wasn't) to my many romantic partners. Hearts broken in many directions, blundering through bad decisions, the wrong lover, the right lover, and the wrong time. All of these complicated dynamics are what these Black women characters offer us if we are paying attention. Shouldn't women have high standards for mates? Shouldn't we honor our own desires and needs instead of ascribing to traditional patriarchal standards of accepting the flaws of men who don't pay enough attention, don't try hard enough, don't offer the same emotional, physical, or financial investment that women are expected to contribute? Females are socialized to first and foremost please males; that is the patriarchal standard. Perhaps these characters offer the viewer a way to celebrate independence, work toward maturity through immature relationships and decisions, fall down and break down and get up and dust off smarter for whatever that experience was. At the end of these narratives, some yet to be written, we see these characters as forging their own path, resisting the white supremacist patriarchal mandate to suck it up and put up with shenanigans because we should never expect to get exactly what we want because Black women never do. Black women are supposed to put everyone else's needs first. Black women are supposed to be strong, have it figured out, not break down, not make mistakes, and not turn away from the "project" that is a man who wants a mother—someone who cooks and cleans and tells him how great he is—a mother he can fuck like a freak. Nah. These characters are showing us a different path. It may be messy, fully of brambles and scrapes, often resulting in wounds that cut deep. But they forge their own path, create their own journey, and resist the role the dominant culture is bent on them living. They refuse to be the Black woman as pillar for everyone else's salty tears, never taking care of her own needs first, always supplicating herself to fathers, boyfriends, brothers, husbands, and sons. These characters, created by and written by women, show us characters who are flawed and struggling, but aren't we all? Isn't that what makes us more interesting and real? Certainly. Certainly.

NOTES

1. As with many of these series, there are several different writers and directors. By Season 3 of *Insecure*, half the episodes are directed by men, shifting the story lines to include the male perspective, a noticeable difference from the first two seasons.

Similarly, with the series *She's Gotta Have It*, Spike Lee directs, but most often it is a woman who wrote the script.

2. Jezebel was a woman in the Old Testament who was said to put on makeup and her best finery for the purpose of either going to her death with dignity or attempting to seduce the king who was throwing her to her death, depending on the telling of her story. The latter theory (one of seduction to save her life) was contorted into contemporary meaning of Jezebel as a woman who wantonly seduces men with her disingenuous desire and wiles. The word "Jezebel" has also been used to stereotype Black women as seductresses of white men, lascivious in their behavior and sexuality. The connection between Christian parables and the judgment of Black women's sexuality is entrenched not only in the word/stereotype of Jezebel, but also in Christian parables that teach girls and women that sexuality, desire, and sexual autonomy are sins. For a fascinating and important article on this topic, please read Brittany Cooper's "How Sarah Got Her Groove Back or Notes toward a Black Theology of Pleasure" (2018).

Chapter 4

Black Women Are Not Always Womanist

The Politics of Empowerment

When *Scandal* first aired on ABC in the spring of 2012, it received immediate attention by fans of *Grey's Anatomy* because of the show's writer/producer, Shonda Rhimes. However, *Scandal* was not just another well-written serialized drama. The featured character of the show, Oliva Pope, was a political powerball, a "fixer" in Washington, D.C., who was literally in bed with the president. And she was Black. A television show starring a Black woman as a power-wielding professional was considered groundbreaking. Not since *Finding Christie Love* (1974–1975 also on ABC) had a serialized drama featured a Black woman as star. As an attorney, Olivia acts as a regulatory force in the white, male world of D.C. politics. But she is an island unto herself. She doesn't have any friends, let alone a Black community. Racism and race issues are rarely addressed, and when they are, typically it is Olivia or others around her who refer derogatorily to Olivia's subordinate position as the Black mistress to a white president. The post-racial approach to story writing and storytelling of a Black woman's reality in *Scandal* reinforces WSCP beliefs of race, class, and gender, giving the primarily white audience easy viewing, but leaving some in the Black female audience experiencing a white-washed version of contemporary identity politics and the realities of racism/misogyny experienced by Black women. Whereas *Scandal* allows a white viewer to consume the storyline without contemplating complex intersections of race, sexuality, and gender, shows such as *BMJ* and *Insecure* do not afford the audience this comfort, forcing audience members to consider complex ways in which race, class, gender, and sexuality shape and oppress their Black protagonists' realities, a decidedly feminist/womanist perspective.

The serialized drama, *BMJ* (BET), first airing the year after *Scandal*, also features a strong, professional Black woman. But Mary Jane Paul, unlike Olivia Pope, is extremely aware of issues of racism and misogyny both as they manifest in her personal life as well as the culture around her (Atlanta, New York City, and the larger North American culture). Mary Jane is a journalist and uses her platform as a television personality to foreground issues of race/gender, acting as a regulatory agent against the white supremacist patriarchy. Similar to *BMJ*, *Insecure (*HBO 2016–2020) features a young professional single woman in Los Angeles (Issa Dee) working at an "inner city non-profit" (code for "white do-gooder organization to help Black youth"). As with *BMJ*'s Mary Jane, Issa also moves the viewer through the brambles of systems of power as they manifest in her personal and professional relationships. The Afrocentric and womanist storylines and the cast of *BMJ* and *Insecure* offer a refreshing and stark contrast to the white-washed, post-racial *Scandal*. The commercial success of *Scandal* indicates the United States' white viewing audience's commitment to a narrative of a post-racial, post-feminist world-view where systems of oppression related to race, class, and gender rarely need to be considered. The dramatic difference between how being Black, female, single, and professional are portrayed on *BMJ*, *Insecure*, and *Scandal* illustrates a distinction between ignoring the complexities of Black female-ness in the WSCP (*Scandal*) and grappling with complex issues of racism, classism, and sexism from a Black feminist perspective (*BMJ* and *Insecure*).

Because there are so few Black female (and even fewer Black feminist) characters in film and television, when two emerge nearly simultaneously, they are worth examining. At their initial premier, the statistics of Black women representations on television represented a tremendous lack.

An overview of the 12 narrative TV shows nominated for an Emmy in 2013 pro-duces an unsurprising chart of white-dominated representation featured in and behind the scenes. Nine shows featured a white female lead, while only three have featured black female characters, even in secondary roles. None of these Emmy-nominated shows had black female leads or creators. (Pixley 2015, 28)

When so few Black women's images in popular serialized dramas create symbolic annihilation (Gerbner 1972), they directly affect the audience. This symbolic annihilation occurs when a person (woman) doesn't see herself in the media she consumes or only sees herself denigrated (Tuchman 1978). Although there are more films and series featuring Black woman since 2015, it is worth analyzing these three shows in relation to each other as they emerged almost simultaneously. Whereas *Scandal*, on the surface, may seem like a break from symbolic annihilation, the character of Olivia actu-ally reinforces it in how she is treated by lovers, acquaintances, and family. Contrasting this, Issa and Mary Jane offer a way into an Afrocentric world of Black feminist identity that acts as a counter-narrative to systematic annihila-tion. Much critical, thoughtful attention should be paid to Olivia, Issa, and

Mary Jane and the shows that house these Black female characters. Because there are so few representations of Black feminist protagonists, the ones we do see have a large impact on viewers. Careful analysis and open discussions regarding Olivia, Issa, and Mary Jane are essential to resisting mindless consumption of damaging stereotypes.

There have been many articles written about *Scandal*, Shonda Rhimes, and her character Olivia Pope in popular press and scholarly publications. Fewer articles address *BMJ*/Mary Jane Paul and *Insecure*/Issa Dee. Whereas *Scandal* and Olivia Pope reinforce tired stereotypes and myths of post-racial, post-feminist cultural ideologies, *BMJ* and *Insecure* grapple with important and complex issues of being a Black feminist/womanist in a white supremacist patriarchy. It is of no coincidence that *Scandal* is the more popular of these series because it allows white viewers to skate over complex issues of power/oppression.

FEMINIST/WOMANIST

Alice Walker (1983) coined the term "womanist" to separate Black female critical consciousness from what she considered to be the racist colorblindness of most white feminists. Whereas historically feminism concerned itself with white women's issues, rarely confronting complex racism within the movement or how Black (and other "non-white") women's perspectives were addressed, Walker's term focused on feminist issues with an emphasis on how race/gender/sex created particular concerns for Black women under the feminist banner. Walker defined a womanist as "a black feminist or feminist of color . . . a woman who loves other women, sexually and/ or nonsexually . . . committed to survival and wholeness of entire people, male and female . . . womanist is to feminist as purple is to lavender" (45). As applied to representation of Black womanhood in media, a womanist representation would address issues of power and oppression in storyline, visuals, music, and tone. In *Scandal*, some of the tired stereotypes of Black women manifest simultaneously in Olivia, whereas Issa and Mary Jane buck stereotypical representations by presenting characters that address, confront, and discuss issues of race, sexuality, gender, and class. Whereas Olivia could be viewed as a Matriarch/Mammy character, a female leader/caretaker in her white-dominated work world, Issa and Mary Jane caretake themselves and other females of color, having little patience for needy whites. Although *BMJ* does include a Black matriarch character in Mary Jane's mother, she is not the sole caretaker of the family. The extended family unit in Mary Jane's world takes turns caring emotionally and financially for individuals in their sphere. Fundamentally, unlike Olivia, Mary Jane's and Dee's "caretaker" roles deviate strongly from a Mammy/Matriarch because they do not focus on caretaking of *white* culture/people/family.

The Matriarch is not the only stereotype disrupted or complicated in these shows. Chaney and Robertson (2016) see multiple stereotypes of Black women in Olivia, arguing she manifests Jezebel and Black Lady as well as Matriarch: "she 'births' her own business" and other characters "seek her advice and counsel, as one would a mother" (Matriarch). Chaney and Robertson continue, "Pope is a sexually aggressive female (Jezebel) who willingly engages in passionate and animalistic sexual relations with the married President Fitz" and she is "physically attractive, has incredible fashion sense, is a hard worker, and is highly respected because she is the best in her field" (Black Lady) (Chaney and Robertson 2016, 142). Although one could also argue that Mary Jane and Issa embody the Matriarch, Jezebel or Black Lady stereotypes, I think they more often disrupt them, defying these tired stereotypes of Black womanhood and instead demonstrate how to be empowered in womanist ways. There is a fundamental difference in being a caretaker of whites (the Matriarch/Mammy stereotypes) and caretaking/being cared for by a Black family and community, those roles ever-changing but *never* caretaking whites. In terms of the "Black Lady" stereotype, some might see that stereotype manifest in Olivia, but the isolated "Black Lady" exercising respectability politics does not manifest on *BMJ* and *Insecure* because Mary Jane and Issa are surrounded by diverse and varied versions of womanhood in other Black and Latina characters featured on these shows. Neither does the Jezebel label fit Issa nor Mary Jane. Whereas Olivia is the sexual temptress for the white man, the mistress that is a threat to his white marriage, Issa and Mary Jane are in control of their sexuality and are not used by men nor are they portrayed as the temptress out to destroy a white family. Issa and Mary Jane are sexually empowered, not seductresses or victims. And their partners are Black men.

Some viewers and scholars tend to judge harshly Black women or characters who seek and have sex, declaring them "promiscuous" (Jeffries & Jeffries 2015, Pixley 2015). However, "promiscuous" is at heart a sexist term reserved for women who engage in *any* sex deemed worthy of judgment, especially sex where she is the power broker or initiator. In considering Walker's definition of womanist, these characters (Issa and Mary Jane) are operating under a self-love and woman-love exploration of sexuality as empowerment. Even if she is monogamous, a woman can be called promiscuous if she has a desire for sex while unmarried. Instead of seeing sexual empowerment as a positive trait, women who have several (even if not simultaneous) sex partners are judged as "promiscuous." The irony of the dueling stereotypes of Black Lady (she must be sexually neutered but professionally powerful) and Jezebel (hypersexual and judged as "promiscuous") create a bind where Black women have no road to positive, empowering sexuality. Characters such as Issa and Mary Jane offer a more progressive and womanist way. Both

Issa and Mary Jane not only take charge of their sexuality, they are meeting Walker's definition of "women loving women:" both have strong, loving relationships with female friends and family members that sustain them. While Olivia's primary relationship with the white, married president puts her squarely in the stereotype of Jezebel or Sapphire (a professional woman who seduces white men for political/social/career power), Mary Jane's and Issa's sexual relationships are almost always with Black men. Both Mary Jane and Issa very briefly engage with a white man, but when they do, the dynamic is a topic of conversation with female friends. Mary Jane even remarks on the novelty of her "first white man" with her confidante. Mary Jane's and Issa's relationships with men are portrayed in complex ways, often with the women as the power broker in these relationships. Issa and Mary Jane also address a myriad of heterosexual dynamics for sexually active women operating within a patriarchal system.

However, there is some critique among viewers regarding all three shows and the topic of romantic love. Some female viewers are frustrated by the implication in Issa, Mary Jane, and Olivia that Black women don't know how to be loved. Eboni, a respondent in my research who is a single female, was critical of the rotating door of lovers and the inability to engage in a healthy relationship as portrayed in *Scandal*, *BMJ*, and *Insecure*. Eboni said:

> The only issue with *Being Mary* Jane and *Insecure* and *Scandal* is there is this portrayal that Black women don't know how to be loved. And I hate that. Like in *Being Mary Jane*, she had her Harvard man, and after five seasons you see her struggle with man after man after man. She finally gets a man that she loves and she can't even deal with it. Without even expressly breaking up with him, she cheats. That is the same thing with Issa Rae [*sic*]. There is this thing out there that Black women don't know how to commit. It's not that way for other races.

For more discussion on this dynamic, see Chapter 3, *All the Single Ladies*. Even if we take *Scandal* out of the analysis, since Olivia is engaging in a dysfunctional relationship with a married man, both Issa and Mary Jane engage with good men—men who love them, who want to commit, who may have flaws but are willing to work on a committed relationship—but they cheat on those men. This dynamic is certainly worthy of analysis and I address this and other issues regarding female sexuality, dating and relationships in chapter 3.

In academic scholarship there is far more discussion of Olivia's sexual/romantic relationship with the white, married president because it is such a fraught, historical model of Black female disempowered sexuality. "Even in communities of color, folks are not certain whether Rhimes' *Scandal* is a progressive step in an anti-essentialist direction or a regressive move backward toward a reconstituted Jezebel-in-bed-with-Massa stereotype" (Mask 2015, 4).

Kerry Washington, the actor who plays Olivia, was quoted in the *New York Times* as rejecting the idea that the character is a Black woman who has any allegiance to race politics. Washington stated, "It's not that [Olivia] rejects the [Black] community; she is not ashamed of being black. She's fully aware of her blackness. She just doesn't identify historically with the burden of blackness because she was raised with a sense of impossibility" (Tillet 2018, 21). Washington's explanation falls short. Not only does Olivia eschew a Black identity, but she embodies racist stereotypes of what the dominant white culture assigns to Black women.

Olivia's very lack of identity as a Black woman with any connection to a Black community represents a comfortable post-racial view for white fans. Olivia's relationship with the president, for example, positions her as the "Jezebel-in-bed-with-Massa stereotype" due to her ongoing disempowered subject position in relation to the white man of power. Olivia's disempowered subject position and the history of white men raping Black women is central to this character's sexuality (Collins 1997 and 2004, Kein 2000, Childs 2005, Washington 2008, Painter 2010). In *BMJ* and *Insecure*, there are no such fraught relationship dynamics because the casts of both shows are almost entirely Black and the women featured on the show almost exclusively engaged with Black men.

Because *Insecure* and *BMJ* are both placed squarely within the context of an Afrocentric community, issues of racism and sexism are discussed, addressed, and confronted in complicated and interesting ways, making the argument for a womanist focus in these shows. In *Scandal*, these issues are not addressed and so the audience is left to their own experience, either deliciously ignorant (white racist audience) or frustrated (audiences who rejects post-racial, post-feminist cultural views). In grappling with her frustration in reading Olivia, scholar Mia Mask (2015) asks, "Is Olivia an impressively complicated black female character struggling with the pressure-cooker of Washington's political machinery and the façade of respectability? Or is she an example of integration-means-capitulation to the white power structure?" (Mask 2015, 7). The viewer, if she chooses to ask such complicated questions, is left to grapple with them on her own.

Olivia—appealing to a primarily white audience—is a clear manifestation of a post-racial, post-feminist ideal. Olivia represents a fantasy of white patriarchal culture: a Black woman who does not have to deal with systemic oppression; she is professionally powerful, but sexually disempowered; she is devoid of Black support/community, a Lone Wolf reaching into a void of "colorblind/gender-blind" white supremacy. The fantasy is of a race-free existence (Iton 2010). "What this absence [of race issues] reveals is not that the United States is a raceless society but that race matters so much that its presence in social relationships has to be erased on screen to make the show successful" (McKnight 2014, 192). The white audience wants to believe in the fantasy of the post-racial world in which Olivia lives and works. While some see this fantasy as a problem, others see it as a positive change. "*Scandal* is a fantastical imagining of an alternate world—one where black women wield great influence, agency, and passion, even up to the executive branch of the U.S. government . . . [it] generates a space for black women to finally partake in fantasy that has long eluded us" (Warner 2015, 19). However, it is a degrading, lonely fantasy that Olivia represents, one lacking a womanist sisterhood and consciousness.

Olivia is utterly alone in her white world of power and prestige; inversely Mary Jane and Issa are surrounded by a Black community of close girlfriends and family. Collins (2000) writes that Black women seek out or create "safe spaces" where they can escape from the dominant culture's oppressive systems. These spaces are created through love relationships, intimate friendships, close family ties, or other self-created retreats. Olivia doesn't have any such spaces, but Issa's and Mary Jane's worlds are full of them.

Because of the womanist/Afrocentric nature of shows such as *Insecure* and *BMJ*, these programs offer an example of a "future text," what is possible when the focus shifts from the dominant white, capitalist, patriarchal, white supremacist culture to something feminist and Black. As defined by scholar Alondra Nelson:

[Future Texts] excavate and create original narratives of identity, technology, and the future . . . [and] represent new directions in the study of African diaspora culture that are grounded in the histories of black communities, rather than seeking to sever all connections to them. (Nelson 2002, 9)

We see in both Issa's and Mary Jane's experiences how independent, highly educated and aware, single Black professional women exist in the WSCP, *not* a post-racial society. These characters offer their audiences a contemporary view of Black female activism and struggle. These female characters are fully aware and address issues of racism, sexism, and classism as they manifest in their daily lives. These dynamics also exist in series such as *Queen Sugar* (Oprah Winfrey Network) but because there is not a protagonist who is a single career woman in *Queen Sugar*, it does not fit as neatly into a comparison with *Scandal*, *BMJ*, and *Insecure*. The tension in *Queen Sugar* is more complicated because two sisters embody different versions of Black womanhood. One (Nora) is womanist, activist, journalist, and a resister; however, she is also engaged with a white lover; her sister, Charley, is an assimilated, light-skinned woman who is invested in the power and privilege afforded her through marriage. *Queen Sugar*'s storyline contemplates the dueling realities of a womanist perspective (Nora) and an Anglocentric alternative reality (Charley). A similar dynamic exists when comparing Olivia's world (white), and Mary Jane's/Issa's world where issues of racism, sexism, and the complex dynamics of Black community are addressed as part of the storylines. Shows such as *BMJ* and *Insecure*, unlike *Scandal*, attempt "to expand what constitutes black female representation on-screen by accepting blackness as a spectrum" (Cartier 2014, 152). In shows such as *Insecure* and *BMJ*, we can celebrate the complexities of a Black womanist identity; *Scandal* offers a white-washed version of a Black assimilated to the dominant culture.

> In appealing to white audiences, Black women/characters in popular media must be "racially specific enough to connote difference, desire, and exoticism, but enough of a colorblind, blank slate to acquire success in the commercial, white-desirous marketplace; be sexy enough to garner desire and media obsession, but be enough of a role model to earn a wide variety of corporate sponsorships" (Joseph 2009, 242).

We see this attempt to neuter the Black feminist identity in Olivia. Olivia rarely confronts or experiences racism or sexism. She is sexy, but also submissive to her white lover, acting in ways that would suggest lack of agency. Olivia "straightens" herself to assimilate to the world of white, patriarchal law/politics. Creating an analogy of "straightening" the unruly "Black"/natural hair to "straightening" one's ethnic markers to be as white as possible, scholar Morrison (2010) argues that Blackness, particularly in female identity, is "processed" like black hair.

> In the way that chemicals or heat are applied to kinky hair to tame it or straighten it out, identity markers more culturally assigned to Whites . . . . Straightening is essentially the assigning of Whiteness to any aspects of our identity that can be construed as positive. (Morrison 2010, 89–90)

Oliviais "straightened" in the way she wears her clothing/hair, by choosing a white lover, in her speech, and in her isolation from any sort of Black community. Protagonists such as Mary Jane and Issa, on the other hand, refuse to be straightened. They date Black men; their friend circle does not include white people; they may have relationship issues with their Black lovers, but they are acting agents, taking control of their desires rather than submitting to white/male power.

These fictional representations of Black women matter, both to white and Black audiences. In studying the effects of representations on Black-oriented reality shows, Tyree (2011) found that even Black audience members believed the stereotypes were accurate representations of Black culture. In case studies and focus groups of young Black women who consumed stereotypical images of Black women on reality television, Coleman et al. (2016)

found that even though the young women identified the behavior they were viewing as stereotypical, it had an impact on their own sense of self and personal decisions/actions. Through consuming narratives such as those on reality television or shows like *Scandal*, Black women come to believe stereotypes about themselves. In addition, white audiences' racist stereotypes or belief in post-racism/post-feminism are codified. Even as Black women live lives of disruption against the white supremacist patriarchy, they see these negative media portrayals and those portrayals inform their bodies, voices, and images (Harris-Perry 2011).

In shows such as *BMJ* and *Insecure*, however, we experience Black protagonists who are empowered and defy stereotypes. These characters represent a space that reflects the complexities of Black womanhood in contemporary U.S. culture. hooks (2014) asked, "What are the spaces we are making? Where do we find our sense of freedom? (especially in the capitalist, white supremacist, imperialist patriarchy?)" When examining the spaces of Olivia versus Mary Jane/Issa, we get two very different perceptions of what it means to be a Black professional woman. The stories constructed about Black womanhood (one decidedly womanist one disempowered Jezebel or Sapphire) are significant in how they affect their audiences.

ROMANTIC RELATIONSHIPS

In all three of these shows, romantic relationships are a large part of the narrative arc. Unlike Issa and Mary Jane who are experimenting with various types of relationships, Olivia is trapped in the role of a mistress. She is the one used/not chosen, at the mercy of her more powerful white male lover. She can't phone him or define the terms of the relationship because he is married (to a white woman). Mary Jane and Issa, on the other hand, freely explore several different types of relationships. They both have problems with men, but they are shown as making their own decisions, engaging and ending relationships on their own terms. Mary Jane and Issa may make bad decisions (they cheat on men who care about them; they can't decide whether to answer calls/texts from ex-boyfriends or potential suitors; they often don't know what they want in a relationship or a partner), but they are the ones making the decisions about their relationships. For Olivia, caught in the dysfunction of loving a married white man who happens to be president, the power she has is extremely limited against her lover's overwhelming institutional power and his marital status to a white woman.

In *Scandal*, Olivia uses disempowering, misogynistic language about herself in the context of her relationship. She is literally the white president's Black whore. Olivia uses the word "whore" in regard to herself (Season 2, Episode

11). When Olivia uses the term "whore" to describe herself, the audience experiences the painfully isolated and unreciprocated dynamic of this relationship. Olivia is at her lover's mercy. The president's wife overtly states that Olivia is her husband's whore (Season 2, Episode 1), saying to him, "I wouldn't need to smile on *Oprah* if you didn't screw your whore every chance you got" (in front of Olivia). Olivia retorts, "I am going to need you to quit referring to me as whore, at least in front of my face." Later in the same episode, in speaking with Fitz (the president, Fitzgerald Gran), his wife says that his ultimate fantasy is "bringing that whore into the White House as your First Lady." Reiterated throughout these episodes, the audience experiences a powerful, educated, strong, professional woman being reduced to her lack of sexual agency. Olivia looks utterly disempowered in her status as presidential whore.

Even when Olivia attempts to rearrange the power structure, she fails and falls back into her role as Black mistress. In Season 2, Olivia says to the president, "You can't treat me like some whore you found on the street" (Episode 19). Yet, in fact, he does, time and again: professing his love, yet treating Olivia in ways that would indicate she is dispensable. Later in the episode, Millie (the president's wife) tells him he can "shack up" with Olivia, but *she* (Millie) won't let it go on forever and when Millie decides the affair must end, she will stand on the White House lawn, and hold a press conference "discussing my philandering husband who can't keep his pants zipped and his whore who has him on leash." Despite these degrading dynamics, Olivia doesn't sever ties with her lover and continues to wallow in her non-status of mistress, devoid of relationship power.

Regardless of how many professional successes Olivia may have, we see in her personal life she is lonely, sexually used, cast aside, and excruciatingly marginalized. She is degraded through language, her own about herself and others' in relation to her. She demonstrates lack of power through her actions. The audience sees her getting raped by the president in a nonconsensual sexual encounter late at night in her apartment. In Season 2, Episode 14, we see a sex scene between Fitz and Olivia that is staged more like a darkly lit stranger assault. While Stevie Wonder croons "I never knew how much love could hurt until I loved you, baby" in the background, Fitz stalks, and assaults Olivia. He throws her into a room where he violently kisses her. She slaps him. They have violent sex. Afterward he tells her "We are done. I may not be able to control my erections around you, but that does not mean I want you." The scene plays out like an acquaintance rape of an entitled, white misogynist.

The racism in the relationship is largely unnamed, but the role of enslaving master/mistress is alluded to. In Season 2, Episode 8, Olivia tells the president that she is his Sally Hemmings. He becomes angry telling her, "You are playing the race card on the fact that I am in love with you?" She replies, "My whole life is you. I can't breathe because I am waiting for you. You *own* me.

You *control* me. I belong to you." The language of slavery resonates in the words "own," "belong to," and "control." The president retorts that she is his whole life, that she controls *him*. "You are nobody's victim, Liv." However, the scene ends with him walking away, leaving her. It is impossible for her to follow. She is left alone. By attempting to cast himself as the victim, the white president deflects any responsibility for Olivia's pathetic position.

In several contexts over the course of the series, Olivia attempts to tell the president that their relationship is over, but every time, he refuses to accept her desire to define the parameters of their interactions. In Season 3, Episode 12, there is a typical interaction where Olivia attempts to gain agency. She says, "I am not a hen. I am not a prize at the state fair. You can't win me." Fitz: "Would you just shut up and let me talk?" She retorts: "I am a person. I am not a hen. I am not a prize." Later in that episode, Olivia says to Fitz: "I can't spend all my time worrying about what you want, what you need." Yet, she does. Time and again, throughout the series, Olivia seems unable to break ties with her abusive lover.

In *BMJ* and *Insecure*, the audience sees Mary Jane and Issa as acting agents in control of their romantic relationships. Unlike Olivia, Mary Jane and Issa engage in several different romantic relationships with different kinds of men, and in each, we see the woman making decisions, choosing how/when to engage with her lovers/boyfriends. The women may have fraught relationships, but the audience watches these women work through these issues in their own ways, not controlled by the men. Mary Jane engages with a married man, Dre, at the beginning of the series, but she doesn't know he's married and when she finds out, she tells him to go away, *and he does*. Mary Jane may still have feelings for Dre, but she resists his periodic advances (her phone displays "Never Answer" when he calls). Another of Mary Jane's lovers, David, provides fodder for strained romance in Mary Jane's life. She loves David and is trying to move on because he is having a baby with another woman. Her phone displays "Let Him Go" when he calls; unlike the interactions between Fitz and Olivia, the interactions between David and Mary Jane are typically respectful even when they are strained. But Mary Jane allows herself to move on from David and Dre, even as she may make some bad choices about how to move on.

During the first season, Mary Jane saves David's sperm from a condom (without his consent or awareness) and puts it in her freezer, contemplating self-insemination without telling David. Eventually, at a gathering of girl-friends, she tells them about the frozen sperm, and they insist she toss it out, that it would be unethical to inseminate herself with David's sperm without his knowledge. She follows this advice. Mary Jane then goes on national television showing the process of freezing her eggs for a future pregnancy. Through this process of Mary Jane's break-up with David, her ongoing desire to have a child, her various approaches to achieve this goal with or without a partner, the audience witnesses a professional woman who knows that she eventually wants to have a child, but on her terms, and so she makes plans for that to happen.

After David and Dre, Mary Jane gets involved with Sheldon, an Black historian, an attorney, an academic and intellectual several years her senior. Sheldon offers himself as a mature, thoughtful, and unconventional relationship partner. Mary Jane assumes the relationship trajectory is one where they will live together, but Sheldon doesn't want to cohabitate, causing Mary Jane to question his commitment. Mary Jane confronts Sheldon about the seriousness of his intentions to couple with her by saying, "You knew I was freezing my eggs." He says, "So have a baby." She replies, "You want me to have a baby with sperm donor?" He tells her he wants a "mutually respectful relationship. You'd have your life and I'd have mine . . . it's not hard to understand, just different." Sheldon is willing to accept her desire to have a child with a sperm donor, but Mary Jane seems unable to alter her image of the conventional relationship. She breaks up with Sheldon, saying, "I will never settle for anything less than what I want or desire." Later Sheldon calls her and asks if they can get back together. Mary Jane says, "I don't know if marriage and kids are in the cards for me, but I do know I want to wake up next to the same person every day" (Season 2; Episode 12). Mary Jane's response to Sheldon indicates she would be willing to embark on a less conventional relationship, but she wants a commitment that he can't provide, so she is moving on. Instead of changing what she wants, putting his desires/needs before her own, or submitting to Sheldon's idea of a relationship, Mary Jane takes stock, defines what she wants/needs, and decides she doesn't want to compromise. By moving on (and moving to New York City), Mary Jane becomes involved with Lee who seems to want the same things she does: a conventional relationship (Season 4). Although Lee already has children, he is open to having a child with Mary Jane, fitting Mary Janes' needs for a partner. By being direct and self-aware about what she wants in a relationship, Mary Jane eventually finds a man who loves her, treats her with respect, and wants the same things from a union.

In both *Scandal* and *BMJ*, the women go through the experience of an unplanned pregnancy and an abortion. Some viewers point to Olivia's response to the unintended pregnancy as a strong feminist message. In a November 2015 episode, Olivia has an abortion and doesn't tell the president. She tells no one. She goes to the appointment by herself. She experiences the pregnancy and subsequent termination absolutely alone. During a question/answer panel at the PaleyFest Film Festival, Rhimes was asked about integrating an abortion into the story line. Rhimes replied, "A woman made a choice about her body that she legally has the right to make" (Wagmeister 2016). There was no trauma or regret. It was a decision she made and moved on. This is a feminist approach to abortion, but the way the abortion is represented only serves to reinforce how alone Olivia is her world, without friends or support. Later, a colleague finds out about the abortion, and Olivia says she has no regrets and refuses to feel ashamed. Abby, Olivia's colleague, is a Republican strategist and she believes she is doing Olivia a favor by refusing to publicly disclose the abortion as a way of gaining a political advantage for Abby's candidate. Olivia seems unfazed by her colleague's attempt to protect her reputation. "My abortion . . . the thing is, I'm not ashamed at all. The only person who would have really been hurt is him (Fitz). It would have hurt him. . . He doesn't know. No one knows" (Season 5, Episode 20). With this statement, Olivia implies that the president would be more affected by the abortion than she was. Because Olivia does not articulate *why* the president would be hurt by her decision to terminate the unplanned pregnancy, the audience is left to speculate. Perhaps he would be hurt because it would be a decision that she made without him, a loss of control over her. By making the decision to terminate the pregnancy, Olivia is deciding for both of them what the best solution is to the situation. But by blocking him out of that decision, she frees herself from his demands on her, on what she should do or what he wants her to do. This is a rare moment in the context of the series and the way their relationship is portrayed. Olivia makes a decision, takes control, decides for herself what she wants to do, and then does it, yet she does it utterly alone.

Contrasting Olivia's self-imposed isolation is the portrayal of Mary Jane's abortion in *BMJ*. In Season 2, David (former lover) and Mary Jane are talking about why their relationship didn't work and Mary Jane mentions an abortion she had when neither David nor Mary Jane were ready to be parents. Mary Jane says, "I made that choice because I wanted to have kids under the right circumstances." The two former lovers share a tender moment, acknowledging the difficulty of the decision and the happenstance of a pregnancy coming at the wrong time. Unlike Mary Jane, Olivia shows no acknowledgment of the difficulty of the decision or that there would be a reason to talk it through with anyone, particularly the man who was responsible for the pregnancy.

Olivia's isolation from friends, family, support, and her inability to gain agency in her primary relationship provides a sharp contrast to how womanhood is portrayed on *BMJ* and *Insecure*. At nearly every point of comparison, Mary Jane Paul and Issa Dee represent an empowered, feminist/womanist, Afrocentric counter-argument to the dysfunctional and damaged representation of Black womanhood that is Olivia Pope. Whereas Olivia is an island of loneliness and isolation, Mary Jane and Issa are surrounded by girlfriends, both at work and in their social circles, women who support them, confront them with honest evaluations of their choices, and act as sounding boards and emotional support. Whereas Olivia's family is dysfunctional, working to thwart her power and sabotage her business/personal life, Mary Jane's family, although not without problems, supports her, relies on her, and represents a positive dynamic in her life. Whereas Olivia's romantic relationship models dysfunction and disempowerment, Mary Jane's and Issa's romantic relationships position them on equal footing with her male lovers/boyfriends, demonstrating not only agency but intellectual engagement and mutual respect.

AFROCENTRISM IN *BEING MARY JANE* AND *INSECURE*

On *BMJ*, from philanthropic galas that the family funds/attends to circles of friends to social clubs, interactions with whites are rare and when they happen, they point to overt racism and white stupidity regarding issues of race. In *Insecure*, the racism, classism, and sexism of the dominant white culture is blatantly addressed, typically in the context of Issa's work world at the do-gooder white nonprofit. In both Mary Jane's and Issa's work world, we see their frustration and literal eye rolls when white coworkers say or do something racist both through microaggressions and bald-faced idiocy. When a white newscaster colleague tells Mary Jane she used to watch a show called *Fame* that featured a "feisty little Black woman," Mary Jane sighs, rolls her eyes and mutters, "Debbie Allen" (Season 2, Episode 13). At work, Mary Jane's manager, Kara, is speaking with a white, male marketing exec who is "concerned" about Mary Jane's popularity with "Hispanic" viewers (Kara is Latin American). The scene then cuts to a woman who is part of a focus group (she could be Latina/she could be "white") saying, "She's (Paul) not relatable" (Season 2, Episode 4). The comments by the executive and the member of the focus group highlight the latent and overt racism/sexism and shift the focus from a white perspective to one of a Black woman. At Issa's work place, she resists admitting to her white liberal boss that the logo for their organization is racist. She endures coworkers who self-righteously say that the Black children "need our help." At one point, we see Issa angrily speak back to racist comments by coworkers, if only in her head. She exclaims: "That is the whitest shit you ever said!" when a white coworker suggests taking the Black children to a white neighborhood to do a neighborhood clean-up (Season 1; Episode 2). Because she is the only Black at the nonprofit, she is often dismissed while simultaneously asked to speak to the experience of all Black people. Although Issa can't directly call out her racist coworkers, we see her confront the racism in her fantasies, giving the racists what they deserve. In addition, Issa has fantastical conversations with her mirror that similarly call out racism/misogyny. These moments allow the audience to hear and see how she *wishes* she could respond to racism and sexism in her work world. These asides destroy the fourth wall of theatre and allow the audience access to insights regarding race, class, gender, sexuality, and other systems of oppression experienced by the characters. This phenomenon of a woman "breaking the fourth wall" to speak and give insights to complex issues is more fully addressed in Chapter 5, *"I'm Talking to You."*

In addition to overt references to racism/sexism, the musical soundtracks in *Scandal*, *Insecure*, and *BMJ* further emphasize the split between a Black woman trapped in a white reality (*Scandal*) and a Black woman who has found "safe spaces" (Collins 2000) that include a rich, affirming Black community and culture (*BMJ* and *Insecure*). Although all three shows integrate Black music in the background (jazz, hip-hop, rhythm and blues), the music in *Scandal* speaks to an oppressed experience of Blackness in a white context. Even as Monk-Payton (2015) argues that the music in *Scandal* points to complexities of racial politics (21), the songs chosen tend to white-wash these complexities. Whereas *BMJ* and *Insecure* features music of socially conscious Black female songwriters/composers like Mary J. Blige, Nicki Minaj, Bittersweet, Stacy Barthe, Ella Fitzgerald, and Me Shell Ndegeocello, *Scandal* uses some classics that may allude to Black politics and perspectives, but just as easily could be seen as mainstream assimilation of Black music acceptable to white audiences and experiences. For example, the tumultuous relationship between the president and Olivia is shown through a sequence where Stevie Wonder sings "Don't Know Why I Love You" and Bill Withers' "Ain't No Sunshine." Other artists included in *Scandal* are Marvin Gaye, Michael Jackson, The Temptations, Bettye LaVette, and Same Cooke, mostly males popular with white audiences.

In *BMJ* and *Insecure*, each episode features classic R&B songs and soundtracks, jazz, hip-hop, and other songs/music by Black artists and most popular with Black audiences. In addition, we see sticky notes throughout Mary Jane's home and in her work space that quote famous workers for social justice and Black women: Ghandi, Maya Angelou, Alice Walker, Audre Lorde, Walter Mosely, Erykah Badu, Susan B. Anthony, Nelson Mandela, Bob Marley; in some cases these quotes also end up as inserts in the storyline, acting as transitions between scenes. In the first episode of Season 2, the series begins with a dinner party/book club where Mary Jane reads aloud from Walter Mosely's book, *Life Out of Context*. What ensues is a political conversation about education, the Black church, activism, "American" culture as a rip-off of Black culture, the economy, meritocracy, and personal responsibility to Black empowerment. In *Insecure*, we see Issa reading *The Turner House* by Angela Flournoy, a book about the Michigan car industry crisis through the eyes of a young Black girl, Cha-Cha. The plot, characters, music, and scene/episode titles are just a few examples of ways the shows keep their Afrocentric and Womanist focus.

In other contexts, the Afrocentric focus is part of the dialogue and story arcs. Mary Jane and her family openly discuss racist stereotypes of Black women as they manifest in Mary Jane's niece (a teen mother with two babies by two different fathers) and brother (a recovering addict who lives with his parents). Niecy, who is Mary Jane's niece and lives with her grandparents/ Mary Jane's parents, remains poor, does not get support from her "two baby daddies," and can't seem to stay in school. Niecy regularly asks Mary Jane and others for financial support. There is clearly affection between the two women, regardless of how different their lives are. Mary Jane's phone displays "Work in Progress" when Niecy calls and Mary Jane rescues and provides respite to Niecy. Even as Niecy relies heavily on Mary Jane and sees her as a role model, Mary Jane becomes frustrated with Niecy's manifestation of cultural stereotype. In one scene, Niecy apologizes to Mary Jane for letting her down by being the stereotypical Black "baby momma." Mary Jane scolds Niecy, "Aren't you tired of being sorry and making promises you can't keep . . . . Your life cannot revolve around a dude . . . . Being a baby momma is *not* a career; *I'm* taking care of your kids" (Season 2, Episode 3). The family— including Mary Jane—rally around Niecy and support her as she cares for her small children and attempts to find her way. The storylines of Mary Jane, Niecy, and the extended family confront the complexities of contemporary Black lives as well as the stereotypes about those lives in various iterations of class, gender, and sexuality.

In *Insecure*, the primary focus of conversations about tacit racism is at Issa's work place, the nonprofit for "inner city" (re: Black) children called We Got Y'all. The executive director of the nonprofit is a Hippy-era white liberal who seems clueless about issues of racism at her organization. In Season 1, Episode 2, Issa's white coworkers are tossing around ideas about how to engage the children. The white coworkers make passive racist comments such as "They [the Black children] would love a drum circle. . . . How about a hip-hop Othello? . . . Because it has an interracial relationship . . . . How about an African American or Latino museum?" Issa interrupts their ideas to suggest something like going to the beach. Her boss calls her out for not listening to her coworkers or caring enough about the children saying, "A leader who takes advice is not a leader. That's from Kenya. Date unknown" (Season 1; Episode 2). In these moments, the audience feels Issa's anger about the whites' perpetual microaggressions and uninterrogated racism. Several of *Insecure*'s episodes have side plots that address issues of racism or being Black in a WSCP. In Season 2, Issa is confronted by a Black principal who has racist ideas about Latinx students, denying them access to an after-school club. Issa is slow to admit that the principal is racist. She tells her white coworker who is consistently calling the principal racist, "Do you know how many racist people there are out there? And truthfully, Black people can't be racist like that. . . . It must be nice to have the privilege to *choose* to be upset over this" (Season 3, Episode 5 "Hella Shook"). In a later episode, Issa is at work when a potential new hire (also a Black female) asks her how it is to work at We Got Y'all. Issa doesn't answer directly, but it is clear by the side-eye she gives and the tone of her, "Well, you know . . ." that she is alluding to a culture of passive racism at work.

By including these moments of what it means to be a Black woman trying to be professional in the WSCP, *BMJ*, and *Insecure* create refreshing counter-narratives to the dominant culture's mythologies of Black womanhood. These shows provide a view of the WSCP from a Black female perspective. hooks (2014) has said, "We [Black women] are so invested in the white supremacy it is tragic. It is more well-paying to remain enslaved . . . . Why don't we have liberatory images of 'What do I look like when I am free?' " *BMJ* and *Insecure* offer one way to answer this question. Mary Jane and Issa may still feel the strain and pain of being Black and female in the WSCP, but they also provide the audience of what a strong, empowered Black woman can be.

Examining what it means to be a Black feminist working within tradition-ally white institutions of power remains unarticulated in *Scandal*. Perhaps this very racism/sexism is why Olivia is so utterly disempowered within the context of her relationships (both familial and romantic). But her lower status as a Black woman is not addressed so the interpretation is left up to the audi-ence. On shows such as *BMJ* and *Insecure,* the reverse dynamic is presented: the audience has concrete examples of how Black women are thwarted, treated differently, denied access to power. Despite these barriers, these characters persist and thrive. Mary Jane and Issa are portrayed as having strong support, whether through girlfriends or family; they are seen as active agents in resist-ing systemic oppression; their worldview is decidedly womanist. In contrast, Olivia is bereft of community. The only central relationship in Olivia's life is a disempowered romantic relationship with a white man. The audience experi-ences Olivia stuck in a degrading position even as she succeeds in professional contexts. Whereas Mary Jane and Issa are shown resisting, defying, confront-ing the white, patriarchal power structure and being successful, Olivia sup-ports, regulates, and is a victim of the WSCP even as she financially benefits. Unlike Mary Jane and Issa, Olivia is a Black woman in a white universe; she is silent in any evaluation of the systems of oppression that affect her.

CONCLUSION

Unlike the sad, lonely island that Olivia Pope finds herself on, bereft of sup-portive family, a core group of friends, and lovers/partners who treat her with respect, characters such as Mary Jane Paul and Issa Dee offer empowering, complex portrayals of Black feminist womanhood in a contemporary setting. Whereas Olivia is belittled, manipulated, yelled at, and bossed around by her married white lover, Mary Jane and Issa find their ways through the bramble patch of contemporary dating lives, but typically find men who respect them and treat them as intellectual equals. Whereas Olivia is rarely (if ever) seen laughing, smiling, and enjoying the camaraderie of friends, Mary Jane and Issa are regularly in social settings that offer positive female friendships, strong bonds of sisterhood, and mutual support. Whereas Olivia's relationship with her family (mother and father) is destructive, dysfunctional, and lacking in any demonstrated love and support, Mary Jane has rich and complicated relationships with her siblings and parents, a line of love, caring, and support running through the family core. Regardless of where they are and what they are doing, the audience sees that Mary Jane and Issa are supported and that they have strong, sure, womanist voices. With Olivia, the take-away is one of loneliness and utter isolation. Why, then, is *Scandal* the more popular serialized drama? Because it is what white audiences want to see. In the white supremacist patriarchy, white audiences do not want to see an empowered Black woman in the context of her community, fighting for social justice and professional success. However, there is reason to hope with shows such as *BMJ* and *Insecure* gaining popularity with both Black and white viewers. The women featured on these shows, offering womanist perspectives, educate audiences and affirm realities that have been missing from mainstream entertainment until recently.

Chapter 5

"I'm Talking to *You*"
Breaking the Fourth Wall

Nola Darling (DeWanda Wise), in Spike Lee's update of his classic film *She's Gotta Have It*, gazes into the camera, speaking directly to her audience, inviting us into her inner thoughts.

> In 7th grade, I woke up one morning and these tiny mounds were occupying my chest. I pinched. I poked. But they wouldn't go away. Overnight, just like that, life was complicated by a quarter pound of flesh: these [points to her breasts]. In school I was tormented, OK, teased, by Rashaad Decker, a horny little punk half my size, but his words cut like a knife. . . . The humiliation was like a dark keloid growing around a wound. Every day I would go home in tears. And every day my mom would say [cut to a close up of her mother's face consuming the screen, eyes wide and serious; Mother:] "Face him down, Nola. Words can't hurt you. Don't give him your power." And, of course, I know that. I mean, I get it. I'm not fucking dense. But today I have something to say to Rashaad and all those other bitches. *Watch. The fuck. Out.* (Season 1, Episode 3: LBD, Little Black Dress)

Fierce. Tone and gaze directed at us, Nola is a prizefighter, dukes up, staring us down. We feel her power. We don't question it. We are thrilled by it. This is not a soliloquy delivered to an unknown audience. She. Is. Talking. To. *Us*.

In the opening example from the "LBD" episode, Nola is narrating to us a moment every person born in a female body can relate to: the moment we are seen as sex objects because of our breasts. Most women can define the exact moment this happens, when we realize we are no longer acting agents, but objects living in a patriarchy. For me, it was my father, horrified and red-faced, yelling at me over the roar of the lawnmower, "Put. Your. Shirt. *On*." I was ten. I had done yard work, like my brothers, without a shirt since I could remember. Now, breasts only beginning to bud, I was inappropriate, sexual-ized, my body needed to be covered. Overnight, my body had turned from child body (sexless) to woman body (sexualized by men for men). This is the moment Nola brings us into, the exact second she, as a female, recognized her worth in the patriarchy: a sex object. The moment when a female moves from agent to object, the moment we realize the horrific inequity we have always lived in, but didn't realize until that moment.

Through these intimate and striking monologues in *She's Gotta Have It*, Nola speaks *to* us, her female audience, about these complicated dynamics she experiences as a Black woman making her way through the brambles of the WSCP. We are her confidantes. We are her target. We can't turn away. *She is talking to US. She is talking to YOU. She is talking to ME.* By break-ing the fourth wall of theatre, her words become personal and specific. There is no other audience, just the viewer and Nola. What she tells us, what she confides in us like a trusted friend, a confidante, a nonjudgmental sister, is essential to understanding her as a deeply complex person. She is no longer a character; she can't be a stereotype or a caricature. She is a sister. We have her back. We *know* her. And we know her more intimately because of these moments where she whispers or snarls or smiles, telling us her inner thoughts. We know much more about her than the characters who orbit around her like bees around a hive: her lovers, her family, her friends. It is *us* she confides in. *We* become part of her world when she breaks the fourth wall.

The phenomena of female characters breaking the fourth wall, a feature of many contemporary serialized shows, takes the place of a voice-over. Sometimes the direct address segues into a voice-over or is used in conjunc-tion with a voice-over. Direct address is more intimate than a voice-over because the character turns to us, gazes at us (sometimes glares at us), and lets us in on her secrets. These intimate moments allow the viewer to connect on a deeper and more personal level with the protagonists. Through these deeper connections, we understand more nuances and complexities of the character. She becomes less of a stereotypical character and more of a friend, someone who trusts us and therefore someone we root for and are drawn to in complex ways. Breaking the fourth wall may not be unique to Black female characters, but when Black female characters allow us into their inner world, it is revolutionary. For decades, Black female characters have been the side-bar characters, the stereotypes, the staid and predictable foils. By putting Black female characters in the protagonist role *and* by allowing them to speak directly to their audience, directors allow the audience to become the characters' intimates. They become friends; they are confiding *in* us. But more importantly, they are able to tell the audience what they are thinking and feeling more deeply than what is offered by watching their interactions with other characters. They can talk openly with us about race, sex, sexuality, gender, class, and complex cultural dynamics, not only offering insights into their personal worlds, but also asking the reader to think more deeply about how Black women struggle against and through the WSCP systems of oppression. In addition, these moments of direct address allow the Black women to take charge. They indicate *they* are in control of the action; *they* are the ones who are driving their destiny and the storyline; it is *their* perspective that counts. By taking control of the narrative, the perspective, and the action, these characters break out of stereotypes, dismantle disempowering positions, and write their own narrative, something that Black female characters have not been allowed to do historically in entertainment media.

HISTORY OF DIRECT ADDRESS/ BREAKING THE FOURTH WALL

The foil of a character addressing the audience directly is not new. It has been part of theatrical productions for centuries and film theorists have identified it in very early film. In theatre, breaking the fourth wall was seen as a rejection of "suspension of disbelief" (Mauer 1982, 25). In film, Charlie Chaplin and Laurel and Hardy, among many other early film stars, broke the fourth wall regularly. These characters addressed the camera with a "comic twinkle," a sort of "I-know-you-know-I-know" (Clayton 2010, 67). These sorts of direct addresses provide a comic aside, a mug to the camera, a shrug of the shoulder, wink to the viewer, fleeting yet important. Today, however, in contemporary series and films featuring Black women, the direct address is more significant. It takes the forms of monologues and voice-overs that drive the plot and provide undeniable depth to the characters. No longer only used for comedic affect, breaking the fourth wall allows the Black woman to have her say, to take her power, to allow us to see how multifaceted her experiences and thoughts are.

When a female character, particularly a Black female character, tells the audience what she is thinking or experiencing, the audience must confront complex issues of race, gender, and sexuality. At the very least, the traditional male gaze is disrupted. In examining prime-time television shows, Lauzen and Deiss (2009) found that far more male characters broke the fourth wall, but that female characters were more likely to address the audience when the writer, producer, or director was female. Female writers, producers, and directors know that using direct address breaks the male gaze. Particularly for female characters, the direct address to the camera/ audience can offer a feminist perspective and deny the comfort of the traditional male point of view. The direct address leaves the audience no way in which to distance themselves from the female character (Mulvey 1992, 33).

Disrupting the male gaze means we have to consider a different perspective; we have to get real with the characters in front of us. "Having a character address the audience directly is a very particular effort towards intimacy with the audience . . . performed for the sake of encouraging our sympathy or some other kind of special connection with the character" (Brown 2012, 13). Typically, direct address is the protagonist, exerting power over the narrative (Brown 2012, 14). However, in some cases other characters are also allowed direct address, a way of providing more insights into the protagonist. In various episodes of *She's Gotta Have It*, lovers, friends, parents, and even Nola's therapist break the fourth wall to tell the audience what *their* perspective is on Nola, always offering insights that are immediately communicated in a monologue or soliloquy, a far more effective strategy than trying to communicate these nuances or inner thoughts through dialogue and action.

Similar to direct address, voice-over narration also functions as a way to explain what a character is thinking or feeling and thus creates more intimacy with the viewer. Allrath et al. (2005) noted that voice-overs are "usually restricted to explaining features of the narrated world, commenting on them, or adding information which is not provided visually" (14). This use of voice-over to explain motive or inner thoughts to the audience is true not only in *She's Gotta Have It*, but *Grown-ish*, and *Mixed-ish*. Direct address and voice-over deepen our empathy with the characters. Brown believes that "direct address often provides a metaphor for a character's vision and, indeed, it is often used to mark a moment of realization or coming-to-consciousness for that character" (2012, 14). These voice-overs/direct addresses provide open and honest expressions of the character (15). Nola Darling's gorgeous and expressive face, her dimples and twinkling eyes when directly staring down the camera lens add to her intimate revelations of struggles with lovers, to her commentary on systematic racism and sexism, and to her attempt to rise above the haters. Zoey Johnson's (*Grown-ish*) side-glances and eye rolls toward the camera add to her charm when she tells us about her strategy to deal with a crush, an annoying peer, or a social faux pas. Rob(yn) Brooks' (*High Fidelity*) heartbreak permeates the sadness behind her eyes, her puffy lips, and her delicate features. When she gazes into our eyes, full face filling the frame, we can feel her. Tracey Gordon's (*Chewing Gum*) perplexed looks or steely glares toward her audience tell us everything we need to know about what she is *thinking* about the scene that just played out. When direct address occurs, typically the camera is zoomed in to the expressiveness of the actor's face. We see the details, the twitches, the smirks, the misty or reddened eyes, the slow tears, the mouths and lips, and eyebrows as they arch or furrow. These details affect how we experience the character, bringing us into her deeper sense of being.

Breaking the fourth wall not only invites more intimacy with the character, but viewers feel more empathy toward the characters who address them directly (Colvin et. al 1997). Audience members become more personally involved with the characters (Auter 1992). "By breaking the fourth wall, characters become more knowable. In turn, viewers may find these characters more empathetic" (Lauzen and Deiss 2009, 384). And when characters are more empathetic, the female viewer keeps watching. When I was interviewing participants about their viewing habits, they would often tell me they really liked a character because she was relatable, because she was "real" or because they felt like they understood her. "I could relate to her," I heard over and over again. When I would follow up with "Why?" or "What do you mean by 'real'?" most had a difficult time articulating why. It was more often than not the empathy they felt for the female character. Direct address and voice-over help build that empathy. And empathy keeps people watching. Lauzen and Deiss (2009) speculated that female characters directly addressing the audience is one of the reason reality shows are so popular. Their research noted that reality shows had more female characters who broke the fourth wall than other types of programming. Lauzen and Deiss wrote, "By speaking directly to the camera, female characters on reality programs are more knowable to their female viewers and thus more dimensional. In turn, this knowledge may lead to greater liking of these characters, increasing the ratings of the programs in this genre" (385). If this hypothesis is correct, it makes sense that more streaming series are having female characters break the fourth wall as a way to increase empathy with female viewers and thereby increasing popularity of the show. It is no wonder that many of the favorite characters referred to by my participants were those that employed direct address.

SHE'S GOTTA HAVE IT

Although *She's Gotta Have It* is produced and directed by a man (Spike Lee), most episodes are written by women. I offer the show here as an interesting text to analyze not only because the protagonist, Nola Darling, breaks the fourth wall but because other characters do as well. Typically, it is only the protagonists who is allowed to address the audience. But in *She's Gotta Have It*, everyone gets their turn, adding to the depth of not only Nola's character but the supporting characters as well. This direct address of several characters (her lovers, her friends, her family, her therapist) are exclusively related to comments *about* Nola and what the characters *think* of Nola, giving Nola dimensions as she is analyzed by, loved by, critiqued by others. Nola herself also addresses the audience, but she often does so *after* others have weighed in. In the first episode, we see lovers and friends address the camera,

articulating pieces of their relationship with Nola and what she means to
them. It isn't until the final scene we hear from Nola herself. Nola gets the last
word with us, the final say. We have heard others' perspectives as they spoke
to us. Now, finally, it is Nola's turn. Sitting on her expansive bed in a crisp,
oversized men's white dress shirt, her hair turbaned, she asks her viewers:

> Have you ever heard of Akira Kurosawa? Well, you should. Kurosawa is
> one of the greatest directors of cinema, Japanese director. One of my favorite
> Kurosawa joints is *Rashomon*. The film came out in 1951 shot in beautiful black
> and white photography. It's about a rape, a murder, and several witnesses who
> all saw the same crime but from entirely different viewpoints. Some might say I
> have a *Rashomon* effect on Jamie, Greer, and Mars [her three male lovers who
> we have already heard from]. They all view me differently, but I will not allow
> them to paint my life, paint who I am. I'm dealing with who I am now, at this
> moment, at this time and space. And I've gotta look within to feel what makes
> *me* happy. And if Jamie, Greer, and Mars wanna deal with me, it's gotta be on
> my own terms. No less. No more. And anyone who *can't* get with the program
> can step. Go with god. [cuts to voice-over as Nola is making a poster and then
> hanging the posters on city walls] One, two or three fingers cannot block out
> the sun. The truth is the truth. I am not a freak, I am not a sex addict, and I am
> damn sure nobody's property. My name isn't "Dime Piece." My name isn't
> "Boo." My name isn't "Baby Gurl." By name isn't "Pssst Shawty." My name
> isn't "Mamacita." My name isn't "Sweetie." My name isn't "Ay Yo Ma." My
> name isn't "Sexy, Sexy, Sexy." My name isn't "Hoochie Mama." My name
> isn't "Honey." My name isn't "Sweetheart." [Cut back to a close-up of Nola
> on her bed, just her mouth and her eyes.] And my name definitely ain't no
> "Motherfuckin' Black Bitch." [Cut to Nola at her art table, paintbrush in hand.]
> My name is Nola Darling. Peace. Two Fingers. Black. Lives. Matter.

With this ending monologue, Nola claims herself. No matter what the other
characters have defined her as, she is owning herself. In this monologue, Nola
says she is more than what men see her as. They see her as a sex object, a
puzzle to figure out, a code to crack so they can gain access. On the street.
In the eyes of men. Random strangers and lovers, they only see her as a sex
object, a prize. She knows this, she is telling us, but she is going to engage
with them on her terms. She will assume power because they will never give
it. Her gaze is searing. Her voice is strong and clear. She is taking *no* bullshit
from anyone. She is telling the audience, "The other people you hear from
are other perspectives of me. But mine is the only perspective that *really* matters." By having the last word, Nola leaves the audience with her perspective
as the prominent, compelling perspective. Through her gaze and words, she
becomes a deeper and more nuanced character than what we have seen in the

previous thirty minutes. Lee can be criticized for his male gaze during sex scenes, his inability to capture realistic female sexual experiences, for not convincing the audience that Nola would waste her time with most of the men with whom she engages, but by allowing Nola to speak directly to the audience, making her voice and perspective the one that resonates through direct address, he offers us a female character who is more dynamic, interesting, powerful, and in control of her own destiny.

The second episode begins with Nola, again on her bed, this time in a lace bra, sitting cross-legged. She is telling us about a woman she is painting, "The Black female form. Wide-hipped and honey dipped under the sun. And under the constant gaze of mennnnn-y. Many. I've always wanted to paint Shemekka (friend). That special brand of Brooklyn brown. BK all day. Never apologizing for the suck of her teeth. For the snap of her neck, or how she moves her Black female form through the world. Zero. Fucks. Given." Nola's perspective sets the tone for the episode. Her thoughts on what is beautiful, what constitutes her art, what catches her attention are clear: Black women. The episode ends with Nola comparing herself to Shamekka:

> She's silky. I'm sexy. I'm Pinot Noir and she's Moscato. But that's my girl for life. True, she comes off as a tough Crown Heights goddess, but aren't the tough ones always a little extra soft on the inside? The Black female form. I've grown protective of it. My foolish attempt to control the gaze of gawkers who think the Black female form is simply here for their consumption, their scrutiny, their grabbing hands, when all the Black female form wants to be is free.

Once again, Nola seizes back the gaze, directing us to what *she* wants us to see, what *she* wants us to understand about the beauty and worth of Black women. She is telling her audience that she is freeing not only herself but the women of her art from the "grabbing hands" and the male gaze. She is reclaiming the literal bodies of Black women and setting them free.

CHEWING GUM

The British series *Chewing Gum* (2015–2017) is told through the eyes of Tracey Gordon (Michaela Coel), a first-generation Brit growing up in low-income housing, daughter of a strident Jehovah's Witness-Caribbean-born mother and sister who is a straight-laced, religious fanatic. The show, written by and starring Coel, is an offshoot of her play *Chewing Gum Diaries*. In the series, Tracey's character is awkward and gangly, trying to navigate breaking out of her strident household's puritanical mores to find sex and romance. Coel's goal is to make her audience uncomfortable through whacky and cringey situations regarding Tracey and her sex life. The audience can't help but feel embarrassed *for* her when Tracey fantasizes about licking her paramour's eyeball, tries (and fails) at being sexy in an African tribal costume, spontaneously experiencing a nosebleed whenever she is sexually aroused, and getting advice from friends at the Quickie Mart where she works on how to survive anal sex ("If he wants to put it in your bum, just breathe through it. Don't start panicking cuz it will hurt and he'll dump you"). The comedic moments are enhanced when Tracey breaks the fourth wall to address the audience, letting us in on how ridiculous she finds herself. She often breaks away from the action to shrug her shoulders while leveling her gaze into the camera or offering a flip comment to let us know she sees how outrageous her life is.

The first episode sets the tone for breaking the fourth wall and audience address. We see Tracey praying with a man. We only see an up-close shot of his lips as he prays; Tracey bites her lip in a lascivious way, turns to the camera and says, "My mother was going to name me Alyssa which means Sweet Angel in India. But when I came out, she took one look at me and named me Tracey." She sneers. "Tracey. It makes me sound like I eat bacon sandies or have sex in the back of the bus. I don't eat pork, man. And I want to have sex with my boyfriend in the bedroom." As her boyfriend continues to pray, Tracey has a sexual fantasy of them having frantic sex. He pulls her away from her fantasy to conclude his prayer about waiting until marriage—or until death—before they have sex. Tracey turns her gaze to the camera and deadpans absolute panic and incredulousness. Thus, her direct address establishes the trajectory of the series. We are taken away from the farcical nature of Tracey's surreal shenanigans by her willingness to let us know *she* is in the on the joke. She *sees* how ridiculous her life is and—along with the viewer—she is in on the joke even as she is leading us through it.

The direct addresses, most often in quick asides and comedic glances from Tracey, heighten the comedic element of the show. Veronica, a woman I interviewed who is a discerning media consumer and prefers foreign series such as Turkish soaps, *Doctor Who*, and *Chewing Gum*, is aware of how the comedic elements are enhanced by these direct addresses. She said:

> I love [Tracey's asides to the audience] because they make me laugh. The way she deals with her life and the situations she puts herself in are funny and true. She doesn't shy away from sexuality and specifically bisexuality and interracial dating . . . . Breaking the fourth wall makes her more human. It makes her seem more like a real human being who we are privileged to witness; she brings us into her world. It isn't reality t.v. but it is the real thing for us. We can see the fullness of her character. I wonder if that makes her less of a caricature. (Veronica)

Veronica may be suggesting this is a question, but I understand it as a statement. Tracey's character moves beyond being the homely, gangly, skinny Black girl to being aware and in control of her reality, even if her mother, sister, and her own naivety act as roadblocks to her pursuit of a sex life and—perhaps—romance. But first sex.

In *Chewing Gum*, we see Tracey in crazy situations where she seems to be a passive participant in relation to a strictly controlling family, lovers who have little interest in her desires, and friends who give lousy advice. Yet when she breaks away from the action to address us, we understand she knows and sees what is going on. She is alerting her audience to the fact that she has awareness and agency; she is not the passive victim. Veronica continues, "There were points in *Chewing Gum* when she was really on the edge, but then she broke the fourth wall and she became less of a trope. She breaks the tension we feel in those moments. She lets us know she is in control." As someone who thinks deeply about these sorts of nuances in the entertainment she watches, Veronica compared the audience address in *Chewing Gum* to being a very different type from audience address in *House of Cards* (Netflix 2013-2018). The reasons for and effect of audience address, prominently used in both shows, were very different. Veronica said:

> When they do it in *House of Cards* it functions less as a character device and more like a plot clarification. It's because they pull you back from the farce. Kevin Spacey's character addresses the audience to say, "This is getting unbelievable." It was to keep the audience engaged because otherwise they would dismiss the plot as being ridiculous. In *Chewing Gum*, it is for character development. She is telling the audience, "I am still human; I'm not going to go that far [to become a caricature or a stereotype]." She addresses it like, "Are you serious right now?"

What Veronica articulated is the difference between how male characters/directors tend to use direct address (to clarify plot or a character's strategy such as is done in *House of Cards)* and how female directors/characters use direct address (to deepen the character and our empathy for the character such as is done in *Chewing Gum, Insecure, Girlfriends, High Fidelity*, and *She's Gotta Have It)*. For example, Tracey uses direct address to let us know she isn't as silly or a stupid as her character seems to be; Rob uses direct address to show us she isn't just a dick on wheels out to break hearts because she is really struggling and conflicted about the way she is acting; Issa uses direct address to let us how she has fantasies about what she *would like* to do, but she ends up doing what she thinks she *should* do. With direct address in *Chewing Gum, High Fidelity, Insecure*, and *Girlfriends* (directed by women), the characters are giving insights into their own agency and inner thoughts. In direct address in shows directed by men, even with female protagonists such as *She's Gotta Have It*, and *Grown-ish*, the direct addresses often relate to strategies of the characters and explain *why* they are doing something. These are important nuances. One uses direct address to deepen our understanding of the character and her agency. The other uses direct address to explain plot and clarify a character's strategy. Of course, there are always exceptions. The direct address in *She's Gotta Have It* (directed by a man, but often written by women) is used both ways: Nola is telling us her strategy, but we also gain insight into her inner thoughts.

One example of how a character uses direct address to explain agency involves Tracey arranging a threesome. In this *Chewing Gum* episode (Season 1, Episode 4: The Unicorn), Tracey arranges to meet a unicorn (a bisexual woman who engages with monogamous married heterosexual couples for sex play). Just when the discomfort of engaging in a "ménage a trois" builds to the ridiculous, Tracey breaks away. She directly tells her audience, "I am going to approach the line, but then I am not doing *that*." She lets us know she is in control of the situation and she won't do anything she isn't comfortable with.

In this episode, Tracey goes on a hook-up app to find a woman to add to her and her partner's sex life. The unicorn, Sasha, is a bit gritty and hard (she has open sores on her mouth), engaging in lots of random sex with many people. There is a hint at judgment in the way she is portrayed. But Sasha gives Tracey and her partner key information, telling them to stop focusing on penetration as the ultimate sex. In following that advice, Tracey has her first orgasm with her partner. Although the episode may cause the audience to cringe in several places, Tracey's asides to the audience provide some relief. She is letting us know, with her look into the camera, that she has everything under control. By indicating to the audience that she is in charge, even if the on-screen action playing out makes us uncomfortable, Tracey is guiding us through the situation, providing nuance and understanding.

GIRLFRIENDS AND *INSECURE*

Girlfriends (2000–2008) and *Insecure* (2018–2020), like *Chewing Gum*, are situation comedies written and directed by women who use direct address often for comedic effect. In the show *Girlfriends*, the lives of four friends of varying lifestyles are featured; the series aired for eight seasons first on *UPN* (seasons 1–6) and then on *The CW* (seasons 7–8) with a variety of directors and writers, most of them women of color. The show was created by Mara Brock Akil who also produced *BMJ* on BET. Tracee Ellis Ross played the protagonist, Joan Carol Clayton; the role provided Ross with a breakout character that segued nicely into Rainbow on *Black-ish*. In the first two seasons of *Girlfriends*, Joan would have moments where her head would float off into a hazy cloud and she would address the audience directly, giving us insights into what she was thinking and feeling. The production quality of the first few seasons was low and these break-away moments were no exception, employing bad digital effects and adding a cartoonish quality to the scene. However, the benefit of these "talking head" asides allowed the audience to be drawn into internal monologues that Joan was having, adding dimension and insight into the character. By the end of the series, these asides had stopped. Production quality increased dramatically when the show transitioned to *The CW* and with that transition, the "bubble head" was no longer used.

In the first episode of Season 1, however, these pop-out moments of breaking the fourth wall happen twice. The first is when Joan's ex-boyfriend shows up at her birthday party as her friend's date. Joan's face pops into a bubble and she addresses the viewing audience of women, specifically, by saying, "Ladies, take note. This is where I turn and pop a wheelie and he is reminded that all this bootie could have been his." In this aside, the female viewer understands that, although she is no longer in a relationship with the man, she wants him to find her attractive and sexy; she wants him to feel regret that he walked away from the relationship. This aside allows the female viewer to understand that as confident as Joan portrays herself to be, she is still caught up tying her worth as a woman to being desired by a man, even if she no longer really *wants* the man. In the context of the patriarchy, Joan needs to seek male attention through sexual worth, even if she does not want to overtly admit this to her friends. In *Girlfriends, Insecure, High Fidelity, Grown-ish, Insecure,* and *She's Gotta Have It*, much of the direct address is about explaining relationship woes often articulating, "I know what I *should* do here, but this is what I am *gonna* do here."

This dynamic of "I know what I am supposed to do, but let me break away and fantasize about what I *want* to do" is also a key part of the direct address in *Insecure*, Issa Rae's HBO series. The protagonist, Issa Dee, often breaks away to address her mirror. Through the mirror, we see her fantasize about what she would say to coworkers or lovers she would *love* to tell off but can't. We see her fantasize about various ways she will respond to advances (from love interests) or racist comments (from coworkers). The effect is comedic, but it is also poignant. She has a yearning to respond to the racist and sexist crap she has to deal with day in and day out as a Black woman. Her release is telling *us* (through her mirror) what she would say or do if she only could without consequences.

Before going out on a date with someone she likes, Issa goes through several iterations of what kind of woman she might want to present during the date. This scene indicates to the audience the choices a woman has to make and the dichotomies of female stereotypes, especially in regard to Black female sexuality that women have to negotiate. In the episode "Insecure as F*ck" (Season 1; Episode 1 2017), Issa stands before her mirror, trying on different accessories and lip stick colors. Who should she play? What persona should she enact? How should she negotiate this first date to keep his attention? She talks to herself in the mirror before going out. The frame closes in on her lips, her face. She changes her lipstick to change her tone:

Fire Engine Red: "Hi, I'm sexy (she says to herself and us, the audience) Let's get out of here. You're *super*," she purrs to an imaginary date.
Fuchsia Pink: (Valley Girl Flirty) "Oh my God! You're a music producer? Do you know Beck?"
Black (Grace Jones Deep Voice): "I don't make love, I *fuck*. You want some of this pussy pot pie? Pop, pop, pop. PRRRR, pop, pop, pop. Pussy pot pie!"
Fuchsia (Sexy British Accent): "Well, hello, Daniel. No, *you* drive on the wrong side of the street."
Black: "Let me sprinkle some pussy parmesan on you."
Red (Fun drunk girl laughing): "OOOOH! Awesome!"
Black: "You hungry?"
Red: "Hey, Tiger. Mmmm." To herself, shaking her head: "So stupid."
Pink: "Take a drink! OOOOH Shots! Shots!"
Black: "You gonna take this nonny or not? Take it! Take it!" She shakes her head, looks in the mirror, tilts her head down: "It's too aggressive." She wipes off the lipstick and puts on some clear lip balm, smiles wryly at herself in the mirror and walks away.

After all her iterations of choices, she chooses to be herself. She isn't going to fall into a stereotype in order to lure a man, attempting to anticipate what he will be attracted to. In the scene, the camera alternates from being the mirror (what Issa sees with her gaze) and the perspective of looking right over her shoulder to see the side of her face and the hazy perspective she is looking at in the mirror. The camera angles and close-ups allow us to get in Issa's head, to feel the playfulness but also the conflict: which version of womanhood should she be? In the end, she chooses herself, her own version, outside all the rigid boundaries and behaviors of a stereotype.

In both *Girlfriends* and *Insecure*, direct address is often used to allow the audience to see the female character imagine what she might do and instead choosing something different because that is the *right* thing to do. In *Girlfriends*, Joan does this another time in that first episode by circling back around to the tension between feeling the desire for male attention because she is a woman trapped in a patriarchal paradigm. At the end of that first episode, the girlfriends are sitting around Joan's living room talking. Joan's head breaks away to address the audience: "So this is where I should probably be talking about friendship and how my girlfriends fill out my life. I hate to admit it, but I am thinking about Charles." Once again, Joan's aside to the female viewer indicates to us that she knows what the *right* thing is to do (focus on sisterhood and female empowerment), but that she finds herself betraying what is right. Instead she focuses on the affirmation from men and seeking heterosexual relationships, however dysfunctional, rather than focusing on her friendships with women. "In the context of romantic relationships, direct address can articulate the attendant problems of knowledge (of one's self, of the motivations and subjectivities of others)" (Brown 2012, 117). In Joan's direct address she is indeed articulating what she knows about herself (self-awareness of what she wants to do) and how that conflicts with what she knows she *should* do. These addresses offer the audience insights to her psyche, cognitive dissonance she suffers, and how those human qualities impact her relationships. The direct addresses highlight her motivations for how she is responding to external actions by others.

For Nola, Tracey, Joan, Zoey, Issa, Rob, and others, direct address allows the characters to communicate the complexities of feelings and choices for Black women in the WSCP. Through their asides that illuminate vulnerabilities or uncertainty in negotiating romantic relationships. These characters can admit to knowing what they *should* do (support the sisterhood, stand strong against desire when a man is not treating her well, not answer a call, be herself instead of a stereotype, speak up against racism/sexism), but they are caught up in the centrifugal force of what the WSCP *tells* them what they should do or be. Even if doing so means selling out herself or acting against her feminist ideals.

INSECURE

Although most of the time we see the character of Issa Dee weigh the alternatives, she typically decides it is important to do what is right, to be herself, to step away from the stereotype. But there are consequences to that strategy. We see the conflict Issa faces: be true to herself and call out the racism (manifesting an Angry Black Woman stereotype) or suck it up and howl on the inside. In "Guilty as F**k" (Season 1, Episode 5), Issa has to endure racist comments from white coworkers about a house in the neighborhood where there is a fundraiser. She hears the white coworkers saying they didn't know there were such nice houses in the (primarily Black) neighborhood. A white coworker says, "I drive past this every day and I didn't know that homes like this existed up here . . . . I hear they call this the 'Black' (whispered)

Beverly Hills. Is that true?" They look at Issa. Issa looks up from her clip-
board, squares her shoulders, and says with simmering anger, "Listen you
gent, Columbus motherfucker. If you don't stay the *fuck* away. I don't know
why I told you about this neighborhood because you all *take* everything.
Can we have anything? LEAVE!" The camera closes in on her face as she
is talking. After her last shouted exclamation, there is a silent beat and the
camera zooms out and over the scene. Issa shifts her weight to her hip, drops
her shoulders and says in a calm voice, "Guys, I really don't know. What I
do know is that we have a lot of work to do. And this bench needs to go over
there." In two clips, we see what Issa *longs* to do (call out her coworkers'
racism in righteous indignation, pointing out the systemic issues of white
oppression) and what she knows she has to do (swallow her anger, be "civil"
and avoid the stereotype of Angry Black Woman). Through these moments of
direct address and close-ups featuring her simmering rage, we feel the tension
that Black women have to face every day as they interact with the WSCP.
These juxtaposing viewpoints offered in shows like *Girlfriends* and *Insecure*
drive home the cognitive dissonance that is a daily part of Black womanhood
in a racist, sexist culture.

GROWN-ISH

Similar to Issa, the character of Zoey Johnson uses this same strategy of letting the audience in on how much self-knowledge and cognitive dissonance
she is experiencing. Zoey will tell the camera, either through mugging for the
audience or direct address, her strategies for getting, keeping, or manipulating
the attention of another character. The character of Zoey breaking the fourth
wall exemplifies a trope that is used across Kenya Barris's body of situation
comedies. In Barris' productions *Black-ish*, *Grown-ish*, *Mixed-ish*, and *Black
AF* the protagonists all use direct address and voice-over to add dimension
to plot and storyline. As Spike Lee's cinematic handprints are his dolly shots
and Lee cameos, Barris marks his shows through direct addresses or voice-
overs that deliver history or cultural lessons or privilege the perspective of
the protagonist. Similar to shows such as *She's Gotta Have It*, *Insecure*,
Chewing Gum, and *Girlfriends* that rely on breaking the fourth wall to deepen
characters, Barris adds a trifecta of direct address (voice-overs, break-away
Schoolhouse Rock-ish history lessons, and talking to the camera) to add
dimensions to characters and plot. In each of Barris-produced shows in the
"ish" suite *(Black-ish, Mixed-ish,* and *Grown-ish)* the trifecta exists to create
a deeper understanding of Black reality in the United States *and* to create
more complex and intimate protagonists for the audience. In *Mixed-ish* and
Grown-ish, both featuring female protagonists, these break-away moments

ask the viewer to not only take a step into the mind and reality of the female character but also understand the complexities of how race/sex/sexuality/class/gender complicate their place in the world.

Barris has a variety of writers and directors (most of them women). In shows such as *Black-ish, Grown-ish,* and *Mixed-ish,* the voice-overs are prominent, offering additional information into the main character's inner thoughts as well as often offering history or cultural lessons to the viewing audience. Here, I will focus on *Grown-ish* and *Mixed-ish* because these two shows feature female protagonists: Zoey and Rainbow Johnson, respectively. When direct address happens, it often is in a scene at the beginning of the episode, allowing the character to cue the audience in on what she is thinking about initial action. The female protagonists in both *Grown-ish* and *Mixed-ish* narrate the action through their female perspectives, asking the audience to empathize or sympathize with the issues they are facing.

In Season 1, Episode 5: C.R.E.A.M. (Cash Rules Everything around Me) of *Grown-ish,* Zoey expresses concern to the audience that her boyfriend, a star basketball player, is not treating her well on social media. When her friends ring in, they tell her to drop him ("cash out!"); the next scene we see Zoey walking across campus, ignoring calls and texts from Cash. She pauses to address the camera and says, "My friends were right. Cash violated my trust and played me in front of the world. I need to cash out." Her voice and eyes drop away from the camera and then she looks back up at the audience, chin tilted down and eyes directly gazing at the audience. We can tell by her face how difficult this is: she wants to listen to her friends; she wants to respect herself; she has conflicted feelings about Cash. One of my interviewees, Karen, noted that Zoey's asides to the audience deepen the connection she has with the character. Karen, a young professional working at a Southern university, said that hearing Zoey's voice-overs and being drawn into her direct addresses "makes it more real . . . . It is like I have a Black friend here who is a very opinionated and we are both looking at each other and in that look we know what the other is going through. It is crazy." Later in the C.R.E.A.M. episode, we see Zoey use the audience as this sort of confidante Karen is referring to. She gets in a car with Cash and turns to the audience to tell them she is a pro at giving the silent treatment. There are flashbacks to her going days without talking to her father until he crumples, weeps, and hands over wads of cash just to get her to talk. Zoey mugs for the audience, "It's not a game I like. But when I play it, I play to win." Without the direct address and flashbacks and voice-overs, we wouldn't understand that she is strategically using the silent treatment as a tried and true method of manipulating men. The voice-over allows the audience to hear what Zoey is thinking and feeling beyond what is happening through the scripted action and creates a sense of intimacy and identification with people like Karen. Karen continued, "I feel more connected to the character. I feel like the character is confiding in me about where they are . . . when Zoey is talking about her heartbreak and she sees her ex for the first time and she says, 'This is awkward,' and you can relate. I know how she feels because I have felt that."

HIGH FIDELITY

The Hulu series *High Fidelity* (2020) also offers a female protagonist Rob Brooks (played by Zoë Kravitz) who uses direct address in similar ways: to share emotional struggles, to articulate feelings of vulnerability. The series is based on a film by the same name released in 2000, but starring a male protagonist. The Hulu series takes the same premise and storyline but flips the sex of the protagonist. Both the film and series use direct address, but they use it differently. In analyzing the purpose of direct address in the film, Brown (2009) writes:

> [The original film] *High Fidelity* [2000, starring John Cusack as Rob] demon-strates further ways in which, in the context of romantic relationships, direct address can articulate the attendant problems of knowledge (of one's self, of the motivations and subjectivities of others). The film also shows that direct address can create a peculiarly intimate link between performer/character and audience *at the same time as* helping to open up a kind of critical distance in the characterization. (Brown 2009, 117)

In the film's DVD extras, the director, Steven Frears, talks about employing the voice-over and direct address in the film as a way of adapting the novel, by Nick Hornby, to the screen. Because the novel allows the reader to hear Rob's thoughts directly through first-person narration, the film mimics this through voice-over and direct address.

In Hornby's book *High Fidelity* (1995), the film adaptation starring Cusack as Rob Gordon, and the Hulu series starring Zoë Kravitz as Rob Brooks, the character Rob begins by narrating his or her five top break-ups. Rob looks for and finds parallels between his or her world of music and his or her love life. Entirely communicated through voice-over narration, flashback scenes, and direct address, the audiences in the film (2000) and series (2020) are told the stories of these break-ups directly through first-person narration. The effect of having Rob address the audience is one that provides context for the ache and longing of the relationships, magnifying Rob's vulnerability and abject befud-dlement as to why he or she can't seem to get a relationship right. Brown notes,

> [Using direct address and voice-over] has the effect of intensifying the isolation and (at times) loneliness of the main protagonist [Rob], and of vivifying the

sense of his [or her] self-obsession. While literary narration is commonly intro-
spective in the manner of Hornby's book, it is certainly more unusual (though
not unheard of) for filmic protagonists to narrate their own experiences inces-
santly to the audience. (119)

Without this first-person address and voice-over, the audience might see
Rob as just a jerk who can't commit, an unsympathetic protagonist. With the
puzzled looks, the sad eyes, and the voice-over tones the audiences of both
film and series see Rob as struggling, trying to do better, parsing out why he
or she was such a jerk. Without these direct addresses and voice-overs, it is
likely the audiences would judge Rob as callous and uninteresting. It is the
intimacy and pain the character can express through direct address that gives
him or her sympathetic elements.

In addition, the direct address and voice-overs establish the distinction
between the world we see Rob inhabit (the record store/friends/apartment/
bar) and the world Rob has and is experiencing in his or her head. When the
director allows the audience access to these two worlds, internal and external,
the character becomes more realistic. The series opens with Rob addressing
the camera. She looks ravaged, as if she has been crying. Her eyes are half-
lidded. She says, "My desert island 'All-Time Top Five Most Memorable
Heartaches' in chronological order are as follows." She rattles off the names
of four ex-lovers and ends on Mac. We suddenly cut to the scene where Mac
is walking out. She is crying, begging him to stay. He leaves and we cut back
to Rob, addressing the audience but also addressing the absent Mac. Her eyes
are wet and red from crying. "Congratulations, Mac. You made the top five."
This is how the audience is introduced to Rob. Because of the direct address,
we feel her pain, vulnerability, and jagged heartache. The flashback takes us
to a moment of the breakup, but looking into her eyes and seeing the ravages
of pain and tears on her face does more than the flashback. We are rooting
for her, feeling for her from that first moment. We know that heartache: a
lover walks out, a relationship we don't want to end ends badly. We feel
those ragged emotions of being desperate and wheedling yet unsuccessful as
a lover walks away, bursting into tears as the latch clicks against a chapter in
one's life. When she turns to address us, laid open like a wound, we feel it on
a visceral level. Her pain enters us through her damp, dazed gaze. She doesn't
have to tell us she is miserable. We see it in her eyes.

In the film version of *High Fidelity*, the initial scene plays out a bit differently, even as the direct address is used. We see Rob's girlfriend walk out first
before Rob addresses the audience, leaving the viewer to interpret the scene
as they wish. Rob slams the door; he is petulant and angry. His tone is not of
grief when he rattles of his "Top Five" list. He seems annoyed and snarky,
almost sarcastic. He is not staring into the camera, but he breaks away and

shifts his eyes, unlike Kravitz who locks in our gaze and will not break it, even for a blink. With Kravitz's version, our intimacy with Rob is tender and concerned; with Cusack this same event has hard edges and features a child-ish male tantrum. We see his struggles to understand his own failings, but we don't feel them as powerfully as with Kravitz's version of Rob. The film Rob asks the audience, "Did I listen to pop music because I was miserable? Or was I miserable because I listened to pop music?" In the Hulu series, this question does not even have to be asked: we feel Rob's misery in her gaze. Although the film also relies on direct address to create these moments of emotional intimacy, these moments are rawer in the series. Whereas Cusack shifts his eyes away from the camera even as he is talking to it, Kravitz will not allow her audience that subtle relief. Her hooded eyes stare us down. The rasp of grief is not only written on her face but in her voice. She will not look away. Whereas Cusack creates his sympathy with the audience through comedic, sarcastic charm in his direct address, Kravitz goes deeper into the emotional landscape, her audience feeling her pain, heartache, and confusion.

CONCLUSION

By looking into the expressive eyes of Zoey Johnson, Nola Darling, Tracey Gordon, Rob(yn) Brooks, and Issa Dee, we come to know them in more complex ways. They become empathetic characters with depth and dimen-sion, their inner struggles and thoughts complicated through direct address and voice-overs. These strategies work to helps us empathize with these Black female characters in important and revolutionary ways. Gone are the stereotypes of S.W.A., Angry Black Woman, Comic Minstrel Foil, and so on. By offering complex and interesting emotional lives, these women defy stereotypes and appeal to our sense of humanity and the struggles of being a Black woman in a WSCP. The nuances of these characters, the struggles they endure, and the bullshit they navigate offer important representations of Black womanhood to audiences of varying demographics. The appeal of these characters is real, which is why they are so popular and emerged over and over in interviews with Black women who remarked on how much they identified with these characters. Characters such as these, created by Black women, push away from stereotypes into representations that feed our hearts, minds, and souls. Through these characters and their direct address, we think and learn more about what it means to be Black and female in the dominant culture. Because they level their gaze and talk *to* us, we become their confi-dantes, their friends, their sisters.

Chapter 6

Funny Women

Laughing With, Not Laughing At

Wicked smart and lightning-quick, like a superhero that you can't quite track with your eyes. This is the timing of comics outstanding at their craft. Phoebe Robinson and Jessica Williams (*2 Dope Queens* 2020), Tiffany Haddish (*Girls Trip* 2017, *She Ready* 2017), Wanda Sykes (*Not Normal* 2019), Robin Thede (*A Black Lady Sketch Show* 2019), and Leslie Jones (formerly on *SNL*, *Time Machine* 2020) are just a few of the many women who are making us laugh *with* them, not *at* them. They aren't pandering to a white audience, manifesting stereotypes such as Sister With an Attitude (S.W.A.), Angry Black Woman, or the exaggerated Black Matriarch Church Lady, all stereotypes popularized by Black male comics such as Flip Wilson, Tyler Perry, and Jamie Foxx. These comics and their contemporaries have found an audience by being smart and addressing issues of race/class/gender/sexuality in ways that do not degrade but uplift. Their comedy causes people to *think* about systems of oppression. To do so through humor is what many of us hunger for when the moments seem bleak. We want and need to laugh. Don't assume they are playing to "yet to be woke" white people; rather, they are talking to other Black women. Their appeal across demographcis proves that funny women can make it without being self-deprecating or genuflecting to the WSCP.

There is a long history of comedic Black women who primarily played to Black audiences. If they gained a following or a few chuckles from the white community, well, that was frosting on the cake. Loretta May Aiken, a.k.a. Moms Mabley, made a name for her character (Moms Mabley) first with Black audiences and later crossing over to white audiences. Aiken began her career in comedy in the 1920s on the Chitlin' Circuit (Vaudeville for/by/about Blacks) and became popular with white audiences from the 1940s into the 1970s. Often her humor was seen as too edgy for white audiences, addressing issues such as racism, female sexuality, and parenthood (Finney

2014). However, she gained enough white appeal to be asked to perform on *The Ed Sullivan Show*, *The Smothers Brothers*, and *The Merv Griffin* Show, all "mainstream" (i.e. "mainly white") talk/variety shows of the 1960s. Whoopi Goldberg reintroduced Aiken's Moms Mabley to contemporary audiences with her HBO documentary *Whoopi Goldberg Presents Moms Mabley* (2013). Aiken provided a way forward for Black women comics; her humor was not self-deprecating and she was *not* the butt of her jokes. In contrast to white female comics of her era such as Phyllis Diller, Joan Rivers, and Gracie Allen, Aiken didn't get laughs at her own expense. Her stories were political and regularly dealt with issues of sexuality, sex, and race. From 1920 to 1973, she was creating a body of political and social humor that paved the way for the women comics of today to follow.

THE GRANDMOTHER OF TODAY'S COMICS

As Aikens herself said, "Moms don't know no jokes. But she knows some facts" (Goldberg 2013). And those facts often related to segregation, the status of women, and civil rights issues. As Mabley, Aiken told stories that had an edge about race relationships that might cause her Black audience a bit of discomfort, but they also laughed. Her humor made a point, but released the tension of the heavy reality of racism/sexism through laughter.

One such bit of Aiken's was about a man who showed up at the Pearly Gates. The man is adamant that St. Peter knows him, but St. Peter seems to not recognize the man. The man says, "Oh, man . . . you *know* me! I was the cat that married that white girl on the capitol steps in Jackson, Mississippi." Saint Peter asks, "How long ago was that?" The man quips, "About five minutes ago" (Goldberg 2013). Here we see Aiken making a statement about the horrors of lynching, of miscegenation laws, of the terrorism that is white supremacy, yet in the end the punch line gets a laugh. This is just a single example of what Aiken's comedy was built upon. She set the standard that comedy needed to be political, and comics had an obligation to speak about the unspeakable, including female sexuality, misogyny, and the horrors of racism.

Another of Aiken's stories about the realities of racism focused on traveling South as a Black woman. "I was on my way down to Miami. I mean *They*-mami. I was riding along in my Cadillac. Passed through a red light. One of those cops pulled me over. I said, 'Yeah, I know I went through the red light. I saw all you white folks going through the green light, I thought the red light was for us." And, "Baby, its rough down there (The South). Some old Klan come talking: 'Mammy. . .' I say, 'No damn Mammy. Mom.' I don't have no Uncle Tom's cabin. Split level in the suburbs, Baby." In these short lines, Aiken as Mabley covers a lot of ground: she is of higher social class than the whites who are attempting to belittle and degrade her (driving a Cadillac; living in a split level in the suburbs). She is also addressing real issues of racism (police profiling; racist/sexist language). Yet she turns the racists on their heads: she is smarter and more cunning than they are; she can use their stupidity against them.

For about forty years, Aiken as Moms Mabley was a star in the Black community, but virtually unknown to whites. During the 1960s, however, social justice was permeating the counter culture and she began to appear on variety shows/talk shows. These shows not only introduced Mabley to a white audience who also immediately loved her, but it was a moment of great affirmation for Black viewers. Goldberg remembered, "Every time there was a Black person on the television, we would gather. [The Black performer] didn't know it, but we were saying, 'Yeah! There is a Black person on the t.v.' " In the 1960s, Aiken as Mabley could address those white audiences for the first time saying, "You don't know me. But let me tell you what is going on." She provided opportunities for white people to think about what it meant to be Black and female in the United States.

It is no coincidence that Aiken made the crossover from predominantly Black audiences to a mixed-race fan base in the 1960s and 1970s. During that time, there were great social shifts regarding race, sexuality, class, and sex—all demanding a voice and power for traditionally marginalized people (TMP). All of these social justice movements, driven by young people, were changing the conversations in the political spheres and by extension changing laws and policies to make the country less racist, homophobic, sexist, and exploitative. In a parallel moment, we are now at the cusp of a similar movement. From women's activists to Black Lives Matter to LGBTQ+ communities, the United States is having hard conversations—and corresponding unrest—about all these social justice issues, fueled by the Trump presidency that represented the most repressive of regime ideologies. At this time, we see Black women comics emerging in ways they never have before. We are hungry, as a culture and a community, for these voices and perspectives. These women are taking the stage and delivering to us a similar sort of socially conscious humor that Aiken used, demanding that we *think* and *act* regarding systems of oppression. And making us laugh along the way.

Even as Aiken's Moms Mabley set the standard for Black women doing comedy, there were few successful crossover Black women in comedy until recently. One might be able to identify Whoopi Goldberg or Wanda Sykes, but other than that, Black female comics were not big names. Now due to the crossover success of comics such as Tiffany Haddish, Leslie Jones, Mo-Nique, Retta, Amanda Seales, Issa Rae, Nicole Byer, Mindy Kahling, and Michelle Buteau (among others) as well as programming such as *2 Dope Queens* and *A Black Lady Sketch Show*, funny Black women are getting more exposure and followers. Although comics such as Whoopi Goldberg, Queen Latifah, Marla Gibbs, and Wanda Sykes have been doing comedy for decades, they tended to be the short list of Black women getting attention. Today, however, streaming services are offering up various Black female comedians in stand-up shows, series, and films. Although sometimes the Black woman is the only Black female in an otherwise white cast [Retta in *Parks and Recreation* (2009–2015) and *Good Girls* (2018–2021); Leslie Jones in Ghostbusters(2016); Tiffany Haddish in *The Oath* (2018); Rihanna in *Ocean's 8*, (2018)] more often than not the funny woman is in a cast/script that features a host of Black women. Offerings such as *Little* (2019), *Girls Trip* (2017), *What Men Want* (2019), *Nobody's Fool* (2017), *Lovebirds* (2020) and *Love Jacked* (2018) provide enough of a change for some people to label the movement a "Black women comedy Renaissance" (Toby 2019), all produced/directed or written—fully or in part—by Black women. But comedic films featuring full casts of funny Black women came much later. Black women began making their audiences laugh first with stand-up and one-woman shows, following in the flat-bottomed footsteps of Aiken.

GOLDBERG AND SYKES

In the tradition of stand-up comedy, both Sykes and Goldberg carried forward Aiken's tradition of talking about politics, sexuality, and race. Sykes began her stand-up career in 1997 writing for and performing on *The Chris Rock Show* (Johnson). By 1999, she was opening for Rock in his stand-up tour (Johnson). At the time, she was known for saying things (primarily about race, sexuality, and gender) that others wouldn't. Her tag line, "Yeah, I said it" was the title of her memoir published in 2004. Once Sykes divorced her husband and married her wife, her comedy became more specific to her life and her relationship (Zinoman 2019). Sykes came out publicly at a Las Vegas LGBTQ+ rally in 2008. For those of us who were queer and following her, we had known for a long time she wasn't straight. But for Sykes this was a public turning point for the nature of her comedy. Her comedy became more openly political and personal. Sykes has said Aiken was an influence on her approach to humor (Johnson).

Sykes most recent stand-up shows are evidence of how she now uses comedy to hit hard on the same cultural and social issues as Aiken. In Sykes award-winning *Tongue Untied* act (Comedy Central 2003), she addresses issues of being Black and female. In talking about the nastiest of the nasty strip clubs in Florida, Sykes says that the women just pose with a leg up and demand, "Look at it! Isn't this what you are here for? Then *LOOK AT IT!*" She continues that it must be "really hard to be a man. That thing up in your head, all the time . . . how do you all hold down jobs, man? You're at work, minding your business, and all of a sudden that thing just kicks in. 'Let's go look at it. Come on, man. When's the last time we seen it. Let's go look at it.' " In this bit, Sykes is playing at sexuality and gender: males who are socialized to objectify women, who need to see women as only one part: their pussy. She skewers heterosexual men's desire to engage in that sort of denigration of women on a daily, moment-by-moment basis. In addition, she is asking us to laugh about that: men are absolutely controlled by their infantile and senseless desire to *see* a vagina. Women may have less tangible power in the culture, she seems to be saying, but at least we are not ruled by an obsession with a singular body part, especially a body part of the opposite sex. Sykes tells us, in so many words, that men are slaves to this obsession, it *controls* them.

In another part of the show Sykes talks about female orgasms. She tells the audience that for men, sex is always good. All they need is an orgasm and it is great for them. Women are more discerning.

> It's like eating in a restaurant. Sometimes it is good. Sometimes you gotta send it back. Sometimes you might get food poisoning. You have those hit and misses, you might want to skip a few meals. "Oh, no. I'm not hungry today . . . . You know, I think I might cook for myself today. Something about the way I cook, it is always filling . . . and I'm a fast cook. The time it takes you to do one meal, I can make three." . . . and then guys wonder why we fake it. It's called time management.

She goes on to simulate an exuberant fake orgasm to the cheering delight of her audience. Thus, Sykes weaves the politics of female sexuality, men's assumed right to orgasm, and the reality of women owning their sexuality and taking care of *themselves* all in a short, laugh-inducing story about sex.

Goldberg's humor also focused on the way women are treated within the context of the patriarchy, with issues of race and class often part of the mix. Goldberg crossed over to mass appeal (read: gained white audiences) with her off-Broadway show that became an HBO production, *The Spook Show* (1983). In it, politics of race, class, gender, sexuality, and homophobia took stage through the monologues of various characters Goldberg created and performed: The Crippled Girl, The Girl with Blond Hair, Fontaine (a junkie), The Raisin, The Surfer Girl, among others. Through each character's monologue, Goldberg hit on issues of race, class, gender, and sexuality. When her second show aired, *Fontaine: Why Am I Straight* (HBO 1988), Goldberg was known for her political comedy (Haggins 2007). Goldberg's political themes in both shows infuse each monologue. Here is a snippet from the character, Fontaine, a swaggering junkie with a head scarf. Fontaine says, "I have a Ph.D. from Columbia." The crowd laughs and he gives them the side eye and continues, "I know you'all didn't think I was *born* a junkie." Here Goldberg calls upon her white audience to imagine another identity (other than poor junkie) for a skinny, swaggering Black man with a head scarf. Goldberg depends on her white audience to be unable to imagine Fontaine any other way than an uneducated street person who has always been using and has always been an addict, jonesing for his next cheap hit. For her Black audience, the humor lies in Goldberg calling whites on their stereotypes, naming their assumptions and mocking them. Goldberg as Fontaine continues, "I have an education," he says with a bit of a condescending sneer at the audience. "I have a Ph.D. I can't do shit with. So, I stay high so I don't get mad." Throughout Fontaine's monologue, Goldberg asks the audience to call into questions white stereotypes about class and race. Fontaine is a junkie, but he travels to Germany, has insights into the fundamental nature of human beings while touring the Anne Frank house, is admitted to a mental institution on his return because he acts out on the plane, and comes to the conclusion that we—collectively—can never know what it feels like, what it is like, to be the "alien" until we are thrust into a reality where *we* are the "alien." In this one monologue, Goldberg is demanding that her white audience consider, think about, and rethink entrenched biases regarding race, class, and national origin. Simultaneously she is affirming the reality of bigotry and bias for her Black audience. Fontaine is not unique in the panoply of Goldberg's characters in this show, engaging whites in humor that also educates and pushes the audience to rethink their own biases and *act* differently in their world.

In addition to the callback to political humor that Aiken established with her Moms Mabley character, Goldberg's dress and mannerisms also reflected the resistance to classic femininity similar to Aiken's Mabley. Haggins (2007) writes:

> Goldberg's consistent choice of baggy unisex clothing corresponds to Moms' attire, which was, arguably, suggestive of a mammy of sorts (frumpy, oversized housedresses, mismatched colorful clothing, floppy hats, socks with slippers) in that neither had made a fashion choice intended to construct their bodies as objects of desire—rather, they had purposefully covered their bodies in ways that made their female sexuality unobtrusive. (148)

I would argue that both Aiken and Goldberg (and newer comics such as Leslie Jones and Mo'Nique) may be atypical (larger?) body types, but decidedly un-mammy-like. The Mammy was a domestic. Her hair was in a kerchief tied on top and her dress was adorned with an apron, both signifying a domestic servant. Neither Aiken's nor Goldberg's attire would cue identity as a domestic servant. Mom Mabley's signature housedress, flat and large shoes, and crocheted hat were not part of a domestic's uniform. She may be a matron, a matriarch, but she was not a servant. Similarly, Goldberg's more masculine choices of attire (*never* a dress) were baggy to conceal her body. Her body was not on display. Through baggy clothing and more masculine dress, these comics are rejecting and defying stereotypes of Mammy, Jezebel, or Sapphire. Aiken, Goldberg, Jones, and others resist the historical mandate that Black female bodies be gazed upon, be available, for white consumption, either as servant or sexual bait. Instead, these comics took/are taking a different tack. Their bodies are *not* the focus; their words and wit are what they want the audience to pay attention to and their choice of attire redirects the white/male gaze from their bodies to their political, social commentary through humor.

THE FEROCITY OF LESLIE JONES

Leslie Jones, similar to Aiken and Goldberg, eschews feminine trappings when performing. Her stance, tone, dress, and mannerism are decidedly masculine, giving her a dramatic and fierce Grace Jones-like presence. Jones, like Goldberg, wears more masculine clothing and combs her hair in a straight-up Mohawk that looks like angry flames shooting out of her head. Similarly, Goldberg and Jones have consistently chosen natural hair styles, never straightening their hair to abide by feminized standards of WSCP-defined beauty. These women are making statements about who they are—and who they are not—through their choice of wardrobe and hair. In contrast to other comics that may feel they need to embody feminine tropes, Goldberg and Jones reject those tropes and instead move into a more masculine pose. Because sarcastic humor, particularly, is more acceptable from men than women (Taylor 2017), it would make sense that female comics engaging in sarcasm would want to present more masculine. By presenting as masculine, the characters may allow the audience to give the female comics more leeway in language, sarcasm, and topics of conversation. Feminine language mandates would manifest as higher and softer voices as well as an avoidance of taboo topics and words such as curses or swears. These comics intentionally resist all of these feminine tropes in speech and language. They are strong-voiced, sarcastic, and using taboo language, taking up space on the stage.

The body language of Aiken, Jones, and Goldberg would also be interpreted as more masculine. They stand with feet planted squarely apart. They take big strides. They often have hands on hips. They do not hold their arms and legs close as a feminine woman would. By taking up space, using lower voice registers, and moving in less-feminine ways, they are claiming the right to speak and be heard. They are commanding the stage in ways that defy lady-like or feminine behavior. In order to engage in the humor they want to engage in (political, blunt, addressing issues of sexuality, gender, sex, and class), they claim the space as a more masculine than feminine presence. And it works.

These comics are highly successful and appeal to a broad audience because they break with feminine traditional tropes of humor. They command attention. Of Jones, one critic noted, "Her approach to comedy can be described as insane, sexually aggressive and almost violent. It might even be scary if she didn't look like she was having so much fun doing it" (Wheaton 2016, 12). The descriptor of "scary" is an interesting one here. Is Jones scary to women? To Black women? Or is she only "scary" to those audience members who are threatened by a Black woman who is taking up space, using her voice, and demanding that people pay attention? Certainly, those residing squarely within the WSCP mindset may be intimidated by such a pose, but *frightened*? Perhaps these audience members (white? Middle class? Male?) would be frightened, except Jones makes them laugh. As Jones propels herself onto the stage during her stand-up show *Time Machine* (Netflix 2020), she yells into the mic as the audience screams back at her. "That is *dope*. Every time I come out and a bunch of a white people scream at me, I just can't. I am like, 'I *made it!*' I mean, I am white people famous, you know?" This is how Jones begins her hour-long comedy set for the audience that looks to be more white than Black. Jones immediately puts her white audience in their place, mocking them by pretending to be a white woman in Starbucks saying "Oh. My. Gawd!" She responds to this fictional Starbucks-swiller of privilege, "You need to *calm*. The *fuck. Down*." For her Black audience, she is affirming their right to put whites in their place. For the white audience, she is telling them, "You annoy me. Check yourself." Michelle Buteau has a similar thread of mocking whiteness in her Netflix stand-up special *Welcome to Buteaupia* (2020). Early in the act, she spies a white woman off to her right who is expressing appreciation by snapping her fingers. Buteau immediately strikes a pose and begins mocking her, "Yes, girl, *Yes!*" she drolls and rolls her eyes. She calls back to this woman periodically, the snapping white woman becomes the butt of the running impromptu joke.

As with Aiken, crossing over to white audiences, being "white people famous," does not mean that the barbs against white people are taken out of these women's humor. Goldberg's, Buteau's, and Jones' humor is decidedly Afrocentric, feminist, and perpetually poking fun at whites. In *Time Machine*, Jones tells her audience that women are *crazy*, but they have earned the right to be crazy because of all the shit the WSCP throws at them. "We should be stark, raving, *insane* . . . we push a human being out of our pussy . . . yeah, I'm gonna *need* more than 6 weeks *off*." She screams at and scolds her white audience. Her face contorts into disgust, pleasure, surprise, and outrage in equal measure; her humor is not just the stories she tells—mostly about her absolute command of her own lived experiences. Jones' humor also centers on the contrast of how pathetic the white audience's experiences must be to the Black experience. Jones' humor embodies the storytelling and physical effects of her screams and facial contortions that punctuate those stories. She picks out a white man in the front row and yells at him, sliding off the stage to get right in his grill, drill-sergeant aggressive. "Do you know that your wife has to take your dick? She cooks your dinner and then she has to take your dick. That's what make her *crazy!*" she screams, inches from the white man's face. She is righteously indignant, outraged, on behalf of all women, glaring into the eyes of this specific white man, but expressing the vitriol seething and simmering in heterosexual women everywhere who have had to "take dick." She defies the stereotype of the Angry Black Woman because she is beyond anger. She is enraged and she is articulating the specifics of why not only she, but also *all* women, particularly Black women, have a right to be enraged living within the WSCP quagmire.

In addition to her larger-than-life movements and vocalizing on stage, Jones also employs a lot of facial expressions in her comedy. These exaggerated grimaces, eye rolls, squints, bug-eyes, and furrowed brows are part of comedic traditions by Black women. Coupling the physical antics with sharp wit, rapid-fire monologue, and topics of sexual taboo, Jones is engaging in a type of comedy historically employed by Black women.

> In terms of composition, African American women's fun making is conveyed through an elaborate combination of repartee, irony, sarcasm, and body language that includes vamping, physical stunts, and erotic flippancy. A mixture that titillates and levies sharp barbs and critical analysis, African American female humor is often rapid-fire, searing, and leveling. (Allen 2005, 99)

Quite literally, Jones stares down and renders the opposition absolutely impotent; when she climbs off the stage to scream into the face of the unwitting, withering white man sitting in the front row, she is turning the tables on the WSCP, putting the white man in a subjugated position, rendering him absolutely powerless and without escape. Jones is ferocious on stage in her strides, in her facial expressions, and in the register of her voice. She is at a superhero level of power. She isn't "The Angry Black Woman." She is much more powerful than that. She is fierce and intense. This persona makes a political statement; she is a Black woman who is taking up space, demanding attention, claiming her right to school the white audience on her reality, her truth. She will not be ignored.

However, not everyone sees Jones' stand-up as political. Some women I spoke with found Jones' more recent stand-up lacking when compared to her work of political satire during her stint on *Saturday Night Live* (*SNL* 2014–2019). As a writer and actor on *SNL*, she often appeared on *Weekend Update* to riff on such topics as abortion rights, Black women deleted from

U.S. history, and the women hockey players who ruled the winter Olympics. Imbedded in the bits were asides remarking on the whiteness, the maleness, the fragility of the Weekend Update host Colin Jost. "Oh, Colin. You always find a way to bring it back to you, don't you, you selfish ass?" she coos in one, rubbing his shoulder. "You delicious coconut milk shake. You will always be my vanilla back up." One of my interviewees found Jones' work on *SNL* much more political and therefore gratifying than her solo work. Donelle, a fifty-eight-year-old self-described butch dyke mother of three grown boys, said:

> Her writing on *SNL* just had more politics in it. I watched her Netflix show (*Time Machine*) and it wasn't as political. It was about sex and growing older, but she didn't have that sharp edge of political humor that she did on *SNL*. . . . I think she probably thinks her white audiences [in the stand-up venue] won't appreciate the political stuff as much . . . .When she was on *Weekend Update*, I would always find those and watch them.

Donelle would seek out and watch Jones' clips on YouTube as she found most of *SNL* to be lacking. "It is for a white audience. Male, mostly. I don't find it that funny," she told me.

Certainly, Jones is aware of the crossover white audience as she performs her stand-up show. Whereas on *SNL* she could go political because the show is known for satire and biting, edgy political commentary, Jones may have reconsidered this approach for a general audience, especially one that might be majority white. The topics she covers in her stand-up (aging, dating, men) do seem decidedly apolitical (more comfortable for a white audience) than her *SNL* work. However, even as the topics are safer, Jones' approach to her white audience is very much maverick and quite literally "in your face."

SKETCH COMEDY

As Jones' own comedy career demonstrates, sketch comedy is a very different genre than stand-up. SNL, where Jones made a name for herself, is the granddaddy of that sketch genre. It has also been historically, glaringly white and male. Although there have been women who were *SNL* stars that went on to comedy careers in film and series (Jane Curtin, Gilda Radner, Tina Fey, Amy Poehler, Kate McKinnon, Molly Shannon, and Kristin Wiig to name just a few), there have been a scarce few Black women featured who then went on to successful careers beyond *SNL*. Leslie Jones, Maya Rudolph, Sasheer Zamata, and Danitra Vance all made a name for themselves through *SNL*, a short list compared to the 150-plus cast members who have appeared on the show since it began airing on NBC in 1975. *SNL*, notoriously liberal politically, couldn't seem to quite practice inclusion when it came to Black women. In 2019, HBO produced *A Black Lady Sketch Show*, created by Robin Thede. *A Black Lady Sketch Show*, similar to *SNL*, is a series of skits that cover cultural and political topics, all through the lens of Black women.

In Thede's telling of how *A Black Lady Sketch Show* was created, she gives credit to Issa Rae for helping her pitch the show. Thede's late night talk show, *The Rundown with Robin Thede* (BET 2017–2018) was canceled; but then Thede got a call from Rae. As Thede tells it, Rae didn't waste any time boo-hooing with Thede over her canceled show. Thede recalls Rae saying to her, "'OK, now is the time we get to work together.' And I said, 'My show just got canceled. You don't want to say, you're sorry?' And she's like, 'For what? No, let's get to work'" (White 2020). *A Black Lady Sketch Show* is unique in in sketch comedy because it is written, directed, produced, and stars all and only Black women, a powerful model of what can and should be done to give voice to a perspective historically silenced in mainstream entertainment media. With Rae's help, Thede was able to pitch the idea to two (women) HBO executives who contracted for the show without a pilot. HBO, according to Thede, had been wanting to create more diverse programming and they saw her show idea as a way to do that (White 2020)

The program is a refreshing thirty minutes of short sketches that skewer WSCP from a Black feminist perspective. One of the most popular skits that originally aired in September 2019, but has generated views through being passed around on social media, was entitled *Courtroom Kiki*, where attorneys, defendant, judge, court reporter, and bailiff are all Black women who are initially surprised and then delighted to find themselves in a courtroom that is entirely Black and female. The humor relies on their immediate sisterhood and camaraderie, much to the shocked and confused defendant (Issa Rae) who doesn't quite seem to understand the lack of decorum. The women take selfies, talk about where they went to school, the judge compliments the stenographer's "goddess locs," and the bailiff twerks as they all chant "Black Lady Court Room! Black Lady Court Room!" "I have sat in this courtroom for 20 years and I have never seen . . . melanin this poppin'!" the judge exclaims. "Cicely Tyson would be so *proud*." The sketch asks viewers to fantasize about a criminal justice system run for and by Black women, a delicious pipedream. But it calls upon real experiences of Black women as well: walking into a traditionally white space and finding another Black woman there, making eye contact, and breathing a sigh of relief. Karen, a young professional working in alumni giving at a mid-sized university in Louisiana, said she immediately identified with that moment of relief, recognizing a sister in the room.

> It is true that you anticipate being the only Black person and then you walk in and there are other Black people or one other Black woman there. It's a relief. You share a look. You feel like, "OK. I'm not the only one." You aren't the only successful Black woman, whatever *that* means. (Karen)

Karen admitted that she had never seen *A Black Lady Sketch Show*, but she had seen this sketch (and others) because they were shared on her social media.

The type of humor on *A Black Lady Sketch Show* is often squarely focused in pop culture vernacular and up-to-the minute cultural references in the context of a world that is entirely Black and female. Because the sketches are typically less than five minutes long, they are easy click bait on social media. Not all of the snappy, snarky pop culture humor is appreciated. Because it is sketch comedy, there is a wide variety (as well as inconsistent quality) to some of the sketches. This is true of most sketch comedy shows: there are some groaners and sketches that fall flat. Veronica, a feminist theologian who identifies as bisexual, was not as pleased with the courtroom sketch, or *A Black Lady Sketch Show*.

> I did watch *A Black Lady Sketch Show*. Some of it I really liked, but part of it seemed ridiculously stupid. I didn't like how they used some of the characters; they made them caricatures. They fed into tropes that aren't funny. One that I remember was the courtroom [sketch] with Issa Rae. These Black women are all happy to be in the same room and being ridiculous like, "Girl, *look!*" and the Issa Rae character says, "This is disrespectful." But they don't pay any attention to her. They are all acting ridiculous, even the judge. (Veronica)

Part of the genre that is sketch comedy is the ridiculousness, the exaggerated scenarios that are based on real situations that people can identify with, spinning them out to the ludicrous. As with any sketch show, some of the jokes will land with an audience member, but not with others. That is the nature of the genre. However, what is important and refreshing with Thede's production is the fact that it is intentionally and entirely Black women, which feels revolutionary. Add to that the focus on *humor* (and not hard stories of struggle and the countless ways Black women have been degraded, demeaned, and denied) and the show feels radical in its scope, focus, and approach. It feels like a relief, a release, a much-deserved thirty minutes of silliness and celebration. Through the sketches, Thede and her writers tell the stories of what it means to be Black and female: to fantasize about Black women being the only group to survive an apocalypse; to learn how to be a better "Bad Bitch" in a support group run by Angela Bassett; to imagine Patti LaBelle showing up amid dry ice fog to sing "On My Own" every time a woman gets dumped ("Oh, my god! Patti La Belle is in your *house* right now!" "I know," the woman who is being dumped replies in deadpan. "She shows up every time"). These exaggerated fantasies may play as ridiculous, but that is the point.

In "Gang Orientation," a garage full of women gang members attend a corporate-style seminar on work environment and benefits: "We are increasing our paid parental leave from four months to six months." One gang member says, "Lowering my risk of post-partum like a mother fucker!" "And just to be clear," the leader continues. "We are not calling it maternity leave anymore because we don't want to be complicit in enforcing a cis-normative agenda." The sketch plays on the stereotype of urban young Black women being gang members, but flips the stereotype because they are smart, educated, concerned for each other's well-being, and engaging in a culture of a corporate work environment with concerns for inclusive language, comprehensive benefit packages, 401K offerings, and getting to know new members through ice-breakers. The "normal" (the stupidity of corporate orientation sessions that are mind-numbingly boring and predictable) becomes ludicrous (a female gang engaging in corporate orientation practices). One must consider Veronica's critique, though. Do these sketches reinforce negative stereotypes or subvert them? In writing about Black female comics on HBO's Def Comedy Jam, some analysts see nothing but tired stereotypes.

> The so-called Queens of Comedy, including Adele Givens, Mo'nique, Cheryl Underwood, Laura Hayes, and Sommore (featured on HBO's Def Comedy Jam, 2001) . . . plays off the persistent stereotypes of black women as domineering, often large, emasculating women who fail to conform to essentialized notions of womanhood. These comediennes consistently focus on the thematic issues of body image, male-female relationships, and racial and gender identities. But they also often reinforce stereotypes of black female sexuality by relying heavily on their own often overly sexualized persona. (Early, Carpio, and Sollors 2010, 34)

Early, Carpio, and Sollors are critical of what can appear at first glance to be comedy based on stereotypes. But I see comics such as Goldberg, Jones, and Thede doing more. They are often taking the stereotypes and then turning them inside out by making them ridiculous. The point these comics are making is to upend the stereotype, show how ridiculous it is, and relate it to something that *real* Black women must address (e.g., having paid parental leave, being the only professional Black woman in the room, or needing a

Bad Bitch support group because they aren't good at being the stereotypical Black Bitch). And even if some audience members or scholars do not buy the argument that the stereotypes are subverted, Thede also does other sketches on her show that have nothing to do with stereotypes. Some of the sketches aren't even supposed to be funny in the way we think of barking laughter and delight. One focuses on a teacher who is called out by her class of girl students for being sad and she discloses her husband left her for an Applebee's waitress (the spot is an advertisement for a lottery); another spot is entitled "Rome and Julissa," a hip-hop version of Romeo and Juliet set in a club; another sketch is about a larger Black woman with natural hair who is "invisible," even to other Black women, and so she is the *perfect* spy. Although such sketches aren't traditionally *funny* in attempting to make the audience laugh, they offer the audience a way to *think* about issues of inequity, discrimination, and day-to-day issues that Black women face in contexts that are light and easy to consume. These sorts of sketches point to real experiences of Black women in the WSCP and cast them in a context that is silly/funny. Through the retelling of these experiences, the stories about being Black and female are relayed to the mainstream audience who, in turn, become more aware; in addition, the Black female audience's experiences and lived realities are affirmed.

THE ORAL TRADITION OF STORYTELLING

Storytelling about how it is to be Black and female in the WSCP has been a strategy of humorists for decades. Thede, Mapley, Sykes, Goldberg, and Jones have all used this strategy of humorous storytelling to illuminate Black women's daily realities of being Black and female in the WSCP. Similarly, Tiffany Haddish, known first for her stand-up and now for her roles in films, focuses her humor on storytelling about her own experiences. All these women use personal storytelling to address issues of race, class, sexuality, and gender. Although Haddish's humor is not as grounded in satire as Thede's, Aikin's, Goldberg's, and Jones' (*SNL* work), her comedy is defined by social commentary based on personal experiences. By connecting her personal experiences with poverty, racism, and sexism Haddish engages in social commentary as her audience laughs. These markers of connecting personal experience to larger political issues through storytelling (making the personal political) are not only feminist but also disrupt stereotypes of Black women by offering more complex identity narratives. As Finley (2016) notes, "Contemporary black women have taken up a brand of satire that privileges emotion and experience . . . permeated with disgust. These representational strategies have the potential to undercut stereotypical tropes that circulate about black women as unruly, incompetent, irresponsible, and interchange-able—tropes so deeply embedded (such as the Angry Black Woman, the Welfare Queen, and the Bad Black Mother) that they often prevent black women from speaking and being heard" (237). Finley is pointing to how sto-rytelling that is sharp, witty, and frank disrupts cultural stereotypes of Black women by complicating the one-dimensional understanding of such mytholo-gies. By virtue of this approach, the Angry Black Women articulates that she has valid reasons for her anger; she narrates the racism/sexism/classism injustices that infringe on her daily right to exist in the WSCP. Storytelling also disrupts stereotypes such as the Welfare Queen; she may have been on public assistance, but she is here to tell you the *reality* of that life.

For instance, Haddish tells the story about growing up homeless with an absent father and a mother who had few coping skills, no education, and was rendered unable to parent due to increasingly extreme mental illness and addiction. At first glance, Haddish's stories seem to reinforce a stereotype of what it means to be poor, Black, and female. But she complicates that ste-reotype by showing the audience details of her life: foster parents who loved her and taught her essential life skills, a grandmother, and a school bully, all characters who give depth to her story so it is no longer just a flat stereotype. In addition, she tells the stories to not only educate but to engage in humor. And she does so quite brilliantly. In her stand-up show *She Ready* (Netflix 2017), she begins by talking about being a foster care kid. She hollers to the audience:

> Anybody else a foster kid?" Silence. "It's cool. It's cool. I was state property. I'm *valuable*. I'm the only one, then? . . . Y'all's mommies and daddies *had* to love you. They didn't get paid or nothing, OK? Everybody's house I walk into from the time I was 11 until I was 18, they got *paid* off me. . . . I came with a *check*. I am valuable. Oh, and I want to say thank you to anyone who paid taxes between 1990 and 1999.

In this segment, she draws a connection to foster care and being enslaved ("The state owned me.") to being a Black girl of value, if only monetarily ("I came with a check"), and flipping the script of foster kids being unloved: "Your mommies and daddies had to love you" (instead of getting money from the government). She spends some time bringing the audience along on her foster care journey where she tells of being with a Mexican family until the father got deported, being in a sex-positive Jewish family, and then being placed with her biological grandmother who told her to guard her sexuality from men. All these stories punctuate her point: "I am not a stereotype; I was loved; I was cared for; I was taught valuable life skills by these adults. It may have been a revolving door of foster homes, but I wasn't a stereotype."

Haddish goes on to talk about getting accepted to New York University (NYU); the audience applauds. She says, "Don't clap. I didn't go. How am I supposed to pay $30,000 a semester? How many dicks do I have to suck to pay $30,000 a semester?" Within this short story, two lines, Haddish is addressing the inequities involving access to quality education (she is smart enough, but the doors are closed to her) as well as the stereotype of being a young Black woman in the WSCP (if she needs to make money fast, she will have to engage in sex work). The audience is laughing, but her point is made: this should not happen; a young woman who is smart enough to be accepted at NYU should be able to attend. Later, Haddish returns to the stereotypes of being poor and Black and female. She is living out of her car and she is working at a comedy club with Kevin Hart. He notices and he tells her, "Tiff, you a pretty girl. You could stay with somebody . . . . Why you not staying with somebody? What's wrong with your pussy?" Haddish brings it back again to the degrading position she is in as a young Black woman: to pay tuition, to avoid homelessness, she is supposed to allow men to use her body. In the next set, she talks about when a census worker comes to her apartment and asks her race. She contemplates the question and her possible answers and then tells him, "Caucasian . . . and ever since then, my life has been so *great!* It is awesome being white . . . Last year I slept with 87 dudes, no one called me a hoe or nothing. I am an entrepreneur. I am a business woman . . . I have a cousin who is a two time felon. She could *not* find a job. I told her to check the 'white' box . . . now she is working for Homeland Security." Again and again, Haddish's storytelling demands her audience reflect on the stereotypes she is supposed to embody but doesn't. She tells about the realities of being Black, female, and how the stereotypes cause real consequences in her life, such as a man's assumption that she will suck dick to pay her bills. For her Black audience, she is testifying; for her white followers she is educating and raising their consciousness.

Not everyone agrees with my analysis of Haddish. Some see her comedy as relying too heavily on stereotypes of Black women (angry, poor and scrappy, sexually free). Aliyah, one of the women I interviewed, is a college student and artist who comes from a family that promoted and educated toward Afrocentric Black pride and cultural awareness. Aliyah had few kind words about Haddish. "I don't like Tiffany Haddish. I feel like she is known for the wrong things. When she is doing comedy, she focuses on negative things; she is a mix of all these negative stereotypes. I don't like the stereotypes. I don't like the character she portrays. I don't want to watch TV and see a Black woman ready to start a fight or do something bad." Certainly, there are those elements in Haddish's comedy (she talks about getting revenge on a cheating man by literally shitting in his Jordans in a very calculated way; she talks about getting in serious fisticuffs with other Black girls and women; she drops in and out of stereotypical poses of Angry Black Woman and S.W.A. and Ghetto Hoe). In my reading of her, dropping in and out of these stereotypes is part of the commentary, as if she is saying, "This might be how some see me, but this is not who I *am*." She complicates the moments with insights and asides that shift meaning.

In her show *She Ready*, Haddish tells the story of Hart, a fellow Black comic, who helps her out when she is homeless by finding her a place to live. Later in the same show she talks of Jada Pinkett-Smith, a star she got to know when they both starred in *Girls Trip*, taking her under her wing, giving her advice, and showing her love. These stories of other Black stars seeing her and helping her on are not only an important part of Haddish's narrative, she wants to make sure they are part of other people's stories, too. In 2019, Netflix launched *They Ready*, hosted by Haddish and giving a platform to new comics, most of whom are Black women. Bringing other women along with her, using her currency to promote others who are earlier in their career trajectory, is part of who Haddish is.

Haddish is not unique in this commitment to helping other Black women enter comedy and finding them audience venues. 2 Dope Queens, Phoebe Robinson and Jessica Williams, are also two comedy stars who are committed to helping other Black women achieve success. These women (Haddish, Robinson, Williams) are providing a hand up to other Black women to succeed. They are telling other Black women comics, "We see you. We love you. We will help you. You are not alone."

2 B 2 DOPE QUEENS

Robinson's and Williams' rise started with a funny, Black woman-focused blog by Robinson. The blog became a local comedy show; the comedy show became a podcast; the podcast became an HBO series. Robinson and Williams' podcast, *2 Dope Queens*, featured their witty repartee about politics, gender, and sexuality among other life issues affecting young, feminist Black women in the Digital Age. The *2 Dope Queens* podcast (WNYC 2016-2018) was based on a live comedy show that Robinson hosted called *Blaria LIVE!* (Desta 2016). The comedy show was a spin-off of Robinson's blog, *Blaria!*, a combination of "Black" and the MTV animated character Daria, a sardonic and smart high schooler. Once the podcast *2 Dope Queens* took off, they shared their platform with lesser known, but extremely talented, women. On the podcast and in the series, Robinson and Williams offer five- to ten-minute segments to new talent, primarily Black women, but also comics from various other traditionally marginalized groups.

Robinson and Williams have a chemistry that includes teasing affection; neither one consistently plays the "straight" part. Traditional comic duos tend to have one who is the naïve "straight" character who sets up the other one's jokes. For Robinson and Williams, they are both ping-ponging the lines back and forth, feeding off each other's comments, each taking turns. Their humor relies far less on the use of facial expression and body language that comics such as Jones and Haddish use, which makes sense since they rose to fame through their podcast. Instead, it is the topics and creative language that sets them apart and adds depth to their comedy.

Because race is often a topic of their rapid banter, including the madness of white privilege, Robinson and Williams have a specific way of pronouncing the word "white" that punches their scorn of the most privileged and powerful "race." When either Robinson or Williams says "white," it comes out "KHWHite people," a guttural loogie-gathering pronunciation that indicates the proper disgust assigned to the demographic. They say it with a smile on their faces, but the audience knows the meaning: you know who you are, KHWH-ite people. And you know *what* you are: as slimy as throat phlegm. "I love the queens. Absolutely *love* them," Donelle told me. "I discovered their podcast, I can't remember whether someone recommended it or I read about it. But I was hooked. Their humor is fairly heterosexist, but not in a bad way. And they do a good job of getting queer comics on their show, so I feel like it is very inclusive. I love how they say 'white,' like it hurts them to say the word. It points to the ridiculousness of white privilege of even having categories of races."

The focus on race is important to The Queens. Williams and Robinson wanted their work "to bust stereotypes about people of color, particularly black women" (Desta 2016). Williams said, "We're awkward and weird and funny and sometimes sad and sometimes happy. We have this whole range" (qtd. in Desta 2016).

A typical example of their rapid-fire repartee is their opening set (Season 1, Episode 3; Hot Peen):

Williams (looking out at the audience): A lot of cocoa khaleesis in the house.
Robinson: Yeah. A lot of interracial couples in the house.
Williams: #IRC. We see you.
Robinson: #Obama'sAmerica. This is great.
Williams: I love that.

In this opening segment, they are intentionally asking us to think about their audience. There are lots of Black women, but white people, too. But the Dope Queens are not about to play to the whites. They will spend time to clarify their comments or points for their white, clueless audience members, but their humor is focused on an audience of young Black women.

Robinson: So great. You know, we've been thinking about what we want the themes to be for each of our shows.
Williams: Really thought about it.
Robinson: Yeah. There is so much going on in the cunt, a.k.a. country.
Williams: You know we got that stuff with North Korea.
Robinson: With everyone, basically, right now.
Williams: With everyone basically right now.
Robinson: We are fighting everyone right now.
Williams: We are fighting a lot of people.
Robinson: Yeah, everyone everywhere. Yeah, women can't be left alone.
Williams: Yeah, the economy, dudes.
Robinson: That is the most G-rated way to say that.
Williams: I know.
Robinson: Women sure are bothered a lot.
Williams: It's nice. It's like the Ellen Degeneres version and I appreciate that. Women are being bothered. And men are doing the bothering a lot of the time.

Here we see Robinson and Williams addressing their audience ("we") of women. They are speaking to the issue of harassment and assault, but they are referring to these assaults on women's bodies and psyches as "bothering," using Ellen possessive' white "family friendly" comedy/talk show as a reference to indicate their language is less accusatory and more careful. Their reference to Degeneres, a notoriously apolitical talk show host that appeals primarily to a white, suburban female audience, and the use of the word "bothering" for assault/rape, is a pointed way of indicating that women aren't supposed to be blaming men for the perpetration of assault on women's bodies. The queens are being polite, to the point of ridiculousness, in naming systemic and pervasive male violence against women.

Robinson: There is so much bothering happening in the world right now, am I right?
Williams: What is the deal with fucking bothering, right?

The Queens never mince words, so it is quaint and funny to have them use "bothering" as a stand in for harassment/assault/rape. It is the height of the #MeToo movement, so the euphemism of "bothering" is sarcastic, meant to tell their female audience, "This is what the dominant culture does: minimizes our experiences of assault and harassment." They know that men are the culprits in most #MeToo stories, but they strike back by focusing this set on "Hot Peens" (sexy penises), reducing men to a body part in the way that men have historically done when they call women a cunt, a pussy, a twat, or when men reduce women to the sum of their vagina, as Sykes played with in her set from *Tongue Untied.*

Williams continues: . . . But we thought about it a lot and we decided the topic would be:
(Yell together): Hot Peens!
Robinson: Objectifying dudes since 1996.
Williams: Yeah, is that when you started?
Robinson: Sure. Yeah. I started at 12.
Williams: Yeah. Wow. That's intense. I was like, 'Wow. Seven. That was such a crazy year for me. Lots of Disney.
Robinson: I have a RRRomance (rolls Rs) . . .
Williams: Don't do that ever again.
Robinson: But before that I was single for two years. I love how someone in the audience just yelled, "That's feminism!"
Williams: Just all of it. It is all feminism. Everything's a feminism. We are all feminisms.
Robinson: Yeah. Right. We are all feminisms.

By naming themselves as feminists, by embracing the mantle that has both been criticized by women of color as being exclusively representative of white privilege and defined by the dominant male culture as angry/bitter/ugly, the queens are redefining what this word means for the audience. Feminisms is everyone. We are smart. We are funny. We are political. And that is what every woman should be, Robinson and Williams say.

Williams: But as we got more famous we started to interact more regularly with really hot peens. Which, for us, was unusual. I felt like it was unusual. We both grew up nerdier girls. From the suburbs. Mostly white communities.
Robinson: So, I started doing some bothering.
Williams: It wasn't even like that. You were so much more thoughtful about it.
Robinson: I was. I was.

Here Robinson is telling the story of maybe "bothering"/harassing a man. But Williams pulls her back: Robinson was pursuing an actor who wasn't into her. She backed off when the actor ignored her advances. Williams was the friend who encouraged her and told her that despite the rebuff, Robinson was still amazing.

Robinson: Yeah. [He was only interested in] Pure friendship. But I like that you had my back.
Williams: Always, baby. I felt like the magical Negro of your movie who was like, "You better believe in yourself, girl! Do it, girl! Hmm-mm. Don't take 'no' for

an answer. Keep going, girl. You believe it, you can achieve it. (singing) It's possible. Impossible things are happening every day."

Here Williams calls upon the cringe-worthy stereotype of the "Black woman as sage/oracle" who tends to show up in films and television shows to save the white person or give meaningful advice. The Queens go on to talk about Williams' love life—she hates PDA, she was raised in a Christian household and she took a virginity pledge at the age of fourteen so sexuality always caused her extreme anxiety. But she has had a bae for three and a half years. She's happy, but still doesn't like PDA.

Williams: You know it's like he said something really romantic to me today. He looked at me and he was like, "Oh, honey. Your edges look so nice." I was like, that is the nicest thing a white man could say to a Black woman. Aside from "Sorry for slavery."
Robinson: And for the white people who are confused about edges.
Williams: Let's catch them up.
Robinson: Black women are conditioned to always pay attention and make sure they are lying flat. Like you wanna have baby hairs. Like on Chili in *TLC*, like you wanna have, smooth it down . . . . So, we get judged a lot. We have to worry about our edges.
Williams: There's an edge budget at HBO so we're happy about it.

Coming full circle on audience awareness—and naming their primary audience as Black women—they make sure their white audience can be in on the joke, stopping to explain the reference to edges. In this dialogue that opens their episode, we see the women taking turns supporting and loving each other. In fact, they often say to each other, "I love you." They tease and laugh, tell the truth, and keep each other honest, but it is all about a deep and abiding friendship, love of each other, demonstrating and testifying to the power of women-loving-women in ways that affirm and uplift. Through their staccato exchanges, we hear the love, the support, and the true delight they feel in each other. There is no degrading taunts or malice, no powerplays or one getting the "upper hand" by playing "smarter." With other classic comic duos (Laurel and Hardy, Burns and Allen, Amos and Andy, Tom and Dick Smothers), one person always played the smarter half to the silly half's bumbling buffoon. Williams and Robinson differ dramatically from this classic dynamic. They are equals in wit and brilliance; they genuinely love, respect, and delight in each other. They model feminist love of women and support while engaging in entertaining banter that keeps their audience engaged and laughing. Their staccato back-and-forths are commentaries on issues of concern specifically regarding Black women. Their use of up-to-the-moment pop culture references and vernacular add to the comic effect.

Williams and Robinson's brand of sisterhood and Black feminism translates into their creating a community of Black feminist comics that they promote and encourage. Their respect and love for Black women is not just evident in the way they speak to each other, but in who they choose to promote and celebrate on their programs. In both their podcast and their HBO series, they promote Black female comics. The women they feature on their shows are allowed access to a national audience, riding the comedy coattails of these two brilliant and funny feminists. They offer their audience evidence that they (Black female comics) are *not* the exception to the rule or somehow unique. They are positioning themselves as hosts to a large body of Black (and other Traditionally Marginalized Peoples) comics who are trying to get the world to notice them. This practice of promoting others is decidedly feminist, creating a sisterhood of comics who have each other's backs, who support and celebrate each other, and who know that success for one does not mean success for all unless there is a concerted effort made. Ruby, a self-described feminist (in her thirties, partnered with a woman, one daughter), said she goes online to find more information about the comics the queens feature on their program.

> I often am laughing so hard I can't stand it. Not just at the 2 Dope Queens, but at the comics they have on. They are all speaking their truths [about race, class, gender, sexuality] and making it funny. It's smart humor, you know. Not exactly cerebral, but *smart*. And feminist. I love that. So much comedy by women isn't feminist. So, I can depend on them to introduce me to other Black feminist comics, some of them queer, so that is also good. (Ruby)

Ruby who performs spoken word and stand-up comedy says she takes heart in knowing Black women are helping each other succeed. "There is a community of us. When I make it, I want to do that, to help other women get a head start. White people have been doing that for each other forever. We need to do it. It is about sisterhood. It is like shopping Black. We have to support each other. We can't really get ahead if we don't pull others up with us."

As 2 Dope Queens, *A Black Lady Sketch Show*, and Haddish's *They Ready* prove, there is no shortage of funny, razor-sharp Black women who are ready to take center stage and make us laugh and *think*. The explosion of Black women doing comedy is not something new, per se, but their access to larger audiences and crossover appeal *is* new. It comes from a few unique cultural dynamics that exist. One is that young audiences are more interested in actively working against racism, thereby offering Black women a new audience group beyond their own community. Research has shown that Generation Z or "The Digital Generation" is much more interested in working for equity, justice, and against systems of oppression than previous generations (Dorsey 2016). The second cultural phenomenal is related to this

Digital Generation: they are astute at self-promotion and using social media to upload their acts, their talent, their performances thereby gaining wider audiences as people view, share, and like. As Peter Kunze (2015), a comedy scholar, wrote in the introduction to an issue of *Comedy Studies* devoted to humor in the Digital Age, "Few subjects have been as impacted by new media to the extent comedy has. One only needs to log on to a social media platform to see a daily barrage of viral videos, memes, blog posts, witty Tweets and Facebook statuses" (100). And one of the benefits of comedy in the digital age is that voices traditionally locked out of access are now set free. Not only that, but Gen Z is adept at liking, passing, and sharing, using social media to promote what snags their attention. Black women comics and humorists, writers and performers, now can make their own space and create a following, circumventing the gate-keepers that are the aged white men who control the entertainment industry. Through digital open-access platforms like YouTube, Black women can create a following. By doing so, they gain access to the white power structures as lucrative talent. By virtue of their voices and perspectives being pushed into the mainstream comedy world, they are educating and raising social consciousness regarding issues of race, class, gender, and sexuality. Issa Rae, who self-published and promoted her original web series *Awkward Black Girl* on YouTube, fully acknowledged the digital world and open access as part of her success. Rae writes in her memoir, "If it weren't for YouTube, I would be extremely pessimistic, but I'm not anymore. YouTube has revolutionized content creation. If it weren't for YouTube, I would still be at the studios trying to convince executives that Awkward Black Girls really do exist" (Rae 2015, 45). Because of the ease in which people can now upload and create content, those traditionally locked out of WSCP entertainment industry now have a chance at gaining an audience and success. Although Rae is not the only Black writer/performer who has gained success in the mainstream through online self-production and self-promotion, she did so to such a great level of success it would be remiss to not discuss her trajectory here.

BEING AWKWARD, BLACK, AND FEMALE

Rae is now not only an established voice of Black feminist comedy through her wildly successful HBO series *Insecure*, she is also a featured star in various genres of films from comedies (*Little* 2019) to action/adventure (*Lovebirds* 2020) to artful romance (*The Photograph* 2020), to drama (*The Hate You Give* 2018). It is safe to say that right now, Rae is *hot*. She makes guests appearances on shows such as *Black A.F.* (Netflix 2020), appears on talk shows, and is often interviewed in mainstream press to comment on the state of Blacks or Black women in the entertainment industry. She is an award-winning writer, producer, and actor. She. Is. *Busy*. And she self-launched her career by offering the perspective of a young Black woman, struggling to make her way in her twenties in Los Angeles, calling herself an "awkward Black girl." In her web series *Awkward Black Girl* (2011), she embodied a new, updated version of the "awkward Black girl" character that was popular on sitcoms in the 1980s–1990s[1] as well as a contemporary young adult version of the sexually and socially awkward young woman as manifested in other female comics and their characters (Tina Fey's Liz Lemon on *30 Rock*, Amy Poehler's Leslie Knope on *Parks and Rec,* Mindy Kahling's Mindy Lahiri on *The Mindy Project*, Lena Dunham's Hannah Horvath on *Girls,* and Abbi Jacobsen's Abbi Abrams and Ilana Glazer's Ilana Wexler on *Broad City*). To this predominantly white, privileged-class list of female protagonists who are anxious and socially awkward, Rae gave her audiences a Black female character with the same sort of social/sexual issues. In addition to having to deal with the typical sexist, misogynist bullshit of the WSCP, Rae's character also has to address microaggressions and full-blown racism in every episode.

The comedy Rae is so brilliant at is one in which her public persona and her inner thoughts are at odds. This self-aware cognitive dissonance between being a polite Black girl in the "real world" and a "don't take shit from anyone, fast and hard talking" Black girl in her mind is communicated to the audience through direct address, through mirrors, and solo rap performances in her car or apartment. Commenting on Issa Rae's *Awkward Black Girl* web series persona (where she raps to herself), media scholar Finley (2016) writes:

> J's (Rae's character on the show) violent raps are citational and provide an intertextual means by which she both critiques a black cultural expressive form that has misogynistically alienated black women, and imitates it as a satirical form of comic relief. J derives catharsis from these moments of satiric performance by accurately citing a black cultural tradition from which she has been forcefully excluded, enabling her to momentarily (if privately and ironically) escape from her Awkward Black Girl status. (260)

These private raps are carried over to great effect from *Awkward Black Girl* to *Insecure*. Rae also uses fantasy break-out moments where she punches a racist in the face, screams at a coworker for a racist aside, or throws and smashes items in a righteously deserved rage. Once these moments are expressed, the camera cuts back to Rae's character in the *actual* moment where she makes a calm or polite comment to or about the white offender, sparing them the much-deserved fallout of Black rage.

Rae's characters intentionally enact awkwardness as a way of setting herself apart. With her awkwardness, she can avoid socializing with the whites in her work group; because of her awkwardness she spares herself negotiating the difficulties of romantic relationships; with her awkwardness she deliberately is playing *against* the stereotype of S.W.A. or Angry Black Woman. One media scholar theorizes that Rae's characters use awkwardness as a way to alienate themselves, as a way of being seen as an individual instead of as a miscellaneous Black woman.

> In the precarious-girl comedy [like *Insecure* and *Awkward Black Girl*], the protagonist embraces the idea that she repels others as a sign of her individuation. If she cannot escape the conditions that make her alienate others, then perhaps she can escape her feelings about her immobility by accepting her abjection as a form of psychological growth and development. (Wanzo 2015, 29)

Wanzo uses the word "precarious" because Rae's characters are not part of a community/social group; they are socially awkward, not manifesting the expected tropes of femininity or even Black womanhood. Because the characters Rae embodies are alienated from others, Rae's characters attempt to adopt "cool" poses, (they fail miserably), which is part of the humor. I would add that the characters, although definitely using awkwardness to alienate or isolate from *whites* and *white* dominant ideologies as much as possible, are embraced within the characters' friend groups, as least in *Insecure*. In this production, unlike *Awkward Black Girl*, Rae's character is not isolated from a friend group, but has a rich community of female friends that are affirming and critical in ways that offer love and support. Her awkwardness in one context (work) keeps the whites at bay; in another context (friend group), the same awkwardness is embraced and loved.

> As a black female comedic writer, Rae's use of awkward does multiple layers of work: it humanizes, visualizes and pushes back against standard performances of (comedic) femininity. That is, Rae's use of humor to self-objectify her awkwardness renegotiates the terms through which her blackness and womanhood are read. (Bradley 2015, 149)

Bradley goes on to say that Rae, "establish[es] a persona that blurs social, political and cultural norms as they relate to popular culture and black women" (149). This blurring of lines between social, political, and cultural to talk about issues of identity harkens back to the comedy employed by Mabley, Goldberg, Sykes, Haddish, Jones, Robinson and Williams, and Thede. These powerfully smart and funny Black women are continuing a comedy tradition that infuses their work with the issues of the day, the reality of their lives, calling upon their audience to think, respond, and react.

WHAT ABOUT THAT AUDIENCE?

These Black women performers have successfully crossed over from a primarily Black audience to a mixed audience. In doing so, they gain access to much-deserved financial success. And we want that success for them. However, the moment they cross-over to that white audience—even if it isn't *all* white—we hold our breath. Will the humor change? If so, how? Will the whites be laughing *with* these women or *at* them? As Black audiences see the nuances in the way these women perform characters or moments that might embody stereotypes such as S.W.A. or Angry Black Woman, will the whites also see those nuances? We hold our breath and anticipate a cringe. Sometimes, however, Black audiences are proud to share their culturally Black comic heroes with white audiences and aren't really concerned with what whites might see as stereotypes. "Black audiences and black people in general have always found the popular stereotypes of themselves to be quite funny, in a certain context . . . Black audiences, during [the 1970s, post-civil rights era], felt more comfortable with [Black humor for Black audiences that sometimes featured stereotypical Black characters] being performed for white audiences. In fact, black audiences were sometimes visibly proud of this" (Early, Carpio, and Sollors 2010, 30, 32.) In their article, Early, Carpio, and Sollars refer to Richard Pryor as a Black comic who crossed over to white audiences by portraying a foul-mouthed "ghetto image" of Blacks. Not everyone in the Black community celebrated Pryor, but for the most part his humor was seen as funny by Blacks even when whites were laughing, too.

One of my respondents was impatient with me asking her to think about whether a white audience or a Black audience made a difference when analyzing Black women's humor. "I don't want to spend any more time thinking about how white folks will react. I tune into comedy to escape white nonsense. That is why I *like* Black comedy. Don't ask me think about how white people see it. Who cares?!" (Lex, fifty-year-old, single and mother of one son, small business owner). Note taken, yet others *were* thinking about this issue and wanted to parse through the complexities of this issue of "who is laughing?" Lex's nonchalance or even annoyance by some Black audience members regarding how whites may or may not perceive Black comics was not necessarily shared by other women I interviewed. Most brought up their concern about how humor created by Black comics for Black audiences would be perceived by whites.

Some Black women in the audience express concern about the *laughing at* versus *laughing with* question. In research interviewing young Black women about *Love & Hip Hop NY* (reality show), the young women expressed concern about how non-Blacks would perceive the characters (Edwards 2016). Edwards (2016) found that the young Black women she interviewed knew that the characters were stereotypes, but they worried that non-Black audience members would not see them as such. Edwards writes, "[The young women] expressed concerned that they do not have control over the fact that people who are unfamiliar with their culture may not be able to see the cast members as individuals who make certain choices based on certain circumstances" (289). This concern of "what does a white audience see or learn about Black women" was also brought up by several of the women I interviewed. Gloria, an academic in the Atlanta area who was single and in her mid-thirties, said:

It is like me telling a story of my crazy auntie. The minute some white person says, "Oh, tell that story about your crazy auntie!" I say, "Nah." It isn't for him to decide. It's *my* story. *My* family. And I'm not telling it so *they* can laugh at it. I own that story . . . . The Black people laugh with love; white people are just laughing. They don't know the love. But with these mixed audiences, I don't know. Maybe the white people see it. They see that Black people are laughing with love. Those whites might get it, that they aren't laughing at a stereotype. I think they can feel it.

Secondary to this issue of who is laughing is whether a performer will change their humor to appeal to that white audience by manifesting the stereotypes the racist white audience enjoys. Laughing *at* instead of *with* was the topic of an episode of *Twenties* (HBO 2020) where Nia, attempting to revitalize an acting career, performs an improv act for a group of white agents (Season 1, Episode 7: What Would Todd Do?). Nia is partnered with a white man who sets the scene: they are coworkers and she just got a new weave and she can't talk about anything else. The man doesn't understand that even this set up is entirely racist and offensive. Nia begins with authenticity, trying to downplay any sort of stereotype, but notices the agents are bored. She makes the decision to adopt the tropes of the S.W.A. stereotype (snarky and sassy, flipping her weave, talking about how the only good baby daddy is the one that pays child support). The white agents sit up and take notice. A Black man in the audience expresses disgust and slowly sinks into his seat. Nia's white improve partner asks if *he* could ever get with a Black woman. She "talks" to her weave as if the weave were a fortune-teller or oracle. "My weave say you are not worthy of being inside a Black woman." The white agents are howling. The Black man in the audience frowns. We can tell by the expression on Nia's face she is disappointed in herself and ashamed and disgusted at the latent racism of the audience. Later, in her yoga class, a Black man approaches her and says there is no shame in "shucking and jiving" to get ahead. He says, "All the greats did. Flip Wilson, Sammy Davis Jr., Tyler Perry. Give the white folks what they need until you are so rich you can do whatever you want." Nia doesn't buy it. She feels ashamed and is determined to take a different approach when she has the chance.

The next time Nia is in her improv class with the same white guy, she gets to choose the scenario. She chooses that he is visiting his old Black nanny at her home for a family BBQ. She skewers him and *he* is left feeling uncomfortable. She talks about his pink, flat butt; his small penis; that he has never been around so many Black people; that he brings a nasty potato salad with raisins and apples that his mother made; that he has an assault rifle in his back pack; that he will smell like wet dog if he gets into the pool.

Given a second opportunity, Nia chooses to not play to the racist stereotypes that appeal to some white people. She chooses to go full-throttle with another version of culturally Black humor: The Dozens (for more information on The Dozens, see page 182). The Dozens insults the rival and, in besting them, emerges victorious. She successfully reclaims her dignity, using cultural Black comedic strategies to do so, and rejects pandering to white racists in order to succeed. This use of The Dozens to gain a foothold even in the context of a white audience speaks to active resistance to a type of humor that her friend calls "shucking and jiving." Instead of giving the white audience what they *think* they want (a S.W.A.), Nia sticks to Black comic traditions and wins over the white audience while honoring her Black roots. The white audience comes over to *her* side of the comic equation rather than Nia changing her humor to accommodate the whites. Haggins (2007) writes about the humor FUBU (For Us by Us)—specifically satire—that Black comedy engages. The FUBU satire may appeal to crossover audiences, but it is especially loved and appreciated by Black audiences who see the layers and celebrate the traditions of Black comedy. Those comics who employ traditionally Black comic tropes and speak to issues of Black identity are proving that FUBU should not be compromised to crossover. Indeed, to examine the work of the Black women in this chapter, one can be true to these FUBU traditions, squarely focus on feminist politics of being Black and female, and *still* be wildly successful to those mainstream audiences, disrupting instead of codifying stereotypes of Black womanhood.

Donelle said when some of her favorite Black woman comics crossed over to white audience appeal (Issa Rae, Phoebe Robinson, Lena Waithe, and Tiffany Haddish) she was nervous, but then she became hopeful.

I didn't think their humor changed. They often would break out to "educate" whites, but for the most part, they were playing to the Black audience. I feel hopeful. I feel a little hope. Just a little. With all the BLM stuff, George Floyd and "say their names," and all that. I go to the rallies and I see a lot of white people there. They are trying. They are working against racism. With the BLM movement, it is Black women, *young* women, doing that work. And those white people are cheering for them. So maybe there are whites who are finally getting it. Maybe. Cuz the cold, hard fact is, we can't do this by ourselves. It's white people who have to solve the problem of racism. (Donelle)

Donelle is making a direct connection between the crossover of some of her favorite comics to the political movement that she sees as hopeful. Perhaps things *are* changing. Perhaps there are *some* whites (enough whites?) to make a difference. What is of note is that, in her analysis, the humor and approach of the Black women she loves hasn't changed much when it crosses over to mainstream audiences. Perhaps this is not new for Black women comics, though. When one examines the work of Moms Mabley, it would seem she did not change her humor to appeal to whites. She remained true to her commitment to politics and Black culture. It was the audience who had to adapt if they wanted to enjoy her show.

The comedy can be Black feminist and political and still bring audiences together. The hope is that the white audience will change by celebrating—and laughing *with*—these powerful, Black women's performances. As Ruby said, "Are they laughing at us? No. They know funny. They know smart. And these women are funny and smart. That is what they are laughing at. And that's good, I think. That's good."

FUNNY FILMS

Although I interviewed over 100 women, the reality is that very few of them talked about women in comedy. That could have been my fault in that I asked them about what they watched and that may have implied film and streaming series, not stand-up. As I was talking to women about their entertainment choices, there were two films that came up over and over: *Little* and *Girls Trip*. Perhaps it was because there are so few comedies that feature Black *women* that these two films were noted. Perhaps it is because, at the time I was interviewing people, we were in the throes of the most horrifically oppressive presidential administrations in recent history, a COVID pandemic, and social unrest regarding systemic racism and modern day lynching of Black citizens, resulting in weekly (if not daily) marches and protests. In the context of that hard reality, we need to laugh. We want to laugh. As one of my respondents told me, "At the end of the day, I don't want to watch the news or a drama or a horror film or anything that is going to make me feel *worse*. I just want to relax and *laugh*" (Lex).

Little (2019) was a Hollywood release written and directed by Black
women (Tina Gordon and Tracy Oliver). The story was said to be the brain-
child of Marsai Martin, the tween who audiences saw grow up on the series
Black-ish playing the youngest daughter, Diane. The storyline of the films
involves a self-centered, high-powered executive (Regina Hall as Jordan
Sanders) who treats everyone horribly. A "Magical Black Girl" curses her
and Jordan becomes "little" (a twelve-year-old, played by Martin) until she
learns her lesson. Issa Rae plays the sidekick assistant. The comedy is a silly
and family-friendly movie of the body-swap genre, similar to *Big* and *Freaky
Friday*. When mentioning the film, the women I talked to acknowledged that
the storyline was predictable, but they wanted to support the Black women
involved in making the film. "I supported it because I wanted to support
the girl who at 14 produced movies. I didn't like the main character . . . I
wish there had been more time that they would have been amicable towards
each other; mostly they just seemed awful. It played a little in the stereotype
that women can't support each other. I didn't like that Black women didn't
get along" (Karen). Another participant said, "There wasn't a whole lot of
depth to it. The lead (Regina Hall) she plays those roles a lot (high-powered
business woman). Once again, she is tough, pretty, and angry. She always
does the men wrong instead of the men doing her wrong. *Little* was entertaining. It was fluff. I don't mind a little light movie every now and then"
(Mashell, health care worker and mother of six). Both Karen and Mashell
were supportive of the film because it featured Black females, but both also
pointed out some tropes that they were not very comfortable with: Black
women who can't seem to get along with other Black women or Black
women who are antagonistic toward each other. In the end of the film, sisterhood prevails, but throughout most of the movie, Mashell and Karen are
right: the women are not supportive of each other.

In contrast to the stereotype that "women can't get along" was the wildly
successful *Girls Trip*, a "buddy movie" where the wild antics in a girls' weekend in New Orleans showcases the tight bond that female friends have with
each other. The comedic elements, witty dialogue, and much physical humor
in the form of pratfalls and precarious situations are guffaw-creating moments.
To have these manifest in an all-female cast and production staff felt fresh.
None of us could remember an all-female buddy movie (as well as all Black)
that tilted toward action/adventure. Sure, there was *Waiting to Exhale* (1995),
but that was more drama than comedy. What has happened in the twenty-five
years since then? Michelle, a college criminal justice major, said:

I liked that *Girls Trip* was more of a fun movie instead of a sad, depressing
movie. Black people always have a sad movie or a historical drama. That
was a fun movie that everyone needed. Every women's shapes and sizes were

represented in that movie. It was literally what Black people needed. We wanted to watch Black people have a *good time*. I am grateful to be reminded of the past, but we should not have to continuously be reminded of what happened that was sad and tragic. *Girls Trip* gave us a time to just relax and be happy. Especially Black women. The friends in the film had a big argument, but then they realized that their friends mattered more. Yes, we are going to argue, but I love my friends. It was real-world stuff. I liked how they portrayed everyone. They included the woman who held a grudge. I like how they put that in there and actually have them talk about it and talk about their feelings and move past it. It showed a really positive portrayal of friendship and sisterhood. We need more of that. (Michelle)

Not only was the film laugh-out-loud hilarious, it showed life-long friendships between a diverse group of Black women who, despite differences and struggles, were able to be vulnerable with each other and end up on the other side with love, grace, and forgiveness. In a world where the representations of Black women are often those of being victims of hardship, of struggle, the elixir of laughter and love that *Girls Trip* provided was something many were ravenously hungry for. We want to laugh; we need to laugh; our lives depend upon it.

CONCLUSION

Without delight, without laughter, without guffaws, without the tear-inducing belly-aches of a good "pee-my-pants" moment, how will we get through the tough stuff? We can't. We *need* humor. Laughter releases endorphins that help us heal from all the wounds the world inflicts upon us. Black women, especially, facing the intersectional barriers of racism, sexism—among other isms—need that laughter most of all. And there are Black women who are doing their work to make sure that much-needed, much-deserved endorphin-rich laughter is available. The Black women comics discussed here are only a small smattering of what is now available through streaming services and social media posts. The Digital Age has arrived and Black women humorists and comics are diving into that medium to deliver their talent to larger audiences. And their work, their commitment to laughter benefits us all. Laughter heals. Laughter helps. Laughter gets us through the hardest times. And, as many of my respondents articulated, in the age of the current political and cultural landscape, laughter and humor are needed now more than ever. If not for humor and comedy, where would we find relief from the systems of oppression, the microaggressions, the overt racism, sexism, homophobia, ageism, and ableism that extract a pound of flesh every day we venture into the dominant culture? Humor should not be taken lightly. The women profiled here know that. Making sure we can laugh is serious business and the Black women doing this work are shattering the boundaries that have been assigned to them. They will not be held back. And our worlds are all fuller and richer because of their ability to make us laugh.

NOTE

1. "Some notable Awkward Black Girl characters in 1980s' and 1990s' television comedy sitcoms include the following: Freddie Brooks (Cree Summer) on *A Different World*, Kim Wayans' characters on the sketch comedy show *In Living Color* and her role as Tonia Harris on *In the House*, Myra Monkhouse (Michelle Thomas) on *Family Matters*, Synclaire James-Jones (Kim Coles) and Maxine Shaw (Erika Alexander) on *Living Single*, and Joan Clayton (Tracee Ellis Ross) and Lynn Searcy (Persia White) on *Girlfriends*. These characters exhibit a wide-ranging spectrum of awkwardness: willingly sexual but inept, economically and/or educationally successful but socially introverted, overly critical of self and obsessive or (multi)talented but in search of self-worth and fulfillment" (Bradley 2015, 151).

Chapter 7

History Lessons

We Are Strong, Independent Women

Some call it "Trauma Porn," those films that cast Black women as victims of slavery, sexual abuse/rape, incest, relationship violence. The audience is primarily white people; the story focuses on unrelenting trauma of Black female bodies. The message is clear: Black women suffer and survive (sometimes). As hooks (1981) wrote, "Usually, when people talk about the 'strength' of black women . . . they ignore the reality that to be strong in the face of oppression is not the same as overcoming oppression, that endurance is not to be confused with transformation" (6). These films serve to reinforce a white supremacist gaze: white folks have a right to look, to call "entertainment" the horrific and graphic representations of Black women's rapes, psychic and physical. Films such as *Precious* (2009) directed by Lee Daniels, *When They See Us* (2019) directed by Ava DuVernay, and *The Immortal Life of Henrietta Lacks* (2019) directed by George C. Wolf fit the definition. Yet these are directed by Blacks. Although the trauma the WSCP wrings out of Black females' lives is real, the graphic scenes of trauma playing out on the screen for a primarily white audience should give us pause. Yes, Black female trauma, systemic rape and abuse, are important issues to address. But when the narrative includes an almost unrelentingly bleak picture of what it means to be Black and female who benefits? In fictionalized true story of Henrietta Lacks and her children, *The Important Life of Henrietta Lacks*, features Sarah (Oprah Winfrey), Henrietta Lacks' daughter, suffering mental breakdowns due to the trauma that is borne of the medical field's exploitation of her mother, her sister's horrific demise at a mental hospital in 1955, and her own life of sexual and physical assault at the hands of Black men who are supposed to protect and support her. The white savior, this time in the form of a young female journalist who is writing a book on Lacks' life, death, and family, is the only person who seems to do right by Sarah and the Lacks family, abused and used by institutional racism as manifested in Johns Hopkins University and the broader field of medical science. A Black con artist also shows up to add to the family's exploitation. The coup de grace is that Sarah dies before the book is published and does not benefit from a foundation established by the book's author, the result of the book being wildly successful and holding for five years on the *New York Times Best Seller* list.

Although these sorts of stories are essential to tell both to honor the Black women who lived these lives and to give name to the depth and destructive power of institutional racism on individuals, families, and communities, we find ourselves hungry for stories of triumph, success, and lasting progress. It is through these empowering stories such as those told in films and series in *Hidden Figures* (2016) directed by Theodore Melfi and based on the book by Margot Lee Shetterly, *Underground* (2016-2017) written and directed by Misha Green and Kate Woods among others, *Bessie* (2015) written and directed by Dee Rees, *Harriet* (2019) written and directed by Kasi Lemmons, and *Self Made* (2020) written and directed by DeMane Davis and Kasi Lemmons that we are allowed a reprieve from the tale of how systemic racism destroys Black women's lives. Rather these films and series, written, directed, and often produced by Black women, move beyond the typical trauma porn. The above films address the trauma of slavery, sexism, and violence inflicted on Black women's/girl's minds, lives, and bodies. But their spirits survive and the films end on an upbeat note, not of tragic death and despair. This difference between "trauma porn" and traumatic experiences that can be survived is key to changing stereotypes of Black women as long-suffering, disempowered victims who die tragically due to racism and misogyny. hooks is right that stories of grit are not the same as overcoming systemic oppression, but some stories of grit also include narratives that triumph over and change those systems in ways that benefit others. Madam C. J. Walker (*Self Made*) gave women the opportunity to become entrepreneurs; blues singer Bessie Smith (*Bessie*) created inroads to a patriarchal, white-dominated music industry; NASA scientists Katherine Johnson, Dorothy Vaughn, and Mary Jackson shattered the myth that girls can't do math, let alone astrophysics. And *Underground* (Underground Railroad drama) and *Harriet* (Harriet Tubman's story) revise white supremacist history, showing us that Black people did have families and communities and romance; even while experiencing the horrors of slavery, these women persevered and thrived. The history of Black women as survivors, as people who not only thrive but succeed, is important. When we experience narratives of triumph and stalwart resistance against the WSCP, we recognize the Black women who forged the trails. And we see a way forward.

SUPERWOMAN IS BLACK

The image of a strong Black woman is one not only perpetuated in entertainment media, but one that is emphasized even in the lives of young Black children. It may be a stereotype, but it serves girls well. Researchers Thomas, Hacker, and Hoxha (2011) found that the representations of Black woman as strong resistors; survivors; and powerhouses within their family, community, church, and workplace were important for Black girls. The girls involved in the Thomas, Hacker, and Hoxha research saw mothers, aunties, and grandmothers as strong and powerful, tireless and hard-working; and this image of their women kin made the girls, in turn, feel strong. This idea of the strong Black woman, similar to lore of Black Girl Magic, helps girls be resilient in the context of a dominant culture bent on destroying them. Thomas, Hacker, and Hoxha write:

> The modern Superwoman image or the Strong Independent Black Woman is the image that is promoted by family and important to adults in girls' lives . . . . The Strong Black Woman image is different from traditional feminine characteristics of submissiveness and passivity, suggesting that the gendered racial identity development of African American women is different from characteristics represented by racial or gender identity constructs [in the dominant white culture]. (532)

The idea or belief of the strong Black woman, the superwoman figure, changes the trope of femininity in significant ways. It allows girls and women to become self-actualized whereas white femininity denies females agency. Instead of femininity being defined as passive, weak, quiet, demure (as are the WSCP characteristics of a "white lady"), Black femininity is celebrated for strength, independence, and grit. Although this could be defined as a stereotype—albeit one that might, in some contexts, benefit some Black females—as with any stereotype, it could disallow a Black woman opportunities to be vulnerable or to rely on others. In analyzing the recent productions featuring strong Black women, it is important to note the nuances in their stories that show them both as strong and vulnerable, independent and able to engage in relationships that offer much-needed support, competent as well as sometimes inept and needing guidance. They are whole humans, resisting stereotypes but rising above and around the barriers placed before them by the WSCP.

These stories, histories, and narratives of powerful and complex Black women of history are essential to creating a canon of representations that belies the lessons taught in school of Black enslavement and disempowerment. Certainly, it is important to learn of the real and systemic ways Black women are harmed and kept down, yet it is also important to offer up models of women who truly worked successfully within the confines of the WSCP and succeeded, changing their own path and the road for all who followed. It is through these important herstories that are being produced and viewed today that we can celebrate a past and use it to define a better future. Many of the women I talked with, especially those who were mothers, spoke with excitement about films and series such as *Harriet*, *Self Made*, *Underground*, and *Hidden Figures* as a way to tell a new story, something to celebrate, an important deviation from the traumatic tales that are the typical lore perpetuated through slave narratives, civil rights era stories, and generational poverty, abuse, and rape. As one of my respondents said, "Yes, we need to hear the hard stories, the bad truths, but we also need to know the other: the heroines in our history, the people who fought and won and persevered, not just those who were beat down into nothing" (Mashell). Mashell was one of many mothers I spoke with who made a point of watching historical films and series featuring Black women *with* their children. Mashell told me she has open conversations with her children as the film/show is rolling, asking questions and answering questions, commenting on the action and engaging in critical thinking as a family. She is not unique in this approach by Black parents. History lessons in films and series provide Black parents with opportunities to engage in "proactive racial socialization" (Adams-Bass, Bentley-Edwards, and Stevenson 2014, 84). Proactive racial socialization includes awareness of racial inequity toward Blacks; parental explanations, examples, and instructions about how to manage both overt and tacit racism; cultural and historical information of Blacks; an affirmation of Afrocentric beauty/attractiveness (Stevenson 1994; Stevenson et al. 2005). Black parents can use films such as *Bessie*, *Self Made*, and *The Immortal Life of Henrietta Lacks* and series such as *Grown-ish* and *Black-ish* to initiate discussions regarding these issues, creating more critical consumers in their Black children.

Mashell's six children range in age from a young elementary school student to a college student. "We talk about everything we watch. There is definitely dialogue the entire time we are watching. Now my youngest is very aware of what is fiction and what is not. I ask her, 'What do you think. What do you think that character thought when she did this or that?' I don't want to persuade her to what I think. I want *her* to think" (Mashell). Mashell's college-aged daughter confirms this, saying, "We can't make it through a movie without talking about it." Mashell is parenting with the goal of critically conscious children, children who are positively racially social.

Mashell offered this story of watching a movie the previous week with her seven-year-old daughter. The movie was a foreign film about an eighty-four-year old African man who was living in his home country, ravaged by war and colonialism.

He had survived the British rule. But he had never learned to read so he had to fight to go to primary school. He did everything he could to attend the school. There was a lot of stuff along the way about politics and history. I kept thinking "Is she even going to like this? Is she going to get this?" But she [the seven-year-old] was totally locked in. At the end she even cried. She said, "Did this really happen? Is this a true story?" Then she had to reassure herself, "They weren't really that mean, were they?" During the movie I paused it because I wanted to get a cup of coffee. She wanted to know when I was coming back. She was totally into it. Totally engaged.

Mashell, like many parents, is not only concerned with the amount of screen time her children have, but the type of screen time. She monitors them closely. Mashell continued:

Absolutely I control what they watch. [The seven-year-old] is very limited with what she watches. Today I was at work. One of my other daughters who was watching her called me and said, "Can she watch Sponge Bob. She says she's not allowed to watch Sponge Bob." That's right. She isn't allowed to watch Sponge Bob. It is masked as a children's show, but it is clearly adult. It is mindless. It isn't feeding her at all.

Mothers such as Mashell are engaging their children in the media they consume, raising a generation of thoughtful, critical consumers. Not only that, but they are focusing their children's attention on stories of Black history, Black culture, Black community, and complex issues regarding race, sex, gender, sexuality, class, and privilege.

But these direct discussions of race/class/gender don't only manifest in films devoted to a specific historical figure. History lessons are also imbedded in contemporary series featuring Black families and characters, offering an additional dimension to feed the knowledge base of the audience. Shows such as *BMJ*, *Black-ish*, and *She's Gotta Have It* imbed history lessons in the script, both the tragic and the celebratory. In *BMJ*, the character Sheldon, a beau much older than Mary Jane who is a scholar/benefactor to Black causes and art, offers an example of how Afrocentrism is integrated into the episode's plot. Sheldon collects slave papers so he can compile "love letters between slaves" in the hopes of creating an exhibit at the African American History/Culture Museum (Smithsonian) (Season 1). Simply by including this aside as part of Sheldon's occupation/research focus, the writers are telling their viewers: enslaved people were literate; enslaved people had romantic relationships with each other; enslaved people felt deep love. These ideas run in direct contrast to the dominant culture's story of slavery where all the enslaved people were devoid of romance and love; as the history books and

Hollywood films tell it, enslaved people certainly weren't literate, unless a white savior taught them how to read.

In another season, Mary Jane Paul gets the opportunity to cover the thirtieth anniversary of Thurgood Marshall being named the first Black U.S. Supreme Court justice. She travels to Atlanta and interviews civil rights activist Dr. C. T. Vivian; Mayor Kasim Reed of Atlanta; and Wyche Fowler, the first African American Ambassador to the U.N. (Season 4, Episode 6). Mary Jane actually speaks to these historical greats, people her viewers may not know exist. By doing so, the show makes the argument that Black history is vast and living; Black history reaches far beyond what is taught during Black History Month or through the mainstream offerings. Black history includes expansive groups, movements, and people beyond MLK and Harriet Tubman. These examples (Mary Jane interviewing living civil rights activists, celebrating Thurgood Marshall, and Sheldon's love letter collection) give an Afrocentric focus to the show, telling a history of triumph and celebration.

In *She's Gotta Have It*, Spike Lee's updated series based on his 1986 film of the same title, an episode is devoted to the outcome of the 2016 presidential election infusing the story with images and references to prominent Blacks in U.S. history (Season 1; Episode 8: #LoveDontPayDaRent). In another episode (Season 1; Episode 5: #AllNegusAndMyBishes ALL WORDS MATTER), Nola Darling visits a middle school and educates the class (and her viewing audience) on the history of "The Dozens," a smackdown word play based in Black culture. In the scene, two boys start back and forth with "Your momma" exchanges. Nola Darling tells the class, "Playing the dozens was a term derived from African enslavement when anyone with a physical disability was sold in a group of 12." These small exchanges, small parts of scenes, allow the audience to access rich details of Black history and culture that are not taught in school. Some critics, however, find these moments heavy handed (Obaro 2017 *Spike*). Since most of the audience may not know these details, it allows the audience to become educated in important ways regarding the richness and complex fullness of Black culture and history. However, it is important to note that the history lectures that Lee puts into his work and those imbedded in Kenya Barris' *Black-ish* production are different from those of Black women directors in two significant ways: Lee and Barris lecture their audience on history that most often comes from a male perspective and neither man portrays Black women as shapers of history.

In *Black-ish*, Kenya Barris infuses these mini-Black history lessons throughout the series in break-out graphics reminiscent of *Schoolhouse Rock* segments. Barris uses these short interruptions with voice-overs to explain topics such as redlining, the politics of colorism, desegregation of schools and HBCUs, Jim Crow laws, and many other topics of cultural and historical significance in understanding systemic racism. The focus on these moments is not so much Black figures in history (rarely Black women), but historical trends and systemic racism. The cartoon graphics that accompany the lessons rarely feature females, even when the cartoons are miscellaneous people. The "lecture style" creates a dynamic in which Dre, the patriarch and narrator of the show, comes off as "schooling" his uninformed/unenlightened audience. Karen, a twenty-nine-year-old college development administrator, said she had learned from these lessons and came to understand the reason behind behavior or beliefs that she knew to be part of Black culture, but did not know the genesis. She offered the example of a *Black-ish* episode that discussed the practice of Black women "plating up" food for their men. Karen said:

> If you are a Black woman from the South there is this assumption that you are supposed to make a man's plate. I was at a social gathering and I brought a man. We hadn't even been dating that long. And someone asked me, "Are you going to make him a plate?" I probably would do that if he were my husband, but not someone I am dating. So, in that case [the *Black-ish* episode] was for the Black community. On that episode Ruby (the grandmother) said that we plate up our men's food because the world treats Black men like dogs. So, you need to treat him like a king when he comes home.

This particular history lesson is interesting in that Barris is convincing his audience that the sexist practice of a Black woman serving up her man (and never the other way around) is somehow a tribute to Black struggle, as if Black men somehow had it/have it harder than Black women. Karen acknowledged, though, that sometimes she felt like the history lessons were for the white audience (she pointed to the Juneteenth episode), but that others were for the Black audience (like the "plating" episode or an episode where the parents discuss name discrimination and what to name the new baby: a Black-sounding name or a white-sounding name). Karen continued:

> There are certain things white people don't ever have to think about like microaggressions such as name discrimination. I remember adding people on LinkedIn [when I was applying for jobs] so they know I am Black and they wouldn't be surprised when I showed up [because my name isn't heard as a Black name] . . . . I oversee someone who doesn't have a super-ethnic name, but it is an unusual name. There are [white] people I work with who refuse to say her name. It is either a refusal and they are determined not to do it. Or it is the inability to try or care about it.

Karen connected the break-out "lessons" infused in *Black-ish* to real issues in her own life and history that needed to be communicated to both white and Black audiences.

Ashley, a mother of four and nurse in her thirties, said she also appreciated the mini-history and cultural lessons in *Black-ish* as it was one of the few shows she was able to watch with her family. Ashley is married to a white man and they have a biracial son together; Ashley also has a child with an ex-husband who is Black; her current husband has two white children. The family of six live together in the same house. Race, she says, is a constant and very real conversation in their house. Shows like *Black-ish* not only educate, but provide fodder for thoughtful discussions. Ashley told me, "Talking about race is something that we have to do in our household. I have a [white] son who is graduating high school. My nine-year-old is Black so we have to have a conservation about that. We are going to have to have these conversations about race in our house. I have a very light skinned baby. I see how these children are treated differently by strangers and co-workers. It is never aggressive in nature, but it definitely there." She said that one of the *Blacksish* episodes that was important to her family was the one about the Ferguson, Missouri, protests after the police killing of Michael Brown. In addition, she said, they watched Ava DuVernay's film *13th*, about the history of the Thirteenth Amendment, mass incarceration, and systemic racism.

> We watched it together. We talked for *hours*. It was very enlightening. I didn't know my children were going to have all these emotions. For my nine-year-old [who is white] it brought up a lot of things we needed to talk about but hadn't yet. We had to have that conversation (about how whites, particularly white cops), see a Black boy. It was tough. Then he was watching a video at his [white] grandparents' house and my son started to cry. There was a Black boy killed the first episode. My mother-in-law was pretty shaken up about it. The first episode he is interacting with the cops and the Black boy is shot and killed. My son started to cry saying, "This could happen to my brother." He was so shaken up. It was a learning experience for my white mother-in-law. "Oh, this is something we have to deal with."

By her opening up the conversation with her family through media such as *Black-ish* and *13th*, Ashley's children become more critical consumers of what they are seeing in other contexts, educating grandparents and others outside the immediate family. In addition, they have become aware of how important historical knowledge is to their immediate lives.

Ashley believes these history lessons are extremely important. The lessons may come to her children through family television and movie nights, but the results of talking about what they are seeing and connecting it to personal and cultural issues help her children navigate the WSCP. "We really have only learned one small perspective of history. So small. It is an educational thing for White and Black. It is almost an acknowledgement for the Black community for a sense of pride . . . . I personally feel a sense of pride and sometimes I learn something new but it is nice to just to see your own history on that screen. We have to learn, as Black people. The history books are written by the people who won. It doesn't mean that other experiences are not valued, but they aren't in the school history books. That's why these shows are important."

BLACK WOMEN'S CONTRIBUTIONS

Hulu and HBO currently offer a plethora of recent films directed or written by Black women portraying important historical milestones that feature Black females: *Bessie* (2015), *Nina* (2016) written and directed by Cynthia Mort, *Toni Morrison: The Pieces I am* (2019) directed by Timothy Greenfield-Sanders, *Moms Mabley* (2013) directed by Whoopi Goldberg, *Say Her Name: The Life and Death of Sandra Bland* (2018) directed by Kate Davis, *Amazing Grace* (2018) directed by Allen Elliot, *The Simone Biles Story: The Courage to Soar* (2018) directed by Vanessa Parise, and *Being Serena* (2018) directed by Noah Lerner, just to name a few produced recently. Netflix continues this trend through titles such as *13th* (2016) directed by Ava DuVernay, *Self Made* (2019), Michelle Obama's story, *Becoming* (2020), directed by Nadia Halgran, *Roxanne Roxanne* (2017) directed by Michael Larnell, *The Death and Life of Marsha P. Johnson* (2017) directed by David France, and *Murder to Mercy: The Cyntoia Brown Story* (2020) directed by Daniel Birman. Each of these films illuminates a Black woman who has played an important role in American history, in the arts, in sports, in science, or in movements of social justice. The "characters," all of them real-life heroines, offer an important version of Black womanhood, one of perseverance, determination, brilliance, talent, and leadership, a sharp deviation from the stereotypes of downtrodden, used, and abused women that are often portrayed when men are behind the camera. These woman-drawn representations engender pride and a way of seeing Black women as not only strong but essential to the path forward. These stories serve to uplift and give dimension to a past that has been largely obscured and ignored by the WSCP. Brought to us by Black women, these stories create a rich and textured history for all of us to hang onto as evidence of the essentialness of Black women to the making of our world. Michelle, who describes herself as an "average Black girl from St. Louis, Missouri," spoke about seeing the film *Selma* (2014), directed by Ava DuVernay, as part of a school field trip.

> In high school they took us to do all the things that Dr. King did. We walked across the bridge and sat in the diner seats. It made me feel like I was there.

That was another thing that played a part in my consciousness. Once I saw that, once I experienced that, it opened my eyes. The movie solidified that. They had these great actors and actresses playing the parts. It seemed so real. They stood up for me, so I should stand up for everyone else. That really pushed me to be that person who stands up. They had all that pain and suffering so we could do this. Especially with me going to college. Without these people going through this pain and suffering I would not be the woman I am.

For Karen, the Netflix documentary about Michelle Obama (*Becoming* 2020) moved her in a similar way.

When I read the book and watched the movie, it affirmed my experience, my life, who I want to be and become. When Michelle Obama says something, it means more because it affirms what our experience is but it also educates whites. I love how real *Becoming* is. She is so *real*. She talks about going to counseling. She talks about the first time she felt love for her country and the fist bump. [Both considered scandalous by many whites, but resonated as authentic to Blacks] All the things that are important to her, she did them, even if she got in trouble or it was something that others told her not to do. I can relate to all of it. I loved the part where she is talking about going to the White House as a wife. I love when she starts to talk about freedom and someone asks her if she misses the White House and she says, "No." She doesn't have to explain or justify it or soften it. I love that.

Through the power of the documentary, Karen was able to find a connection with a powerful, self-assured, accomplished Black woman, someone to help her navigate who she wants to be. For women like Karen and Michelle, these stories, told through the camera lens by Black women filmmakers, offer important and affirming perspectives on Black women's role in history, one that makes their world, identity, and life goals tangible.

Karen, Michelle, Ashley, and Mashell all spoke to the power of having these Black feminist/womanist representations available. In recent years, Hollywood production companies and streaming services such as Hulu and Netflix have put money and effort toward telling more histories of Black women. This could be because of shifting beliefs that these stories need to be told—a cultural shift that some attribute to the election of Barack Obama and a Black family in the White House. But more likely these films emerged because marketers have realized stories about Black women of history make money. Perhaps due to the success of films such as *Selma* (2014) and *Hidden Figures* (2016), movie producers saw an advantage in Black woman bio pictures. In addition to the Hollywood release of *Harriet* (2019), streaming services have offered up similarly feminist versions of historical Black women.

All of these productions by women/for women tell the women's stories from a decidedly feminist/womanist perspective creating a new canon of Black feminist histories that are essential to the development of Black girls as cultural leaders. Without their history, they are destined to absorb the stereotypes.

LESBIAN SIDEBARS

In 2013, Whoopi Goldberg created a documentary about Loretta Mary Aiken and her comedic character, Moms Mabley. In a segment within the documentary, Norma Miller, a dancer who worked with Aiken, talked about Aiken's lesbian identity.

> She was the one woman amongst these men. She was the best . . . . She and I shared a dressing room for two weeks. She and I and her girlfriend. She was real. I mean, she was Moms onstage, but when she walked off that stage, she was Mr. Moms [she wore men's clothes and had a female partner.] And there was no question about it. No question about it. I mean, she was Mr. Moms. On stage she was really Moms and she was always after the great Cab Calloway. But you never saw her with a young man. You saw her with young girls. And there was no question. She was the first complete . . . . I don't know, we never called Moms a homosexual. That word never fit her. We never called her gay. We called her Mr. Moms. (Goldberg 2013)

Goldberg includes this information as part of telling Aiken's story. It is a fact, a dynamic, like so many others, about who Aiken was. Goldberg's inclusion is a short sidebar, refreshingly non-judgmental or controversial. It was neither sensational nor salacious. It was a fact. Aiken was a lesbian in the Black community during 1940–1970. Similarly, two biopics of 2020 released exclusively on streaming services told the story of famous Black women who also were not entirely heterosexual. Their sexuality is part of who they were; a part of all the other many characteristics that made their lives interesting. Bessie Smith and Madame C. J. Walker made their way through the antebellum/ Jim Crow era despite being pushed back due to race and sex. *Bessie* (HBO) told the story of Blues singer Bessie Smith and *Self Made* told the story of Madame C. J. Walker. Walker, with the help of her husband and daughter, created an empire based on hair and beauty products for Black women. Both films focus on discrimination the women experienced in their own communities (colorism, sexism) as well as systemic discrimination from WSCP. However, these films also offered something interesting in their inclusion of lesbian and bisexual plot lines, moving beyond the heteronormative narratives of most biopics.

In *Bessie*, Writer/Director Dee Rees wastes no time in integrating a bisexual/lesbian narrative. When Bessie Smith meets up with Ma Rainey in Rainey's traveling show, showgirls wander in and out of Rainey's elegant room in various stages of undress, offering kisses and caresses to her. Smith's eyes widen, but more in recognition of what she has, until that moment, no way of articulating: it is possible for women to love other women in the ways that women love men. Although Smith is portrayed as engaging in both heterosexual and lesbian relationships, there is little moralizing regarding her sexuality. Her liaisons with women are presented as fact, drawn as fully or as superficially as her heterosexual relationships. In the movie, she takes a female lover. One of the few times we see Smith weep is when Bessie's paramour announces that she is getting married—to a man. The next scenes show Smith spiraling down into addiction. She seeks out her mentor's, Ma Rainey's, help. Rainey offers Smith comfort, compassion, and a place to heal. Rainey tells her, "You just take care of you right now. Get your head straight." Smith has never experienced someone looking out for her in this way. Breaking down, Smith weeps, touched by the love of a woman.

Even as the movie ends with Bessie and a male lover, Richard, her openly romantic and sexual love of women is not portrayed as less than or superficial. In fact, the men who are supposed to love her are often portrayed that way. Early in the movie, she takes a man, but it is shown as a business arrangement. He accompanies her as her partner, but his function is as a protector in rooms of men. Smith is portrayed as not needing much help. She is quick to physically (and sometimes violently) defend herself as needed. When racist whites terrorize her tent performances in the South, riding up in white hoods, attempting to set the tent on fire and shooting at her train car, Smith runs out of the tent and stands her ground, facing off the lynch mob. The terrorists leave.

Rees draws Smith as a strong and self-reliant figure, one who easily loves and stands up for herself and other females in a hostile world. After becoming famous, Smith is invited to events of white liberals who want to rub elbows with her greatness. At one such party, a white man bloviates, "Langston Hughes is the best Negro poet of our time." Bessie doesn't skip a beat before replying, "Oh, well. Who's the best *poet*?" rendering the man lacking a rejoinder. At another moment, a white academic, Carl Van Vechten, brags to her that he is writing a book called *Nigger Heaven*.[1] Smith knocks him off his Northern, "more evolved white man," high horse with a smirk and slyly says, "The difference between white folks in the South and white folks in the North is that white folks in the South care how close you get and that you know your place. White folks in the north don't care how close you get as long as you know your place." These short exchanges, often limited to smirks, one-liners, and side-eyes provide moments of glee as Smith bests the whites and colorist Blacks at their game. The film portrays Smith as standing toe-to-toe with the patriarchy, racism, and classism in the form of various individuals; yet Smith always comes out on top, trouncing them at their own game. It is also significant to note that Rees ends the film on a happy note, a picnic with a man Smith loves, as opposed to the tragic end of Smith's life. By doing so, Rees asks her viewers to remember Smith as strong, smiling, and victorious, a powerful image of Black womanhood.

Similar to Rees' version of Bessie Smith, DeMane Davis and Kasi Lemmons draw Madame C. J. Walker as a powerhouse who builds an empire despite the racism, colorism, and sexism she has to endure. Colorism and classism are central to Davis and Lemmons' version of Walker. The host of Black female writers for the short series (three hours in total) depicts the primary barriers to Walker's success as that of being a larger, darker woman attempting to become an entrepreneur. Despite barriers of being female, Black, and dark-skinned, Walker builds an empire of Black beauty products and gives back by sponsoring schools, scholarships, and supporting other Black women entrepreneurs. Walker is driven and won't take "no" as an answer whether that no comes from a light-skinned female business owner who locks her out of sales, white bankers who refuse to lend her money for a factory, or Black activists such as Booker T. Washington who won't deign to address women's concerns of sexism and struggle.

In addition to Walker's struggles against sexism, we see a struggle of Walker's own homophobia meted out against her daughter, Leila. Although the homophobia is portrayed as mild and Walker comes around to acceptance, this side story offers a way out of trifling heteronormative relationships that stymie women. Similar to *Bessie*, the lesbian side bar in *Self Made* allows women to escape some of the most disconcerting limitations of compulsory heterosexuality on women. In both films, men are mostly portrayed as being millstones around women's necks. In *Self Made*, Walker's daughter, Leila (played by Tiffany Haddish) initially gets married to an aimless man, even as she does so to please her mother. Soon we find out that Leila is more interested in taking women for romantic/sexual partners. At first her mother ignores these relationships other than to say her daughter is "playing at" something. Walker tells Leila, "You need to promise me you will settle down," telling her daughter she needs children (although she stops short of saying Leila needs a husband as husbands tend to be more of burdens and barriers in this version of Walker's story). As the series progresses, so does Walker's attitudes about Leila's lesbianism. When Leila chooses to move to Harlem with her lesbian lover, Walker accepts and embraces her daughter's choice of mate. Walker tells Leila she needs to be who she is. "You have always been different . . . I am proud of you. You have done a great job with the Harlem Salon . . . you are my legacy. My most precious gift. The beauty of my whole world and I will always love you. Always."

This affirming message of mother love, women-loving-women, and sister-hood is explicitly made at the end of the series. The final episode closes with Walker addressing her phalanx of saleswomen, apostles looking to her, wait-ing to absorb her wisdom. She stands before them as a savior, the women who are following her path, striving to earn their own way, make their own mark. She tells them they are so much more than employees.

> I had a dream, but you made it a reality . . . . Precious few of us reach our des-tiny. We are dismissed, undermined, ignored, stepped on, beaten, or even worse, killed. That is why I decided to pull out of the drugstore deal. I don't need a chain to grow my business. I have you, an army of strong, powerful women. Take control of your lives. Take control of your destiny.

This call-to-action is not just for the workers before her, but the viewing audience as well. What can happen if Black women take control of their lives, their destiny, despite or even in the face of the WSCP? In this spirit of success despite the dominant culture's oppression, the Netflix documentary *She Did That* (2019), directed by Renae Bluitt and Sterling Milan, profiles several Black women entrepreneurs who are defying cultural barriers that block Black women. They are the very legacy that is Madame C. J. Walker's work. She paved the way so that, today, 80 percent of small business owners are Black women entrepreneurs (Bluitt and Milan 2019). In *Bessie, Harriet, Underground*, and Walker's story, the productions end on a scene, a state-ment, a note of hope, resilience, and success in building a world in which Black women can thrive.

HARRIET AND *HIDDEN FIGURES*

Ashley, an E.R. nurse with four children, said the historical films about Black women are family events. But she seeks out films that offer something beyond Black struggle. She pointed to *Harriet* and *Hidden Figures* as films that told stories "beyond the struggle" of Black women who "live and have families and identities beyond the stereotypical downtrodden Black woman." She continued:

> We went to see *Hidden Figures* with the whole family. I loved what *Hidden Figures* did for the ladies, but it is also a film that males need to see. My husband said, "Let's take the boys and see it." My husband really loves anything about aero-engineering. My son wants to pursue that in college. It was so good to see

my son researching the women after we got home. It opened up that world to them. And our boys were able to see the females as historical figures. We were ready to see that movie before it came out. (Ashley)

The powerful representation of Black women as scientists spoke to many, especially young people, who had never thought of Black women as scientists before. Marta, single/no children insurance agent, said, "These women (Jackson, Johnson, and Vaughan) did what they did so I could do what I wanted to do. These women fought to make it OK to do the same thing as a white person and get the same equal rights."

Harriet (2019) and *Hidden Figures* (2016) were mentioned and discussed by nearly every woman I talked with. The women I interviewed saw these films as revolutionary for the way Black women were portrayed. *Hidden Figures* portrays the women scientists (Katherine Johnson, Dorothy Vaughan, and Mary Jackson) who worked at NASA during the 1960s. Although the film is directed by a man, it was based on a book by Margot Lee Shetterly and the screenplay was written by Allison Schroeder. The film tells the story of three Black women scientists who worked at NASA, facing discrimination but contributing significantly to the space program. Unlike *Harriet*, *Hidden Figures* tells the story of women who were not generally known, offering Black women and girls new heroines to admire. Similar to *Harriet*, *Self Made*, *Bessie*, and *Selma*, however, the women in *Hidden Figures* are multidimensional. The audience sees them as scientists, but also as typical women within the context of family, with friends, living within a Black community and church, and not only as isolated people trying to forge a way in the WSCP. These women had support and supported each other, their friendships and families portrayed in interesting ways throughout the film. Mashell offered this as one of the reasons she loved the film. "I thought it was great to see behind the scenes, the women that don't get talked about. These women who were working for NASA and no one ever knew them. I do like to see how strong we are. I feel like a lot of people work in that environment where you are treated so poorly . . . all that they endured and they knew their worth" (Mashell). Films such as *Harriet* and *Hidden Figures* offer different versions of Black womanhood beyond the stereotypes that have plagued Hollywood characters for decades. These films, the women who are writing and directing them, offer an important representation to disrupt stereotypes and break open new versions of what it means to be Black and female in the United States.

These powerful, competent, and dynamic versions of Black womanhood are a refreshing change and immediately noted. Aliya, a nineteen-year-old artist, said, "Films like *Hidden Figures* are much needed because we didn't know who these women were . . . . The film was a positive representation of Black womanhood. We got to see their families, their work, their community.

It is easier to relate to them. They acted differently depending on whether they were with their family or at work. I can relate to that. We got to see them act like themselves." EJ also expressed how important the film *Hidden Figures* was to her and other women in her family.

> There haven't been many movies about Black women that did anything in history. My mom was in tears that I was able to see something like that . . . . My mom made me go see it with her. There seems to be more films about powerful Black women. I had never heard of [the scientists in *Hidden Figures*] before. I was so shocked that I hadn't heard about them. After I saw the film, I even researched them . . . . I started to think "What else do I not know?" That would be a movie that I would show if I ever had girls. I loved their determination. Black women are so determined. When I was growing up there were so many films where Black women were portrayed as not smart and not knowing much. But in *Hidden Figures* and *Harriet* it is different; they were so smart. They were the smartest people in the room.

To have Black women portrayed as "the smartest in the room," the most competent, and the strongest breaks the shackles of stereotypes. However, women also noted an annoyance that most Hollywood films that feature Black women include some sort of white savior. In *Hidden Figures*, the white savior manifests to solve the problem of segregated bathrooms on the NASA compound. The bathroom issue was one that nearly every woman talked about: the female scientists having to walk great distances while at work to find the "colored" bathroom in a different building. The women I spoke with pointed to the detail that a white man is portrayed as being the person who changed that for them so they could use the restroom in the building where they worked. It is the white man who dismantles the "Whites Only" sign and the women I spoke with cried foul. Michelle said:

> I cannot imagine the Black restrooms being in another building. The white character who helps them, I saw that he actually cared. And I thought, "Well, maybe not all white people are bad." But then my sister did a research paper on one of the women. She said she didn't like that the man was shown as helping them. She didn't think it happened that way. In these Hollywood films it is always a white man helping to pave the way for a Black person, when the whole time it was the Black person and they did it themselves.

The trope of "white savior"—a white character who advocates for the Black character, becoming the hero of the Black person's story—is regularly present in Hollywood films. Ashley told me it was her husband, who is white, who pointed out the white savior in *Hidden Figures*. She said:

The white man saving the day, it is a thing. My husband pointed it out. That man probably didn't do that [facilitate an integrated bathroom] in real life. He might have. But I feel like that they have to do that for the white audience. It was an amazing story without that. They always have to have something that is like, "They weren't all bad." They always they have to put that. My husband said, "Here comes the white man to save the day."

Mashell also said she noticed the white savior thrown in for good measure. "I notice the white savior in every movie, but I kind of expect it. I figure it is a white director and it is going to happen like that. I don't mind it as much now. I get used to it. Some of it makes you mad. It softens the blow [for white audiences]. It makes [white people] think, 'Not all white people are bad.' "

Despite the standard addition of "white savior" moments in these Hollywood films, the depiction of Black women as cultural heroines is worth celebrating these films.

This theme of hope is one prevailing in films and series about Black women, makers of history. In *Hidden Figures* (2017), the film ends with photos and short bios of the women on which the film was based, uplifting the audience. These women had full careers and rich lives. *Harriet*, directed by Kasi Lemmons who also directed *Self Made*, stars Cynthia Erivo in the title role. The film tells a fuller story of Harriet Tubman than the typical paragraph of middle school history books. Tubman's story takes the viewer from the plantation where she was raised and the family she left behind, to her return to help others escape, and the plight of moving people into Canada to avoid the reach of the Fugitive Slave Act of 1850. Although there are many liberties the Hollywood film takes with details of Tubman's life (Breen-Tucci), the main elements are relayed accurately, creating a multidimensional version of Black womanhood. Lemmons' version of Tubman shows her as smart, determined, unwilling to be cowed, and committed to her family, community, and social justice. We see Tubman not just as a one-dimensional historical figure but as a woman who loves, fights, struggles, and prevails. She wields weapons and uses her smarts to carry out her mission, over and over again, risking her life to lead others to freedom. She rarely relies on whites or men to complete her missions. Painting Tubman as a complex and dynamic woman felt revolutionary to some viewers who only knew Tubman from a photo and a mention in grade school history classes during Black History Month. EJ, a college sophomore, was moved by the way Lemmon brought a historical figure to life. EJ told me, "I loved *Harriet*. We hear about Harriet Tubman, but I had never seen a movie about her. It was my first time. I watched with my grandma and it moved her to tears." These cross-generational movie-going moments are meaningful. EJ and her grandmother bonded over a story about a powerful Black woman of history. EJ also noted who was in the audience at the theatre. "It was not just people who *had* to see it [not just a Black audience]. They wanted to see it. The story was more complex compared to what we learned about in her history class. Her personality, her emotions. It gave her a depth that we didn't know. She is a real person and she has real emotions. It was tough to watch, but it was also exhilarating. She is a powerful woman." For EJ, Lemmons' depiction of Tubman offered her a more complex and real person to refer to, a powerful reminder of who fought and won against systemic oppression.

The depiction of Tubman as powerful is only one element of how and why she was revolutionary. This film creates Tubman as a woman who has many dimensions, who has a family, who has smarts and savvy, but at times is vulnerable and scared. She acts within and through the support of other women, but she defies the systemic racism that is determined to break her. These connections of community, the portrayal of Tubman as a woman with a life, a family, a support network offer a fuller representation of Black women in history. We see the importance of women-loving-women within a community of sisterhood, not just in *Hidden Figures* and *Harriet*, but in *Self Made* and *Bessie* as well as the series *Underground*.

UNDERGROUND

In the second season of *Insecure*, the writers spoof a serialized slave narrative, *Due North*, that all the *Insecure* characters seem to be watching and discussing. These asides written into Issa Rae's production are veiled references to *Underground*, a popular series on WGN (2016–2017). Written by Misha Green and directed by various people including many women (WGN, 2016–2017; now on Hulu) *Underground* rejects the traditional slave narrative (trauma porn) in that it focuses on communities, families, and other relationships and the various ways resistance to slavery manifested. The main characters in the series include the runaway Rosalee, her house enslaved mother, Ernestine, and their communities of family, friends, abolitionists, and activists. In the promotional ads, Rosalee faces the audience wielding a gun, raised as if prepared to protect herself and others, a powerful image of defiance and strength. In *Underground*, Rosalee is the character driving the action, but there are also the "house slaves" that provide a counter-narrative of passive/aggressive resistance. Rosalee, born of her enslaved mother Ernestine, and their white master, escapes and helps others make it to freedom, providing the primary action of the series. There are also white abolitionists who work in Washington, following politics and speaking out in formal systems of power. The narrative arc is established with the constitutive white saviors, but as the series progresses, the whites recede into the background and the lives of the

Black characters develop, telling a view of slavery that may have traumatic elements but is more about Black women seizing agency and kicking ass in various directions. The focus of family, relationships, and maverick women is similar to the themes in *Harriet*.

Unlike so many other slave narratives, *Harriet* and *Underground* focus on relationships and resistance instead of just the subjugation and horrors of slavery. Ernestine (and others) are used as concubines by white owners, but they are not defined by that identity, allowing the female characters to be seen as whole people. Previously, the only role for Black females in slave narratives was that of the sex slave who birthed babies that were sold from them. "In the latest spate of Hollywood films that thematically have taken on African and African American slavery, including *12 Years a Slave*, the 'concubine,' not surprisingly, remains the most important black female character" (Stevenson 2014, 112). By focusing on "Black woman as sex servant for white men," a tragic role of anti-agency, films such as *12 Years a Slave* reinforce the myth that Black women did not resist, could not resist, and were at the mercy of (or saved by) men. In the case of Eliza in *12 Years a Slave*, she is trapped in the role of concubine and further suffers abuse by being sent out as a "field slave" when the master's wife can't stand her in the house. The audience understands Eliza to be an absolutely agentless person, whereas the Black men are resisting and escaping. It is true that most enslaved women were raped as part of their experience, but the film offers no other perspective of Black women. Contrasting this characterization of Black women during slavery with the Black women in *Harriet* and *Underground,* one immediately sees a stark difference: one of agency and self-determination in the films directed by women.

Underground provides a narrative in which the women are not defined by their rapes. Although scholars such as Stevenson have not yet written about *Underground,* the critiques of other films and the role of enslaved Black females in those films seems to not hold up in *Underground*. Stevenson notes, "Yet this [sexual] abuse [by white men] did not define [the women's] entire lives. This point is one that [director Steve] McQueen repeatedly fails to make in [*Twelve Years a Slave*], and offers no counter or additional images of bondwomen's lives" (113). To portray Black women only as disempowered sex slaves is to deny them the dignity of their history that involved active resistance, organized escapes, and communal acts of leadership (Stevenson 2014, 114). *Underground* and *Harriet* provide a different, fuller view of Black womanhood during slavery.

A key difference in how women are portrayed seems to hinge on the directors. Male directors often produce slave narratives that deny women agency. In these films, women are relegated to sex slave identity/concubine, whereas the men are the activists, pushing against domination. In slave narratives written by or directed by women (Kari Skogland's *The Courage to Love*, 2000; Haile Gerima's *Sankofa*, 1993; Kasi Lemmon's *Harriet*, 2019; and Misha Green's *Underground*, 2016–2017), we see women as acting agents, refusing to be defined by sexual slavery. Instead the protagonists in these films/series are competent, strong resisters, and foundational members of their Black communities.

The appeal of *Underground* for many of my participants was the portrayal of women's lives during slavery. The women who spoke of *Underground* all spoke of it favorably, commenting on the relationships (romantic, familial, community, church) among the Black characters and how women were central to those relationship stories. Although the brutality of antebellum South is part of the series, viewers appreciated that it wasn't all about the horrors of slavery. Amber, a forty-nine-year-old mother of four ranging in age from toddler to teenager, told me that although she doesn't like movies about slavery, she did enjoy *Underground*. She said:

> *Underground* was sometimes difficult to watch because of the racism and how some of those scenes play out. . . . For some people there is an appeal, an interest in or a need, to see that type of history. But I don't need to see it. But I liked the show for other reasons. I don't know if it is historically accurate, but to see that history portrayed [the deeper parts of relationships, communities, and lives outside of the identity of "enslaved person"] is nice. We have so many films about war and other topics but I feel just recently we are able to see what it meant to be Black and a slave. Even if those shows are difficult to watch, we shouldn't look away. We are yearning for that piece of history. We have heard about the history of slavery, but we don't get the details. We have to seek it out. It is not easily available as other histories.

Amber is noting that *Underground* is more than a slave-era dramatic series. Woven into the story line are the politics of slavery, the incremental steps made (and lost) by abolitionists on the federal level to engage in the fight. In the first episode, the viewer learns about the U.S. Supreme Court hearing arguments about the Fugitive Slave Act, a heinous piece of legislation that allowed bounty hunters to pursue those who had escaped to the North and return them to slavery, torture, and sometimes death. In the second season (Episode 6: Mint) the entire fifty-minute program is devoted to a monologue of Harriet Tubman talking to a group of abolitionists, narrating her life from being an enslaved child to underground engineer/activist. This episode has the feel of a short one-person play with no reference to the characters or plot in the existing series, although some characters are seated in Tubman's audience. Acting as a mini history lesson, the first-person fictionalized account of a major figure in Black history, this episode educates the audience on the details of Tubman's life, creating a more dynamic and nuanced narrative for this historical icon.

In *Underground*, female characters drive the action. The two major protagonists, Rosalee and her mother Ernestine, offer distinct perspectives on living, thriving, and creating family/community during slavery. The life of activist Rosalee provides a sharp contrast to her mother, the "house slave." During the series, the audience sees Rosalee come of age and take charge in various situations, often saving the day for enslaved people who are on the run. She fights off slave catchers, she gets medicine for those who need it, she moves runaways through the underground, she falls in love, she gets married, she has a baby. Unlike Ernestine, the "house slave," Rosalee has agency and grit, driving the action of most episodes and making choices that determine the course of her freedom as well as those she interacts with.

Ernestine, on the other hand, vacillates between urging other enslaved people to not take risks and doing what she can in subtle, less-obvious ways to protect her children, family, and friends from the master's cruelty and whims, but her strategies sometimes backfire. In contrast, Rosalee is regularly successful. Ernestine openly laments her lot, stating that it is a myth "house slaves" have it better than the enslaved people who work in the fields. She says, "Everybody out there in the fields, they think they want to be in the big house. The closer you are to white folks the better. Safer. What they don't know is that living in their world, it starts to change you. We start actin' like them. Do things we never thought we could" (Season 1; Episode 6: Troubled Water). Eventually, the jealousy of the master's wife earns Ernestine a spot on the sale block. The wife is jealous not because her husband is having sex with Ernestine but because the children love Ernestine more than her. In the second season, Ernestine schools a young woman on how to keep the master interested through sex, emphasizing that the white man has to think that he is in control, the teacher/master, even as she is manipulating him (Season 2; Episode 5: Whiteface). However, Ernestine is still caught in the cliché of only being worthy or interesting as a sex slave, something that Rosalee has escaped. Rosalee is the contrasting woman of agency to Ernestine's identity as a sexual trope for the master, manipulating him but also suffering because of her status as the house concubine. Ernestine turns to opioids to numb her psychic pain, whereas Rosalee finds love and marriage and motherhood, even as her life is action-driven, full of near-death experiences and adventure.

The representations of Rosalee and Ernestine, although offered up as a contrasting perspective, also incorporate elements of day-to-day life, relationships, and community that are important to the audience. Trinity, a political advisor in Chicago, said she liked the series because it shows dynamic and interesting details about women's lives.

[Underground] was personal. It was like they were actual people. They were human. Sometimes a slave movie is just that. They are just slaves. But *Underground* is different. It shows all the ins and outs of the relationships. Yes, they are struggling, struggling all the way around, but not just about the struggle to be free. It shows the mother and her children and them butting heads. It shows a whole person. She wasn't just a slave. Slavery did not define her. It was a side of her, but there was so much more to her as a human. I loved it.

More than one respondent who talked about why they enjoyed *Underground*, in the same conversation mentioned why they didn't like the film *12 Years a Slave*. Ta'Nisha said although she liked *Underground*, she could not watch *12 Years a Slave*. "I could not finish *12 Years a Slave*. I have tried to watch *12 Years a Slave* a couple different times. It is a hard story to watch. It is jarring to my soul. I haven't been able to get through it. I can't bring myself. I am still trying to figure out how I feel. I don't think we need to see the horrors. I can't get past the graphic nature. I know that type of thing happens so we have to watch it . . . . Do we have to actually watch that?" (Ta'Nisha) Scholars and critics have been vocal about their negative assessment of these graphic depictions of "trauma porn." Some scholars, however, celebrated the film as "fully and accurately depict[ing] the brutality and dehumanization of slavery and without white saviors being foregrounded" (Drake 2019, 171). Drake does lament exactly what my participants also critique: the focus on trauma and graphic horrors of slavery instead of the humanity of Blacks, the diversity of lives and experiences, and the relationships that were also part of the Black experience. Drake states, "Why is it that trauma and pain can be claimed as the quintessential black experience, while the experiences of . . . exclusively black social groups and bonds, not be a black experience?" (171). At what point doe graphic horrors of slavery become Black snuff films? How much graphic violence is needed to evoke empathy from an audience? For the Black women I interviewed, the graphic violence was disturbing, not empathy-evoking. The difference between *12 Years a Slave* (Black male director) and *Underground* or *Harriet* (Black women directors/creators/writers) seems to point to a difference between how men will treat the use of violence, especially in regard to rape and violence against women, and how women treat the same topic. Women foreground relationships and resistance not rape and trauma. Some of my interviewees critiqued slave narratives written by men, especially in their treatment of women, as too graphic. This complaint is echoed by more than one scholar of Black cinema. Stevenson, a scholar of Black cinema, takes issue with the way Ridley and McQueen (*12 Years a Slave*) portray the Black experience during slavery as one where men are the resisters and Blacks are portrayed as having no community. She writes, "As a result, the film's viewing audience is left to believe, mistakenly, that the slaves on the various plantations and farms . . . did not have close ties to one another, or function as communal units; that slave resistance was rare and an experience largely confined to the actions of men; and that 'free' men and women in the antebellum North were, indeed, free and equal to their white neighbors" (Stevenson 2014, 109). *Harriet* and *Underground* provide an alternative narrative, one where the focus is the women and the way they make community, forge relationships, and outsmart the systemic oppressions of slavery and racism.

CONCLUSION

Black women shaped this country. Their work, their intellect, their perseverance, their passions, their love created science, systems of government and policies, art, music, literature, and much more. Their legacies need to be uncovered and told. Black feminists who are making art and entertainment today are doing this important work. With streaming venues and executives who see that these stories, these histories, are not only important but popular with wide audiences, more Black women's stories are getting attention. Through the telling of these stories, Black girls (and boys) are provided a history that the WSCP denied them; Black women are given a lore that includes and encourages them: Black women matter. And they have mattered. Black women such as writer/director/producer Kasi Lemmons, Ava DuVernay, Oprah Winfrey, Dee Rees, Margot Lee Shetterly, and Misha Green are only the short list of what is possible. Black women are directing, writing, and producing the histories of their mothers and grandmothers, offering us legacies of what it has meant to be Black and female but also the contributions these women made to the building of our world. These history lessons, told through the eyes of Black women, change how we perceive ourselves—blowing apart stereotypes and shattering the trope of "trauma porn." They not only offer the audience a rich snapshot of the past but also allow us to imagine the possibilities yet to come. These superwomen are Black. Thanks to the work of women, we no longer have to think of Black women of history as enslaved, powerless victims.

NOTE

1. Van Vechten (a white man) published his book *Nigger Heaven* in 1926 about a "great Black walled city" that was the neighborhood of Harlem in Manhattan. The book was controversial even in its day, a white man's version of Black life during the Harlem Renaissance.

Conclusion

A Reason for Hope

"The point was to really open a book that's about black people, or by a black person, me or anybody."—Toni Morrison, on why she wrote books

"[Watching films/shows from a Black perspective] makes white people uncomfortable; we are asking white people to smell their own shit. This is the experience white people have when they watch Black films . . . In the movie theatre, one of the things I love about seeing the movies, it is ALL Black people in here and sprinkles of white. And I know [the white people] are thinking, 'We came on the wrong day.' Black people start talking back to the movie; we do the call-and-response. White people who choose to attend will learn something. Something in addition to what is on the screen."—Drayah, college student

Although the quote by Morrison is about writing books, in the Digital Age, it is also true of visual texts. As the world's culture shifts from communication based on written word to visual and digital communication, Black women are creating texts that are informing and educating as well as reflecting their lived realities, a lens for the world to understand what it means to be Black and female. As I embarked on this project, I believed there would be a finite number of shows/women to analyze. I had, at the outset, limited myself to shows/films, no older than 2015, that were directed, written, or produced by Black women. Easy, right? How many can there be?

What I quickly discovered was that I had excruciatingly underestimated however many I thought there were. Due to streaming services and Black women taking charge and creating their own content and posting on social media, due to larger companies such as HBO, Netflix, and BET actively *seeking* Black women writers/producers/directors, due to a cultural shift with Digital Age young people who are adamant that they want to consume a diverse panoply of characters/programming (not just those that represent the dominant culture's demographic), Black women are getting work done and seen. They are busy creating shows, programming, and ideas that have a ready and hungry audience. For the first time in history, Black women's stories are being told in ways, formats, and at a volume that has never existed before. Some have called this a Renaissance of Black women in entertainment (Wicker 2018, Toby 2019, Cieszki 2019), a rebirth, a renewal. No, that can't be right. In fact, this is not a rebirth, but a birth. It is not a renewal, but a fresh start. Black women have never had a time when their voices and perspectives were given privilege, honored, and celebrated in the mainstream media. At least not in the U.S. dominant culture. Sure, there was the Harlem Renaissance that celebrated and proliferated the art, music, and literature of Blacks in the United States. But even that I would say was not a "Renaissance" (literally "rebirth")—Blacks have always made art, literature, and music. They were just systematically denied access to systems of power in the United States to be recognized for their work, within the WSCP.

I would not term this trend of Black women's creativity, art, and media productions getting play as a Renaissance but as an "explosion." Black women have always produced art and film and performances—and they succeeded with niche audiences outside of Hollywood's channels since arriving, enslaved, on this continent. But now it is different. There has been a sea change. For one thing, these Black women writers, producers, and directors are putting their stories, the lives of Black women, at the center, not at the periphery. The stories, the narratives, the gaze are about them, through them, in the mainstream avenues, not art houses nor in subculture venues. As Morrison once said, "What was driving me to write was the silence – so many stories untold and unexamined. There was a wide vacuum in the literature and I was inspired by the silence and absences" (Als 2020, 25). The work of the women examined in this book are answering Morrison's call. They are offering to the world a way to break open the silences and absences of Black women. They are filling a historical void. "Look at us. We are here. These are our stories."

For the first time Black women are making in-roads to popular and powerful media outlets. They are getting play. And because of the popularity of such shows and films as *Hidden Figures, Girls Trip, 2 Dope Queens, The Black Lady Sketch Show, Insecure, Twenties, Harriet, The Underground, Queen Sugar, Lovecraft Country*, and so many, many more, we can be hesitantly hopeful. Because we know how this works. It's capitalism. Popularity makes bank. And bank gets attention. And these women are making *bank*. Even as I write, I feel like I can't keep up. There are too many shows, too many films, all by Black women telling their stories. On *Quibi* there is Tyra Banks in her series called *Beauty*; Queen Latifah launching a murder series called *When the Streetlights Go On*; Lena Waithe's docuseries on sneakers (of all things!) called *You Ain't Got These*, and Gabrielle Union's *Black Coffee*. As I write, there are films by Black women that were redirected from theatre release due to the Covid-19 pandemic, including Janicza Bravo's *Zola*, an honest look at sex work within the genre of a road trip movie. And by the time this book is in your hands, there will be so many more films and shows by Black women. Every time I open the *New York Times* or *The New Yorker*, every time I log into Hulu or Netflix and look at "What's New," Black women are there, creating/producing/directing.

These offerings by Black women feel like an explosion in the same way that a rainstorm in the desert erupts in the sky. Because of this explosion of Black women's work, we see—or at least I see and I believe I am not alone—a dismantling of those tired stereotypes that for too long have defined Black womanhood. It isn't that the stereotypes no longer exist, only that when Black women are behind the camera, they blow those stereotypes to smithereens.

What I hope to have argued here is that this is a moment of hope. That representations of Black womanhood are changing, stereotypes that for hundreds of years destroyed Black women's lives, minds, and bodies and deprived them of agency are being destroyed—by Black women who are writing, directing, producing, and performing on their own terms. And that is a good thing. When Black women are behind the camera, they create characters that are complex and hopeful, interesting and important. As "The Bechdel Test" changes our awareness and throws down a gauntlet of responsibility (Does the film have women in it? Do they have names? Do they talk to each other about something other than men?), I have proposed a similar challenge: let us celebrate, promote, and clamor for more films and series that pass "The Black-del Test" (Is the production written/produced/directed by Black women? Does it feature Black female protagonists who operate within a Black community, who have Black friends and lovers? Does it tell the story of Black women's realities, addressing issues of race, sex, sexuality, class?). By supporting these shows, by putting the films/programs in our Quibi, YouTube, Netflix and Hulu cues, by paying money to go see them in the theatre, we can make the industry understand that telling these stories is important *and* lucrative. We can do the work to help these Black female voices by pushing, liking, sharing, posting about, and recommending these works on social media, streaming services, and digital forums. This revolution is in our hands, literally at our fingertips at the reach of our keyboard and mouse clicks.

This book and the women I interviewed are arguing that Black female characters and programming created by Black women reflect the realities of Black womanhood. We need more Black female characters acting from places of power, agency, and autonomy. When Black women are allowed to create, they can resist presenting narratives, films, and series that "always [portray Black women as] acting from the position of powerlessness" defined by the white supremacist capitalist patriarchy (hooks 1995, 269). The work and words of the Black women profiled in this book represent a sea change. Their work is a testimony affirming Black womanhood. As Dillard (2016) said, "We are still here as Black women in a place that has never affirmed Black womanhood. So we affirmed it for ourselves" (210). These women, Lena Waithe, Della Rees, Viola Davis, Ava Duvernay, Issa Rae, Robin Thede, Tiffany Haddish, Misha Green, Oprah Winfrey to name just a *few*, are affirming for themselves and others what Black womanhood is and what Black women have done and can do.

It is mind-boggling and overwhelming (in a very good way) once one begins looking. Because of those algorithms that keep track of past "likes" and give us more of what we want, my "Suggestions for You" list in Hulu, Netflix, and YouTube quickly became full of films and shows I had never even heard of, featuring actors I had never encountered, all pointing to the same area of interest: Black women in leads, Black women in charge, Black women producers. On occasion in this book I included shows or films that had male producers or directors (*Black-ish* by Kenya Barris and *She's Gotta Have It* by Spike Lee) only because there were women who were directing and writing those shows. Because it typically takes a team of writers and directors to produce a series, women are behind the scenes even if the producer is male. Primarily I stuck with female producers, directors, and writers, only deviating when there was a deliberate need to do so. And still, weeding out any films/shows involving men in power left me with more shows/films than I could possibly analyze in one book.

The most glorious part of this process was interviewing women. I started out with students I had worked with as a professor. These young women knocked my socks off with how intelligent and insightful and smart they were about the media they were consuming. They referred me to other women, who referred me to other women. In research, this is called "snowballing." The interview base was not entirely random, but it was far reaching in demographics. I interviewed aunties, mothers, grandmothers, colleagues, and friends. I interviewed women of all sexuality identities including women who identified as pan, bi, butch, dyke, lesbian, and trans. I interviewed professors, medical doctors, nurses, and EMTs. I interviewed women who were stuck in generational poverty and those who are among the working poor. I interviewed women as young as eighteen and those as seasoned as sixty-five. And every time I interviewed someone, they would tell me about more shows or films they liked that featured Black women, by Black women, about

Black women, programming that I had no idea of, but would then look up and sample. By the ways in which the interviewees talked about what they consumed, it was clear they were critical consumers, thinking carefully and thoughtfully about representations of womanhood in these entertainment venues. The interviews typically look about ninety minutes, but most times longer. And many times, I wanted to keep having conversations with the women to whom I spoke. In some cases, I also wanted to become their friend: so smart, so engaged, so amazing.

I would find myself watching a film or program and think, "I wonder what _____ would have to say about this?" or "I've got to see if _____ has seen this." The richest and best part of this project was hearing what women had to say. I hope that I am able to represent their smart thoughts and their incredible personalities in the quotes I chose to use. There are pages and pages (hundreds of pages) of quotes that I couldn't use because there simply was not enough space. That is the hard part. Dear reader, you are only getting a glimpse of these women's thoughts. There were so much more that I simply couldn't squeeze in.

In the same way that I had to make difficult cuts regarding quotes, I also had to make difficult cuts regarding genres. As women told me about what moved them, I quickly discovered that no matter what the genre, there were Black women producing, directing, and writing it. Genres such as science fiction, psycho-thriller, action adventure, dystopia, mystery series, reality television, and talk shows were all genres that were discussed, but I didn't have time to investigate. And what to do with Beyoncé's *Lemonade* (2019)? Or Wangechi Mutu's *The End of Everything* (2013)? These sorts of texts are outside the traditional, typical genres. So, I made the decision to focus on genres that came up consistently across many interviews: comedy, serialized dramas of Black women's lives, and historical dramas. And after doing several interviews, I knew I had to also address topics of hair, colorism, and sexuality as they emerged over and over again in interviews.

The voices represented here are of Black women: both those who I interviewed and those whose work I analyzed. As I talked with the critical consumers, they would often tell me about their lives and how their own stories intersected with what they were watching. They readily pointed out what was authentic to them and what was ridiculously unauthentic. They told me stories of being a girl in a family of boys, being light-skinned (or dark-skinned) in a family unlike them, of being sexually assaulted or being denied scholarships or funding for education, of being told they couldn't do it (whatever it was they wanted to do) because they were just a Black girl, just a Black woman. And for these women, the work of other women, telling *their* stories, meant a great deal. They were being represented. They were. Their lives.

What is hopeful is not just these life-affirming stories that are making their way to the mainstream, thanks to Black women, but that there are almost too many of these new productions to keep up with. Whenever I spoke with a woman, she would alert me to two or three or four more programs or films that I was absolutely unaware of—but they were meaningful to her. These are all real reasons to celebrate, to feel hopeful, to be heartened. There are *good*, thoughtful, interesting and complex representations out there. Too many for one book. And that is a terrific statement to make.

This is the challenge for other scholars: keep doing this work. We need to document what is going on. Even if you do not agree with my analysis here or feel the voices in these pages do not represent you, please go on. Even if you believe that as a white woman academic, I have no right, no place in recording these voices or engaging in this analysis, please continue and do what you think needs to be done. Please write another book and set me straight. Please keep analyzing, thinking about, and celebrating the work that is emerging. These women deserve that. And we all *need* that. Every time an academic or a journalist writes an article or a book, every time a young woman or girl writes a blog or tweets or engages in online fan bases about this type of programming, Black women win. They are legitimized and they get the press they deserve. Similar to the Black Lives Matter movement's "Say Their Names" that creates a litany of people who have senselessly died at the hands of whites with guns, I want to give these women attention and start the list. The New BLACK Criterion List (What should it be named? Who will name it?). We need to know their names, to say their names. They are adding much needed perspective and voice to our culture, thereby shifting attitudes and beliefs. We need to teach them and discuss them and write about them. We need to see their work as the beginning of a new version of Black woman-hood, created by and for Black women.

And to the women producing, writing, and directing I say this: keep going and bring others along with you. We need more queer voices, for one. We need voices about and from the perspective of women who are differently abled.

Because of time and space limitations that I had to face, there were a couple of very popular genres that my interviewees regularly mentioned that I didn't include: science fiction/dystopian fiction and reality television. As I am readying this book for publication, Misha Green's fascinating production *Lovecraft County* is airing on Hulu (2020). Someone else will have to analyze that production and Green's work; it is worthy of analysis. I didn't include reality television because Jervette Ward has already published a terrific book about Black women in reality television (*Real Sister* 2015) and I didn't want to be redundant. Read Ward's book. It is thoughtful and fascinating with chapters written by several different women who *love* reality

TV and the women on reality TV. It's smart and fascinating and wonderful. Reality television, especially series such as *Real Housewives of Atlanta* and *Basketball Wives*, were very popular with my participants and they often said deeply insightful and fascinating things about these shows and the genre in general that I would have loved to include, but I wasn't writing about that genre.

The other genres I didn't include that many participants talked to me about were science fiction/dystopian fiction and psycho-thriller/horror. I didn't include these because I didn't have time to investigate them. But here is a call to the scholars out there: look into this! There is no scholarship written (that I could find) on Black women who are directing, writing, and producing these genres. And there are films/shows by those women. They deserve to be talked about, written about, and named. The women I talked with had fascinating insights into characters or shows in these categories and this is where I hand the baton off to other scholars interested in this area of research: take a look at Black women in science fiction and horror. There are some interesting things going on there in programs such as *Lovecraft County, Watchmen, Doctor Who* (the 2020 season where a Black woman shows up as The Doctor), *This Is Us, Black Panther*, and *The Old Ones*.

In addition, there were shows/films starring amazing Black women, embodying a narrative told from a Black, female perspective but in investigating them, I would discover they were written/directed by men and therefore outside the scope of this book. *Atlanta* is one such series; there are female directors and writers on the series, but they are outnumbered by men. Or there would be an interesting film or show, but I wasn't quite sure where it would fit, the genre seemed outside the scope of what I was looking at. Two productions that immediately come to mind are *Queen Sugar* (a family drama) and *The Hate You Give* (is this a young adult film? Or something else?). There are gaps and holes in what I was able to do within the time and space I had here. However, I am loath to leave out some of the thoughts my participants had on these missing genres. I want to include their voices here as a way to get others started. There are some young scholars reading these words right now who will be able to take these ideas and run with them. Please. Help yourself. Here are some smart insights to get you started:

THE HATE YOU GIVE

This film, based on the award-winning young adult book of the same title by Angie Thomas (2018), was often discussed in my interviews. Especially by the younger women. Those who lived in large urban areas, such as Chicago, St. Louis, Kansas City, and Washington, D.C., locked into the moral and

ethical dilemma of staying within the historically Black part of town or moving out to another area. Are there more films about these real, hard choices
that Black women have to make? The screenplay was written by Audrey
Wells, a white woman who tragically died of cancer the day before the film
was released. The film was directed by George Tillman. Many of my young
research participants had first read the book by Angie Thomas and then saw
the film. In talking about the film, they would sometimes conflate the book
with the film or speak simultaneously about both book and film.

> It is so real. The experience of having to decide what to do: support the Black
> community or move out of the community. I *know* that feeling. It is happening
> to me right now. I'm at college. I got out. But should I go back? Am I betraying
> my community if I don't go back? It could be Atlanta, Birmingham, Detroit, St.
> Louis. All of these places have a traditional Black community that is not doing
> well. Do we go back? Do we try to rebuild? What is happening in the Black
> community was shown in this film. It is so real. Showing the brutality of what
> people have to experience if they choose to stay. (Drayah)

Another twenty-something college student who has worked as an EMT and is
currently studying biology with the hopes of becoming a doctor, had much to
say about her lived reality of growing up on the east side of St. Louis and her
experience at a predominantly white university in rural Missouri. Michelle
moved away from her Black neighborhood in St. Louis for college to get
away from the reality of violence in her neighborhood. She connected in a
direct way to the book/film *The Hate You Give*.

> The movie [*The Hate You Give*] gave me a visual, but with the book I felt it. I
> felt the reality of her pain of seeing yet another Black boy die. The movie was
> more of detached, but you still feel [the boy who is shot by police] is one of your
> own. I was thinking 'This could be my brother and this could be my cousin." It
> shows things you couldn't see just reading the book. In the movie they moved
> out of the Black part of town and took the kids out of the Black school. She
> was in a good neighborhood and a PW (predominantly white) school. She was
> saying, "When I am at home, I am one person. When I am school, I am another
> person." She changed what she was for the kids at her school. I have done that
> here (in college). I came from a Black community, a Black high school and all
> of a sudden, I am here and whites are looking at me like they don't know how to
> act. My freshman year I did that, I tried to act more white. I felt uncomfortable
> when I did it, but it was like a survival strategy. But I felt I was not myself. I
> felt like I should not have to change who I was to be around anyone. I shouldn't
> change who I am to please someone who is not the same color as me. Now (in

her third year) I don't care. I am who I am. I am outspoken about race issues. I tell it like it is. I need to be who I am. (Michelle)

FAMILY PROGRAMMING

I interviewed a fair number of mothers. Some of them were very young mothers (late teens and early twenties); others had children who were grown (mothers and grandmothers in their fifties and sixties). Even as none of my questions specifically asked about media consumption and children, most of the mothers I spoke with talked about the media their children consumed and trying to steer them toward Black-centered shows and characters. One mother of small twin girls told me about *Black Lightning* (CW 2018–2019) a series about a Black supergirl. Another young mother said, "I loved *Wrinkle in Time*. It was amazing to see young girls in STEM. And to add in the fantasy element. It was a perfect film for both my daughter and my son: girls can be great at science and math! They can be interesting heroes in an adventure movie." These mothers wanted their children to not only see positive and complex representations of Black people on the screens, but they wanted to create critically aware consumers by talking with their children about lack of representation or stereotypical representation. I also had several women talk to me about how their mothers had made sure they had access to powerful Black girl representations, steering them toward shows that featured Black girl protagonists.

When Disney came out with a Black princess, it was a big deal. It was 10 years ago (*The Princess and the Frog* 2009), but why did it take Disney so long? She was a princess. And she was Black. My mom was the mom who made sure I had Black baby dolls. When it came to Disney, the princesses were always white. So, it was radical when the Black princess came out. Even watching it now I really liked it. She gets the restaurant she always wanted and she didn't take the easy way out. The bad guy shows her she can have everything in the easy way, but her morals didn't allow it. That is what my mom taught me: don't take the easy way out. Because the easy way out is going against your morals or causing you to do something unethical. I did notice that. I loved that. She had the best friend, the white girl who was really rich. She was a poor Black girl and the white girl was really rich. Usually when you see this dynamic, you see them butting heads. The white girl was still humble. She went to the friend's little diner. It was a positive relationship between a white and Black girl. The white girl supported her. I liked that even for younger girls, you have to be conscious and aware. (EJ)

Mothers were able to tell me, in detail, what children's shows they found acceptable or positive. Clearly, these women had been thinking about the programming their children were being exposed to and were very committed to steering them towards positive, non-stereotypical representations.

> As a parent, I now focus more on programming that I watch around my children. We watch more YouTube when it is the family. I also use YouTube because there is a lot of diverse content and they are interested in it. Some of it is I want them to watch more balanced [diverse with Black characters] programming than what is on regular T.V. YouTube has those things . . . . With my children's programming, I watch with them. Some of the kids' shows have some problematic examples [stereotypes of Blacks, especially Black boys] in there. Sometimes I am watching with my son, who is 8, I sit there and watch it and I think, "No. We need to watch something else." When the Black boy is slow or stupid or naughty, it makes me turn my head. Or even if the Black kid is the sidekick, not the main character. I don't like that. We need to be the focus. *Craig of the Creek* (Cartoon Network 2018) is a really cute show that I like. He is a Black boy and he has two friends. They go on adventures in the woods. And not only is it his character and his adventures, but he has a really cute family as well. I like that we see the whole family. I also like that his mom and dad are dark-skinned. He has an older sister or brother and their banter is very funny. It shows a normal Black family and that is something I like to see. (Ashley)

On Black superheroes:

> Black Lightning is *SO DOPE*. They give them artificial superpowers. Black people have superpowers in real life. We make something out of nothing. I love my culture. We are so innovative. People have surgeries to look like us. I grew up seeing my mom grinding, working all the time. You have to know that Black women are superheroes. We need a movie like that: a Black woman superhero. (Dena)

> When we got out of *Black Panther,* we were driving home and my dad just started crying. Crying! I had never seen him cry before. He said, 'You have no idea how different my self-worth would have been if I had been able to see films like this as a boy. (Grace)

PSYCHO-THRILLER AND CRIME FILMS

One of the women I interviewed talked at length about the genre of psycho-thriller and crime dramas. This genre featuring Black female-driven storylines was clearly a big hole in my knowledge. When I interviewed EJ, a vivacious and driven campus leader, I listened with interest as she talked about the details of films such as *Lila and Eve* (2015) with Viola Davis and Jennifer Lopez, *The Call* (2013) with Halle Berry, *Kidnapped* (also with Berry, 2017), *Breaking In* (2018) with Gabrielle Union, and *Seven Seconds* (2018) with Regina King. EJ told me she likes these films because the Black women are powerful and unrelenting.

A lot of times, Black women are portrayed as poor and helpless. The implication is that they are beat down that they don't try hard enough. So, people have that stereotype of Black women. I like to see these characters who are doing everything. The Black female character in the thrillers and action films do have the drive and determination. They don't give up. They aren't victims. They are the counterargument to being complacent or passive . . . . Black women have that determination. For their loved ones. They are in control and they have self-control. These characters are like the women I grew up around. I would see my mom upset, but she wouldn't lose control. She was always so professional. Even in the films, they can't blow up because it is a stereotype (Angry Black Woman). They have every right to rage, but they can't because it is a stereotype. When a Black woman or man does something like that, they are seen as animal-like characteristics. (EJ)

FAMILY DRAMAS: *EMPIRE* AND *QUEEN SUGAR*

Empire: "I love the actress who plays Loretha "Cookie" Lyon (Taraji Henson), but her character is a stereotypical Black woman from the hood. She's coarse. She's been in prison. She is snappy, rude, funny, but then she would blow up in your face. Her morals are me, me, me. I wish she could have played it in a different way. She was ringleader so those characteristics are part of being that kind of character. Eventually they showed us her backstory. We saw her childhood. We saw the relationship with her husband and so we know why she was the way she was. Because she went through all she did, we understand why she is so ruthless. I was appreciative of that, but still, it didn't have to be that way." (Patrice)

Queen Sugar: "There aren't a whole lot of shows, especially dramas, that are centered around Black families and the intricacies of all those dynamics. But when I think about *Queen Sugar*, a lot of the activism that is happening is their home town is what is happening in the U.S. And then you get the history of Black farmers in the South. [The series] could be a pushback against the dominant culture. It depicts a Black family fighting against the wealthier white family and how that dynamic brings out everything in their family: infighting, jealousy, power grabs. Also, I like that Mariana (an attorney) works in a company that is male-dominant and she shows women how to fight for equality in a setting like that. And then the Black girl on the show is seen with Black Lives Matter women and she is doing her activism work in a very public way. So, they not only cover the family drama, but the politics as well." (Stacy)

The two examples of *Queen Sugar* and *Empire* create a Black-centric version of the nighttime drama series that are similar to the typical daytime soap opera genre. However, with these family dramas, the directors/writers also infuse issues *specific* to Black communities and families. The portrayal of Black families has more depth than the typical white version of family dramas or the Latin American Telenovelas.

WHY THESE SHOWS AND FILMS ARE IMPORTANT

Those scholars outside the fields of Media Studies, African American/Black studies or even Gender Studies might argue, "It's just television. It's just movies. It's just entertainment. Who cares?" What we know is that media representations *do* matter: they affirm and teach stereotypes or disrupt them and those actions have real-world consequences. Social Science scholars and psychologists have known, through research since the 1970s, what a powerful educator television is. We learn about others through our screens; we learn who we are; or we learn who we aren't. Black women in the United States have long been denied dynamic, interesting, and complex versions of themselves. Instead of being By Whites, For Whites, the entertainment programming analyzed here suggests there is a body of work that is For Black Women, By Black Women, answering the call of so many great Black women, including Morrison, who have argued that the erasure of Black women's lives cannot and should not be tolerated.

In interviewing women, I heard story after story of how powerful it was for them to see Black women on the screen, telling the stories of Black women's lives. The women I talked with often immediately brought the conversation back to how these programs and films reflected their lived reality in important and affirming ways. What follows is a story that Michelle shared with me after she talked about the importance of films such as *The Hate You Give:*

I began being critically aware when I was really young. When my oldest brother passed away (he was killed in a drive-by shooting) I was 7 and it really opened my eyes to a lot of stuff. The police said there was a robbery, and that is why he was shot. But he was shot in front of our house. My mom pushed the police to investigate what happened. They were not doing anything. He was just another Black boy. She called the police department every day. They didn't do *anything*. That is when I realized there was no justice for a Black man. I realized these inequities not only because of what was going on around me, but what was going on in the world. It opened my eyes and I had to grow up. I learned first-hand what the pain and the hatred towards another Black person can do; you may not even know the person that well or at all. That pain and hatred could *kill* another Black person. It continued to happen. My friend's cousin—he was in middle school—was killed by a white cop and there were no consequences. And I knew that wasn't right. At a young age I knew that wasn't right and that something was wrong. Seeing whites get away with murder, it made me realize how bad it was for Blacks. And if I was riding around with my brother and we would get pulled over, I'd get scared. He drove an average Black car, a Monte Carlo, and on top of that he had dreds. I saw the difference between riding with him and riding with my mom. She appears white, she would never get pulled over. When I am with my brother, it is always something. At first, I was thinking it was something with gender, but as I grew up, I thought it wasn't just gender because it happened to Black women, too. The police would pull me or my brother over for nothing, just making an excuse. Once we got better cars, then we were stopped because the cars were too nice and they thought they were stolen. In middle school I knew a girl and her boyfriend who got pulled over and the cop was asking for their stuff. And a cop shot him because he said the boyfriend was reaching for a gun. At a young age, I learned to watch my sur-roundings and think. Don't be blind; *think*. I have learned to not feel safe until I am in the house.

For women such as Michelle, the films *The Hate You Give* (2018) and the series *Queen and Slim* (2019) speak to her of her lived experience of growing up in a city, under the thumb of the WSCP. These films and series tell the story of being young, Black and female in a world where Black communi-ties are under siege. These stories reflect Michelle's and others' realities; they address complex issues such as whether to stay or move; how police brutality and gang violence are destroying families; and how to emerge as a Black woman who lives and thrives. These programs and films are more than just entertainment. They speak multiple and complex truths, focusing on the reality of what it means to be Black and female in this country. The complex intersections of race, class, gender, sexuality, privilege, education, ability, age, and family structure are what these women behind the camera are help-ing us understand. Kimberlé Crenshaw (1989) dubbed this web of complex and inter-connected identities "intersectionality." Years before Crenshaw coined the term "intersectional," Audre Lorde (1983) wrote about this same dynamic of multiple oppressions. Lorde, a self-defined "Black, lesbian, mother, warrior, poet," wrote, "There is no hierarchy of oppression . . . . I cannot afford the luxury of fighting one form of oppression only. I cannot afford to believe that freedom from intolerance is the right of only one particular group. And I cannot afford to choose between the fronts upon which I must battle these forces of discrimination, wherever they appear to destroy me" (1).

The traditional stereotypes of Black women and girls perpetuated by the dominant entertainment industry aimed to destroy the individuality, the beauty, the humanity of Black females. We are currently experiencing a moment when Black women are seizing control of some parts of that industry to, in turn, destroy those stereotypes. This book is an attempt to celebrate those warriors, those writers, those directors, and those women. Their work is important. It has the power to change our worlds. We need to do our part: watch, share, like, push, recommend, discuss, teach these works. And all the works that are emerging after these words are written and published. As Fannie Lou Hamer and Toni Morrison both famously said, "It's in our hands." In the Digital Age, it is all at the tips of our fingertips, our keyboards, our clicks. Answer the call of Hamer, Lorde, Morrison, and so many others: there is work to be done.

Appendix I

Quoted Participant Demographics

(* after a name denotes a participant-selected pseudonym; all other names are authentic)

Aliyah, twenties, single, no children, Midwestern college student, graphic art major, Kansas City.

Amber, forties, married to a man, mother of four ranging in age from toddler to teenager, bus driver, East coast.

Ashley, thirties, married to a white man, two children (one Black and one biracial/2 white step children), nurse in the South.

*Bettina**, forties, married to a man, two children, director of a nonprofit and outspoken activist in her community, South Carolina.

Coretta, sixties, divorced, grandmother to six/mother to four, postal worker, living in Iowa.

*Courtnee**, thirties, trans, partnered/no children, social worker, Arizona.

Dena, nineteen, living with her boyfriend and eighteen-month-old son, Certified Nursing Assistant, hopes to attend community college to become a nurse, Nebraska.

Donnelle, fifties, partnered with a woman, mother of three grown children, self-described "butch dyke," police officer, Illinois.

*Drayah**, in her twenties, single, no children, college student studying film production, Missouri.

Eboni, thirties, a single, no children, entrepreneur who has a social media presence celebrating bigger female bodies (Identity of She), Arizona.

*EJ**, nineteen, single, no children, college student, undeclared major, described herself as "always wanting to dig deeper," Missouri.

Gloria, thirties, single, no children, professor of English, Atlanta area.

Grace, eighteen, single, no children, first-year college student (undeclared major); first-generation college, raised by a single mother in the Detroit area.

Janae*, twenties, single, no children, college student finishing her creative writing/publishing major at a mid-sized Midwestern University while working at a nursing home, Kansas City.

Karen*, twenties, single, no children, administrator in an alumni office of a medium-sized university in Louisiana, opera singer.

Lex*, fifties, single mother of one son, small business owner, Oregon.

Marta*, in her thirties, partnered with a man/no children, insurance agent, Nebraska.

Mashell, fifties, married to a man, mother of six ranging in age from seven to twenty-two; college degree, works as an administrator in a nursing home, Kansas City area.

Michelle*, twenties, single, no children, EMT and college student, describes herself as "an average Black girl from St. Louis."

Michele, twenties, single, no children, college senior majoring in criminal justice and social justice activist on her campus, Missouri.

Patrice, forties, mother of two teenagers, absent husband/father, stay-at-home mother in the Minnesota.

Ruby*, thirties, partnered with a woman, one daughter, stand up/spoken word artist, self-described "feminist," Portland, Oregon.

Shayna*, forties, divorced, teenage daughter, academic at a large university in Texas.

Stacy*, thirties, married to a man, mother of baby twins, college administrator/program director, Missouri.

Tania, twenties, single lesbian, mother of two "fur babies," stylist, St. Louis.

Ta'Nisha, sixties, married to a man, grandmother of two/mother of three, accountant, Ohio.

Trinity, thirties, partnered with a man, no children, political advisor, Chicago.

Veronica*, forties, single mother of two boys (ages thirteen and seven), minister, identifies as bisexual, describes herself as "a Black feminist theologian whose emphasis is on philosophical constructions of god in the Black church," Southeastern Nebraska.

References

Adams-Bass, Valerie, Keisha Bentley-Edwards, and Howard Stevenson. "'That's Not Me I See on TV': African American Youth Interpret Media Images of Black Females." *Women, Gender, and Families of Color* 2, no. 1 (2014): 79–100.

Akbar, Na'im. *Breaking the Chains of Psychological Slavery*. Tallahassee, FL: Mind Productions and Associates, 1996.

Allen, Carol. "'Shakin That Thing' and All Its Wonders: Female African American Comedy." *Studies in American Humor* 3, no. 12 (2005): 97–120.

Allrath, Gaby, Marion Gymnich, and Carola Surkamp. "Introduction: Towards a Narrotology of TV Series." In *Narrative Strategies in Television Series*, edited by Gaby Allrath and Marion Gymnich, 1–43. New York: Palgrave Macmillan, 2005.

Als, Hilton. "Ghosts in the House." *The New Yorker* 66, no. 21 (July 27, 2020): 30–39.

Arogundade, Ben. *Black Beauty: A History and a Celebration.* London, UK: Thunder's Mouth Press, 2000.

Ashburn-Nardo, Leslie, Megan Knowles, and Margo Monteith. "Black Americans' Implicit Racial Associations and Their Implications for Intergroup Judgment." *Social Cognition* 21, no. 1 (2003): 61–87.

Auter, Philip J. "TV That Talks Back: An Experimental Validation of a Parasocial Interaction Scale." *Journal of Broadcasting & Electronic Media* 36 (1992): 173–181.

Badillo, Casandra. "'Only My Hairdresser Knows for Sure.' Stories of Race, Hair and Gender." *NACLA Report on the Americas* 34 (September 26, 2007): 35–38.

Baker, Christina. *Contemporary Black Women Filmmakers and the Art of Resistance.* Columbus: Ohio State University Press, 2018.

Barker, Ciril Josh. "Black Worker Told Her Hair Too Urban' for Banana Republic." *New York Amsterdam News.* October 10, 2017. http://amsterdamnews.com/news/2017/oct/10/banana-republic-manager-ny-sent-employee-home-over/.Barr

Barris, Kenya. @funnyblackdude, *Twitter.* December 21, 2019.Battle, Juan, and Anthony Lemelle. "Gender Differences in African American Attitudes Toward Gay Males." *The Western Journal of Black Studies* 26, no. 3 (2002): 134–139.

Bias, Employment, Discrimination, and Black Women's Hair: Another Way Forward. J. Reuben Clark Law School, Brigham Young University, 2018.

Blair, Cynthia. *I've Got To Make A Livin':Black Women's Sex Work in Turn-of-the-Century Chicago.* Chicago: University of Chicago Press, 2010.

Blair, Cynthia. "African American Women's Sexuality." *Frontiers: A Journal of Women's Studies* 35, no. 1 (2014): 4–10.

Bluitt, Renae and Sterling Milan. *She Did That.* Netflix (2019).

Bobo, Jacqueline. "Reading Through the Text: The Black Woman as Audience." In *Black American Cinema*, edited by Manthia Diawara, 272–287. New York: Routledge, 1993.

Boylorn, Robin. "As Seen on TV: An Autoethnographic Reflection on Race and Reality Television." *Critical Studies in Media Communication* 25, no. 4 (2008): 413–433.

Bradley, Regina. "Awkwardly Hysterical: Theorizing Black Girl Awkwardness and Humor in Social Media." *Comedy Studies* 6, no. 2 (2015): 148–153.

Breen-Tucci, Elza. "Things *Harriet* Got Wrong About Harriet Tubman's Life." *Grunge.com.* November 4, 2019. https://www.grunge.com/173225/things-harriet -got-wrong-about-harriet-tubmans-life/.

Brooks, Siohban. "Black on Black Love: Black Lesbian and Bisexual Women, Marriage, and Symbolic Meaning." *Black Scholar* 47, no. 4 (2017): 32–46. DOI: 10.1080/00064246.2017.1368065.

Brown, Rachel. "Michelle Obama's Hairstylist Johnny Wright Gives Her Bounce for DNC Speech." *Los Angeles Times.* July 26, 2016. Accessed 30 July 2020. http://www.latimes.com/fashion/la-ig-michelleobama-hair-20160726-snap-story .html.

Brown, Shaunasea. "'Don't Touch My Hair': Problematizing Representations of Black Women in Canada." *Africology: The Journal of Pan African Studies* 12, no. 8 (December 2018): 64–85.

Brown, Timothy A., Thomas F. Cash, and Robin J. Lewis. "Body-Image Disturbances in Adolescent Female Binge-Purgers: A Brief Report of the Results of a National Survey in the USA." *Journal of Child Psychology and Psychiatry* 30, no. 4 (1989): 605–613.

Brown, Tom. "Introduction: Direct Address in Film History, Theory and Criticism." In *Breaking the Fourth Wall: Direct Address in the Cinema*, 1–21. Edinburgh: Edinburgh University Press, 2012.

Buchanan, Kyle, and Reggie Ugwu. "The Criterion Collections 'Blind Spots.'" *New York Times Arts and Leisure Section.* August 23, 2020, AR6.

Butler, Judith. *Gender Trouble.* London: Routledge, 1991.

Cartier, Nina. "Black Women On-Screen as Future Texts: A New Look at Black Pop Culture Representations." *Cinema Journal* 53, no. 3 (2014): 150–157.

Celious, Aaron, and Daphna Oyserman. "Race from the Inside: An Emerging Heterogeneous Race Model." *Journal of Social Issues* 57 (2001): 149–165. DOI: 10.1111/0022-4537.00206.

Chaney, Cassandra, and Ray Robertson. "Chains of Psychological Enslavement: Olivia Pope and the Celebration of the Black Mistress in ABC's *Scandal*." *Africology: The Journal of Pan African Studies* 9, no. 3 (2016): 126–153.

Childs, Erica Chito. "Looking Behind the Stereotypes of the 'Angry Black Woman': An Exploration of Black Women's Responses to Interracial Relationships." *Gender and Society* 19, no. 4 (2005): 544–561.

Cieszki, Cameron. "Welcome to Hollywood's Black Renaissance." *The Pointer*. February 6, 2019. https://thepointeruwsp.com/2019/01/30/welcome-to-hollywoods -black-renaissance/.

Clark, Cedric. "Television and Social Controls: Some Observations on the Portrayals of Ethnic Minorities." *Television Quarterly* 8 (Spring 1969): 18–22.

Clayton, Alex. "Play-Acting: A Theory of Comedic Performance." In *Theorizing Film Acting*, edited by Aaron Taylor, 62–80. New York: Routledge Press, 2010.

Coleman, Nicole, Eboni Butler, Amanda Long, and Felicia Fisher. "In and Out of Love with Hip-Hop: Saliency of Sexual Scripts for Young Adult Black Women in Hip-Hop and Black-Oriented Television." *Culture, Health & Sexuality* 18, no. 10 (2016): 1165–1179.

Collins, Patricia Hill. "Mammies, Matriarchs, and Other Controlling Images." In *Gender: Key Concepts in Critical Theory*, edited by Carol Gould, 76–106. New York: Humanity Books, 1997.

Collins, Patricia Hill. *Black Feminist Thought: Knowledge, Consciousness, and the Politics of Empowerment*. New York: Routledge, 2000.

Collins, Patricia Hill. *Black Sexual Politics: African Americans, Gender and the New Racism*. London: Routledge, 2004.

Colvin, Randy, Dawn Vogt, and William Ickes. "Why Do Friends Understand Each Other Better Than Strangers Do?" In *Empathic Accuracy*, edited by William Ickes, 311–340. New York: Guilford, 1997.

Cooper, Brittney. *Beyond Respectability: The Intellectual Thought of Race Women*. Urbana, IL: University of Illinois Press, 2017.

Cooper, Brittney. "How Sarah Got Her Groove Back, or Notes Towards a Black Feminist Theology of Pleasure." *Black Theology* 16, no. 3 (2018): 195–206.

Craemer, Thomas. "An Evolutionary Model of Racial Attitude Formation: Socially Shared and Idiosyncratic Racial Attitudes." *Annals of the American Academy of Political and Social Science* 614, no. 1 (2007): 74–101.

Crenshaw, Kimberlé. "Demarginalizing the Intersection of Race and Sex: A Black Feminist Critique of Antidiscrimination Doctrine, Feminist Theory and Antiracist Politics." *University of Chicago Legal Forum* 140 (1989): 139–167.

Cruz-Gutiérrez, Christina. "Hair Tangled with Politics: Michelle Obama's Tale of Strategic Resistance and Accommodation." *Continuum: Journal of Media and Cultural Studies* 34, no. 1 (2020): 59–72.

Cunningham, Michael, Anita Roberts, Alan Barbee, Perri Druen, and Chen Wu. "Their Ideas of Beauty Are, On the Whole, the Same As Ours: Consistency and Variability in the Cross-Cultural Perception of Female Physical Attractiveness." *Journal of Personality & Social Psychology* 68, no. 2 (1995): 261–279.

Dasgupta, Ninanjana, Mahzarin Banaji, and Robert Abelson. "Group Entitativity and Group Perception: Associations Between Physical Features and Psychological Judgment." *Journal of Personality & Social Psychology* 77, no. 5 (1999): 991–1003.

Dawson, Gail, Katherine Karl, and Joy Peluchette. "Hair Matters: Towards Understanding Natural Black Hair Bias in the Workplace." *Journal of Leadership and Organizational Studies* 26, no. 3 (2019): 389–401.

Desmond-Harris, Jenee. "Michelle Obama's Hair: For African-American Women, Hair Commands Great Interest and Carries a Lot of Cultural Baggage." *Time.* September 7, 2009. Accessed 30 July 2020. http://content.time.com/time/photogallery/0,29307,1919348,00.html.

Desta, Yohana. "Jessica Williams and Phoebe Robinson's Unfiltered Comedy Podcast Will Be Your New Favorite." *Mashable.* April 5, 2016. https://mashable.com/2016/04/05/dope-queens-podcast/.

Dillard, Cynthia B. "We Are Still Here: Declarations of Love and Sovereignty in Black Life Under Siege." *Educational Studies* 52, no. 3 (2016): 201–215. DOI: 10.1080/00131946.2016.1169737.

Dolan, Paul. *Happily Ever After: Escaping the Myths of a Perfect Life.* London: Allen Lane Press, 2019.

Donnelly, Matt, and Brent Lang. "Hulu Snatches Justin Simien's 'Bad Hair' as Sundance Wraps Up." *Variety.* January 31, 2020. https://variety.com/2020/film/news/bad-hair-hulu-justin-simien-sundance-1203479899/.

Dorsey, Jason. "National Study on the Unexpected Viewpoints of the Generation After Millennials." *The Center for Generational Kinetics* (2016): 5–7. https://genhq.com/generation-z-research-2018/.

Drake, Simone. "The Marketability of Black Joy: After 'I Do' in Black Romance Film." *Women, Gender, and Families of Color* 7, no. 2 (2019): 161–181.

Early, Gerald, Glenda Carpio, and Werner Sollors. "Black Humor: Reflections on an American Tradition." *Bulletin of the American Academy of Arts and Sciences* 63, no. 4 (2010): 29–41. Accessed 23 July 2020. www.jstor.org/stable/41149267.

Edwards, Erica. "'It's Irrelevant to Me!' Young Black Women Talk Back to VH1's Love and Hip Hop New York." *Journal of Black Studies* 47, no. 3 (2016): 273–292. Accessed 13 July 2020. www.jstor.org/stable/43926943.

Entman, Robert M., and Andrew Rojecki. *The Black Image in the White Mind: Media and Race in America.* Chicago: The University of Chicago Press, 2000.

Finley, Jessica. "Black Women's Satire as (Black) Postmodern Performance." *Studies in American Humor* 2, no. 2 (2016): 236-265.

Finney, Gail. *Look Who's Laughing.* New York: Taylor and Francis, 2014.

French, Megan. "Michelle Obama Sports Her Natural Hair and the Internet Loves It." *US Magazine.* April 4, 2017. Accessed 30 July 2019. http://www.usmagazine.com/stylish/news/michelle-obamasports-her-natural-hair-and-the-internet-loves-it-w474999.

George, Rosemary. "From Expatriate Aristocrat to Immigrant Nobody: South Asian Racial Strategies in the Southern California Context." *Diaspora* 6, no. 1 (1997): 31–60.

Gerbner, George. "Communication and Social Environment." *The Scientific American* 227, no. 3 (1972): 153–160.

Giannino, Steven S., and Chrystal R. China. "A Critical Look at Certainty Adverbs and the Essentializing Discourse of Black Female Identity in the Reality Television Show, Girlfriend Intervention." *Howard Journal of Communication* 29, no. 1 (2018): 18–32.

Glassman, Jonathon. "Slower Than a Massacre: The Multiple Sources of Racial Thought in Colonial Africa." *American Historical Review* 109, no. 3 (2004): 720–754.

Goldberg, Whoopi. *Whoopi Goldberg Presents Moms Mabley.* New York: HBO, 2013.

Gray, Herman. "Anxiety, Desire, and Conflict in the American Racial Imagination." In *Media Scandals: Morality and Desire in the Popular Culture Marketplace*, edited by James Lull and Steven Hinerman, 85–98. New York: Columbia University Press, 1997.

Haggins, Bambi. *Laughing Mad: The Black Comic Persona in Post-Soul America.* Piscataway, NJ: Rutgers University Press, 2007.

Hall, J. Camille. "No Longer Invisible: Understanding the Psychosocial Impact of Skin Color Stratification in the Lives of African American Women." *Health & Social Work* 42, no. 2 (2017): 71–78. DOI: 10.1093/hsw/hlx001.

Hannon, Lance, and Roberta DeFina. "Just Skin Deep? The Impact of Interviewer Race on the Assessment of African American Respondent Skin Tone." *Race and Social Problems* 6 (2014): 356–364.

Harris-Perry, Melissa. *Sister Citizen: Shame, Stereotypes, and Black Women in America.* New Haven, CT: Yale University Press, 2011.

Henderson, Carol. "Introduction: On First Ladies, Duchesses, and Bawses—Black Womanhood Rebooted." *Journal of American Culture* 42, no. 1 (2019): 3–9.

Higginbotham, Evelyn Brooks. *Righteous Discontent: The Women's Movement in the Black Baptist Church, 1880–1920.* Cambridge, MA: Harvard University Press, 1993.

Hochschild, Jennifer, and Vesla Weaver. "The Skin Color Paradox and the American Racial Order." *Social Forces* 86, no. 2 (2007): 643–670. DOI: 10.1093/sf/86.2.643.

hooks, bell. *Ain't I a Woman: Black Women and Feminism.* Boston, MA: South End Press, 1981.

hooks, bell. "Straightening Our Hair." *Zeta Magazine* 1 (September 1988): 33–37.

hooks, bell. *Black Looks: Race and Representation.* Boston: South End Press, 1992.

hooks, bell. "Feminism in Black and White." In *Skin Deep: Black Women and White Women Write About Race*, edited by Susan Shreve and Marita Golden, 265–277. New York, NY: Doubleday, 1995.

hooks, bell. *Are You Still a Slave?: Liberating the Black Female Body.* New School Eugene Lang College [Video File]. May 7, 2014. https://www.youtube.com/watch?v=rJk0hNROvzs.

Hudson, Shawna. "Re-Creational Television: The Paradox of Change and Continuity Within Stereotypical Iconography." *Sociological Inquiry* 68, no. 2 (1998): 242–257.

Hughes, Michael, and Bradley Hertel. "The Significance of Color Remains: A Study of Life Chances, Mate Selection, and Ethnic Consciousness." *Social Forces* 68, no. 4 (1990): 1105–1120.

Hunter, Margaret L. "Colorstruck: Skin Color Stratification in the Lives of African American Women." *Sociological Inquiry* 68, no. 4 (1998): 517–535.

Hunter, Margaret L. "If You're Light, You're Alright: Light Skin Color as Social Capital for Women of Color." *Gender & Society* 16 (2002): 175–193. DOI: 10.1177/08912430222104895.

Hunter, Margaret L. *Race, Gender, and the Politics of Skin Tone.* New York, NY: Routledge, 2005.

Hunter, Margaret. "The Persistent Problem of Colorism: Skin Tone, Status, and Inequality." *Sociology Compass* 1, no. 1 (2007): 237–254.

"Inside the World of P-Valley: STARZ." *YouTube.com.* June 18, 2020. https://www.youtube.com/watch?v=pzDKajKh2f0.

Iton, Richard. *In Search of the Black Fantastic.* New York: Oxford University Press, 2010.

Jackson, Angelique. "Justin Simien, Kelly Rowland and the Cast of 'Bad Hair' on the Realities of Black Hair in Hollywood." *Variety.com.* January 24, 2020. https://variety-com.ezproxy.missouriwestern.edu/2020/film/news/bad-hair-kelly-rowland-justin-simien-elle-lorraine-1203479097/.

Jackson, Ronald L. *Inscripting the Black Masculine Body: Identity, Discourse and Racial Politics in Popular Media.* Albany, NY: SUNY Press, 2006.

Jeffries, DeVair, and Rhonda Jeffries. "Mentoring and Mothering Black Femininity in the Academy: An Exploration of Body, Voice and Image through Black Female Characters." *The Western Journal of Black Studies* 39, no. 2 (2015): 125–133.

Jere-Malanda, Regina. "Black Women's Politically Correct Hair." *New African Woman* 479 (December 2008): 14–18.

Johnson, Allen. "Wanda Sykes-Hall Writes for Chris Rock and Does Her Own Stuff, Too." *Chicago Tribune.* February 12, 1999. Accessed 30 July 2020. https://www.chicagotribune.com/news/ct-xpm-1999-02-12-9902120214-story.html.

Jones, Charisse, and Terry Ellis Niecquel. "Banning Ethnic Hairstyles 'Upholds This Notion of White Supremacy.' States Pass Laws to Ban Hair Discrimination." *U.S.A. Today.* October 14, 2019. https://www.usatoday.com/story/news/nation/2019/10/14/black-hair-laws-passed-stop-natural-hair-discrimination-across-us/3850402002/.

Jones, Jacquie. "The Construction of Black Sexuality." In *Black American Cinema,* edited by Manthia Diawara, 247–256. New York: Routledge, 1993.

Jones, Lisa. *Bulletproof Diva: Tales of Race, Sex, and Hair.* New York: Doubleday, 2004.

Joseph, Ralina. "'Tyra Banks is Fat': Reading (Post-)Racism and (Post-)Feminism in the New Millennium." *Critical Studies in Media Communication* 26, no. 3 (2009): 237–254.

Jost, John T., Mahzarin Banaji, and Brian Nosek. "A Decade of System Justification Theory: Accumulated Evidence of Conscious and Unconscious Bolstering of the Status Quo." *Political Psychology* 25, no. 68 (2004): 81–919.

Kahn, Katy. "Critical Debates on the Politics of Representing Black American Women in Musical Video Productions." *Muziki: Journal of Music Research* 5, no. 2 (2009): 263–270.

Kambon, Kobi. *Cultural Misorientation: The Greatest Threat to the Survival of the Black Race in the 21st Century.* Tallahassee, FL: Nubian Nation Publications, 2003.

Kein, Sybil. *Creole, The History and Legacy of Louisiana's Free People of Color.* Baton Rouge: Louisiana State University Press, 2000.

Keith, Verna M., Karen D. Lincoln, Robert J. Taylor, and James S. Jackson. "Discriminatory Experiences and Depressive Symptoms Among African American Women: Do Skin Tone and Mastery Matter?" *Sex Roles* 62 (2010): 48–59.

Kunze, Peter. "Introduction: Laughter in the Digital Age." *Comedy Studies* 6, no. 2 (2015): 101–106.

Landor, Antoinette M., Leslie Simons, Ronald Simons, Gene Brody, Shalondra Bryant, Fredrick Gibbons, Ellen M. Granberg, and Janet Melby. "Exploring the Impact of Skin Tone on Family Dynamics and Race-related Outcomes." *Journal of Family Psychology* 27, no. 5 (2013): 817–826. DOI: 10.1037/a0033883.

Lauzen, Martha, and Douglas Deiss. "Breaking the Fourth Wall and Sex Role Stereotypes: An Examination of the 2006–2007 Prime-Time Season." *Sex Roles* 60, no. 5–6 (2009): 379–386.

Lemi, Danielle C., and Nadia Brown. "Melanin and Curls: Evaluation of Black Women Candidates." *The Journal of Race, Ethnicity and Politics* 4 (2019): 259–296.

Lerman, Amy E., Katherine T. McCabe, and Meredith L. Sadin. "Political Ideology, Skin Tone, and the Psychology of Candidate Evaluations." *Public Opinion Quarterly* 79, no. 1 (2015): 53–90.

Lerman, Amy E., and Meredith L. Sadin. "Stereotyping or Projection? How White and Black Voters Estimate Black Candidates' Ideology." *Political Psychology* 37, no. 2 (2016): 147–163. DOI: 10.1111/pops.12235.

Lewis, Gregory. "Black-White Differences in Attitudes Toward Homosexuality and Gay Rights." *Public Opinion Quarterly* 67, no. 1 (2003): 59–78. DOI: 10.1086/346009.

Littlefield, Marci. "The Media as a System of Racialization: Exploring Images of African American Women and the New Racism." *American Behavioral Scientist* 51, no. 5 (2008): 675–685.

Loiacano, Darryl K. "Gay Identity Issues Among Black Americans: Racism, Homophobia, and the Need for Validation." *Journal of Counseling & Development* 68, no. 1 (1989): 21–25. DOI: 10.1002/j.1556-6676.1989.tb02486.x.

Lorde, Audre. "There Is No Hierarchy of Oppressions." In *Bulletin: Homophobia and Education.* Council on Interracial Books for Children, 1983.

Lorde, Audre. *Sister Outsider: Essays and Speeches.* Berkley, CA: Ten Speed Press, 1984.

Maddox, Keith B., and Stephanie Gray. "Cognitive Representations of Black Americans: Re-Exploring the Role of Skin Tone." *Personality and Social Psychology Bulletin* 28, no. 2 (2002): 250–259.

Mask, Mia. "A Roundtable Conversation on *Scandal*." *The Black Scholar* 45, no. 1 (2015): 3–9.

Mauer, Warren R. *Understanding Gerhart Hauptmann*. Columbia: University of South Carolina Press, 1982.

McKnight, Utz. "The Fantastic Oliva Pope: The Construction of a Black Feminist Subject." *Souls: A Critical Journal of Black Politics, Culture, and Society* 16, no. 3–4 (2014): 183–197.

Mercer, Kobena. "Black Hair/Style Politics." In *The Subcultures Reader*, edited by Ken Gelder, 420–435. London: Routledge, 2005.

Miles, Tiya. "Black Hair's Blockbuster Moment." *New York Times*. February 27, 2018. https://www.nytimes.com/2018/02/23/opinion/sunday/natural-hair-black -panther.html.

Miller, Mitzi. "Natural Wonder." *Ebony* (December 2013–January 2014): 133–137. Johnson Publishing Company.

Monk-Payton, Brandeise. "The Sound of *Scandal*: Crisis Management and the Musical Mediation of Racial Desire." *The Black World Scholar* 45, no. 1 (2015): 21–27.

Morgan, Joan. *When Chickenheads Come Home to Roost: My Life as a Hip Hop Feminist*. New York: Simon & Schuster, 1999.Morrison, Adele M. "Straightening Up: Black Women Law Professors, Interracial Relationships and Academic Fit(ting) In." *Harvard journal of Law & Gender* 33, no. 1 (2010): 85–98.

Moultrie, Monique. "Putting a Ring on It: Black Women, Black Churches, and Coerced Monogamy." *Black Theology: An International Journal* 16, no. 3 (2018): 231–247. DOI: 10.1080/14769948.2018.1492304.

Mulvey, Laura. "Visual Pleasure and Narrative Cinema." In *The Sexual Subject: A Screen Reader in Sexuality*, edited by John Caughie and Annette Kuhn, 22–34. London: Routledge Press, 1992.

Muscio, Inga. *Cunt: A Declaration of Independence*. New York: Seal Press, 1998.

"Music and Arts: Performances at the White House." (2016). *The White House: President Obama*. https://obamawhitehouse.archives.gov/performances.

Ndichu, Edna G., and Shika Upadhyaya. "'Going Natural': Black Women's Identity Project Shifts in Hair Care Practices." *Consumption Markets & Culture* 22, no. 1 (2019): 44–67. DOI: 10.1080/10253866.2018.1456427.

Neil, Latisha, and Lafiya Mbilishaka. "'Hey, Curlfriends!': Hair Care and Self-Care Messaging on Youtube by Black Women Natural Hair Vloggers." *Journal of Black Studies* 50, no. 2 (2019): 156–177.

Nelson, Alondra. "Introduction: Future Texts." *Social Texts* 20, no. 2 (2002): 1–15.

Norwood, Carolette R. "Decolonizing My Hair, Unshackling My Curls: An Autoethnography on What Makes My Natural Hair Journey a Black Feminist Statement." *International Feminist Journal of Politics* 20 (2018): 69–84.

Nosek, Brian A., Mahzahrin R. Banaji, and Anthony G. Greenwald. "Harvesting Intergroup Implicit Attitudes and Beliefs from a Demonstration Web Site." *Group Dynamics* 6, no. 1 (2002): 101–115.

Obaro, Tomi. "'She's Gotta Have It' Is Spike Lee at His Lecturing Worst." *Buzzfeed*. November 28, 2017. Buzzfeed.com. https://www.buzzfeednews.com/article/tomio-baro/when-will-spike-lee-stop-lecturing-us.

Orey, Byron D., and Yu Zhang. "Melenated Millennials and the Politics of Black Hair." *Social Science Quarterly* 100, no. 6 (2019): 2058–2077.

Painter, Nell. *The History of White People.* New York: W. W. Norton Press, 2010.

Pixley, Tara. "Trop and Associates: Olivia Pope's Scandalous Blackness." *The Black Scholar* 45, no. 1 (2015): 28–33.

Pickens, Theri A. "Shoving Aside the Politics of Respectability: Black Women, Reality TV, and the Ratchet Performance." *Women and Performance: A Journal of Feminist Theory* 25, no. 1 (2015): 41-58. Rae, Issa. *The Misadventures of Awkward Black Girl.* New York: Atria, 2015.

Rae, Issa. *The Misadventures of Awkward Black Girl.* New York: Atria Press, 2015Rainwater, Lee, and William Yancey. *The Moynihan Report and the Politics of Controversy.* Cambridge: The M.I.T. Press, 1967.

Redd, Nancy. *Bedtime Bonnet.* New York: Penguin Random House, 2020.

Reliable Source. "Michelle Obama's Bangs: Are Their Days Numbered? See How They Grow (Photos)." *The Washington Post.* April 9, 2013. Accessed 1 August 2019. https://www.washingtonpost.com/news/reliable-source/wp/2013/04/09/michelle-obamas-bangs-are-their-days-numbered-see-how-they-grow-photos/?utm_term=.b42365221647.

Rich, Adrienne. *Blood, Bread, and Poetry: Selected Prose 1979–1985.* New York: Norton Publishing Company, 1986.

Roberts, Robin. "Music Videos, Performance and Resistance: Feminist Rappers." *Journal of Popular Culture* 25, no. 2 (1991): 141–152.

Robinson, Cynthia. "Hair as Race: Why 'Good Hair' May Be Bad for Black Females." *Howard Journal of Communications* 22, no. 4 (2011): 358–376. DOI: 10.1080/1046175.2011.617212.

Roundtree, Cheyenne. "Photo of Michelle Obama Goes Viral as Internet Praises the Former FLOTUS for Wearing Her Hair Natural." *Daily Mail.* April 4, 2017. Accessed 1 August 2020. http://www.dailymail.co.uk/news/article-4377536/Michelle-Obama-pictured-wearing-natural-hair.html#ixzz4q0sTFhZz.

Rowe, Kristin D. "'Nothing Else Mattered After that Wig Came Off': Black Women, Unstyled Hair, and Scenes of Interiority." *The Journal of American Culture* 42, no. 1 (2019): 21–36.

Rudman, Laurie A., and Meghan McLean. "The Role of Appearance Stigma in Implicit Racial Ingroup Bias." *Group Processes and Intergroup Relations* 19, no. 3 (2016): 374–393.

Russell, Kathy Y., Midge Wilson, and Ronald Hall. *The Color Complex: The Politics of Skin Color Among African Americans.* New York: Harcourt, 1992. Revised 2013.

Salamon, Hagar. "Blackness in Transition: Decoding Racial Constructs Through Stories of Ethiopian Jews." *Journal of Folklore Research* 40, no. 1 (2003): 3–32.

Samudzi, Zoe. "Queer Bait and Switch: She's Gotta Have It Fails LGBTQ Viewers—Again." *BitchMedia.* July 11, 2019. https://www.bitchmedia.org/article/queerbaiting-in-shes-gotta-have-it.

Sankofa, Jasmine. "From Margin to Center: Sex Work Decriminalization is a Racial Justice Issue." *Amnesty International.* 2015. https://www.amnestyusa.org/from-margin-to-center-sex-work-decriminalization-is-a-racial-justice-issue/.

Saro-Wiwa, Zina. "Black Women's Transitions to Natural Hair." *The New York Times*. May 31, 2012. http://www.nytimes.com/2012/06/01/opinion/black-women -and-natural-hair.html?_r=0.

Sawyer, Mark. *Racial Politics in Post-Revolutionary Cuba.* Cambridge, MA: Cambridge University Press, 2005.

Scott, A. O. "Daughters of the Dust (1991). *New York Times Style Magazine* (April 13, 2020): 89-91.Sewell, Christopher J. P. "Mammies and Matriarchs: Tracing Images of the Black Female in Popular Culture 1950s to Present." *Journal of African American Studies* 17 (2013): 308–326.

Sewell, Christopher J. P. "Mammies and Matriarchs: Tracing Images of the Black Female in Popular Culture 1950s to Present." *Journal of African American Studies* 17, no. 3 (2013): 308-26.Sidanius, Jim, Yesilernis Pena, and Mark Sawyer. "Inclusionary Discrimination: Pigmentocracy and Patriotism in the Dominican Republic." *Political Psychology* 22, no. 4 (2001): 827–851.

Smith, S. "And Still More Drama!: A Comparison of the Portrayals of African-American Women and African–American Men on BET's *College Hill*." *The Western Journal of Black Studies* 73, no. 1 (2013): 39–49.

Soloski, Alexis. "The Sex Worker as More than Set Dressing." *New York Times Arts and Leisure*. July 12, 2020, 11.

St. Felix, Doreen. "I Will Survive: I May Destroy You on HBO." *The New Yorker* 66, no. 19 (July 6 and 13, 2020): 66–68.

Stevenson, Brenda. "*12 Years a Slave*: Narrative, History, & Film." *The Journal of African American History* 99, no. 1–2 (2014): 106–118.

Stevenson, Howard. "Validation of the Scale of Racial Socialization for African American Adolescents: Steps Toward Multidimensionality." *Journal of Black Psychology* 20, no. 4 (1994): 445–468.

Stevenson, Howard. "Influence of Perceived Neighborhood Diversity and Racism Experience on the Racial Socialization of Black Youth." *Journal of Black Psychology* 31, no. 3 (2005): 273–290.

Stokes, Lynissa R., and Leslie R. Brody. "Self-Silencing, but Not Sexual Relationship Power Associated with Condom Use for Black College-Aged Women." *Behavioral Sciences* 9, no. 2 (2019): 13. DOI: 10.3390/bs9020013.

Tate, Shirley. "Black Beauty: Shade, Hair and Anti-Racist Aesthetics." *Ethnic and Racial Studies* 30, no. 2 (2007): 300–319. DOI: 10.1080/01419870601143992.

Taylor, Charlotte. "Women are Bitchy But Men Are Sarcastic?: Investigating Gender and Sarcasm." *Gender and Language* 11, no. 3 (2017): 415–445.

Telles, Edward. *Race in Another America: The Significance of Skin Color in Brazil.* Princeton, NJ: Princeton University Press, 2004.

Terkildsen, Nayda. "When White Voters Evaluate Black Candidates: The Processing Implications of Candidate Skin Color, Prejudice, and Self-Monitoring." *American Journal of Political Science* 37, no. 4 (1993): 1032–1053. http://www.jstor.org/ stable/2111542.

Breen-Tuchi, Ezra. "Things *Harriet* Got Wrong About Harriet Tubman's Life." *Grunge,* November 4, 2019. grunge.com/173225/things-harriet-got-wrong-abou

Thomas, Anita J., Jason D. Hacker, and Denada Hoxha. "Gendered Racial Identity of Black Young Women." *Sex Roles: A Journal of Research* 64, no. 7–8 (2011): 530–542. DOI: 10.1007/s11199-011-9939-y.

Thompson, Cheryl. "Black Women, Beauty, and Hair as a Matter of *Being.*" *Women's Studies* 38, no. 8 (2008): 831–856.

Tillet, Salamisha. "New Voices for a Dwindling Middle." *The New York Times.* January 8, 2017, 15.

Toby, Mekeisha Madden. "Meet Some of the Black Women Leading a Comedy Renaissance." *Shondaland.* October 14, 2019. https://www.shondaland.com/watch /a29442027/black-women-comedy-renaissance/.

Treviño, A. Javier, Michelle Harris, and Derron Wallace. "What's So Critical About Critical Race Theory?" *Contemporary Justice Review* 11, no. 1 (2008): 7–10. DOI: 10.1080/10282580701850330.

Tuchman, Gaye. *Making News: A Study in the Construction of Reality.* London: Free Press, 1978.

Tyree, Tia. "African American Stereotypes in Reality Television." *Howard Journal of Communications* 22 (2011): 394–413.

Unbought and Unbossed. (December 21, 2019). "@Brax6Jackson." *Twitter.*

Wagmeister, Elizabeth. "Shonda Rhimes on Fitz Learning About *Scandal* Abortion: Does He Have To? A Woman Made a Choice About Her Body." *Variety.com.* March 15, 2016. https://variety-com.ezproxy.missouriwestern.edu/2016/tv/news/ scandal-abortion-shond-rhimes-reaction-fitz-olivia-1201731223/.

Wagmeister, Elizabeth. "Saying 'So Long' to Scandal." *The New York Times.* April 15, 2018, 21.

Walker, Alice. *In Search of Our Mothers'' Gardens.* San Diego: Harcourt, 1983.

Wanzo, Rebecca. "Black Love Is Not a Fairytale." *Poroi* 7, no. 2 (2011): 1–18.

Wanzo, Rebecca. "Precarious-Girl Comedy: Issa Rae, Lena Dunham, and Abjection Aesthetics." *Camera Obscura* 31, no. 2 (2016): 26–59.

Ward, Jervette. *Real Sister: Stereotypes, Respectability, and Black Women in Reality TV.* New Brunswick, NJ: Rutgers University Press, 2015.

Warner, Kristin. "If Loving Olitz Is Wrong, I Don't Want to Be Right: ABC's *Scandal* and the Effect of Black Female Desire." *The Black Scholar* 45, no. 1 (2015): 16–20.

Washington, Harriet A. *Medical Apartheid: The Dark History of Medical Experimentation on Black Americans from Colonial Times to the Present.* New York: Anchor Press, 2008.

Weaver, Vesla M. "The Electoral Consequences of Skin Color: The 'Hidden' Side of Race in Politics." *Political Behavior* 34, no. 1 (2012): 159–192.

West, Caroline, and Kalima Johnson. "Sexual Violence in the Lives of African-American Women." *National Online Resource Center on Violence Against Women.* 2013. VANET.org. https://vawnet.org/sites/default/files/materials/files /2016-09/AR_SVAAWomenRevised.pdf.

Wheaton, Ken. "Creativity 50." *Advertising Age* 87, no. 24 (2016): 12.

White, Peter. "'A Black Lady Sketch Show': Robin Thede on Predicting the Apocalypse and New Writing Talent for Season 2." *Deadline.* July 6, 2020. https://deadline.com /2020/07/a-black-lady-sketch-show-robin-thede-season-2-interview-1202978600/.

White, Shauntae Brown. "The Big Girl's Chair: A Rhetorical Analysis of How Motions for Kids Markets Relaxers to African American Girls." In *Blackberries and Redbones: Critical Articulations of Black Hair/Body Politics in Africana Communities*, edited by Regina Spellers and Kimberly Moffitt, 17–27. New Jersey: Hampton Press, 2010.

Wicker, Kay. "It's Official: We are Experiencing a Black Renaissance." *ThinkProgress .org*. March 16, 2018. https://archive.thinkprogress.org/black-renaissance-2018 -93d8b3981e28/.

Wilder, Jeffrianne. "Revising 'Color Names and Color Notions': A Contemporary Examination of the Language of Skin Color Among Black Women." *Journal of Black Studies* 41, no. 1 (2010): 184-206. Wiltz, Teresa. "The Evil Sista of Reality T.V." *Washington Post*. February 25, 2004. https://www.washingtonpost.com /archive/lifestyle/2004/02/25/the-evil-sista-of-reality-television/cb22c1dd-b4b9 -4ba8-9785-925d998a7312/.

Wolf, Naomi. *The Beauty Myth: How Images of Beauty Are Used Against Women*. New York: William Morrow, 1991.

Wyatt, Jean. "Patricia Hill Collins Black Sexual Politics and the Genealogy of the Strong Black Woman." *Studies in Gender & Sexuality* 9 (2008): 52–67.

Yancey, George. "Skin Deep: Race and Complexion Matter in the "Color-Blind Era." In *Skin Deep: How Race and Complexion Matter in the "Color-Blind" Era*, edited by Cedric Herring, Verna Keith, and Hayward Derrick Horton, 1–21. Chicago, IL: University of Illinois Press, 2004.

Zinoman, Jason. "Tell a Joke, Risk Your Life." *New York Times* (April 10, 2019): C1,C6.

Index

About the Author and Artist

Kay Siebler, PhD, is a queer feminist who can't shut up about social justice. And this has gotten her into more than one mess. Oh well. She began her teaching career thirty-five years ago as a Peace Corps volunteer in Morocco. Currently she is a professor of English at the University of Nebraska Omaha. She has taught at several universities and community colleges in the U.S. and abroad. She is a scholar and teacher of English, rhetoric, media, and gender studies. Siebler has published articles and books on the topics of feminist pedagogy, the rhetoric(s) of Black women, neo-burlesque, queer identities, and pedagogies of social justice/civic engagement. The things that make her heart sing are to teach and to write. A day outside the classroom better be on the porch reading and writing—otherwise, what is the point? You can reach her at kay.siebler@gmail.com or ksiebler@unomaha.edu.

ABOUT THE ARTIST

Katharen Wiese (b. 1995, Lincoln, Nebraska) is an artist, curator, and a community arts organizer living and working in the historic Everett Neighborhood of Lincoln, Nebraska. Ms. Wiese graciously provided the cover art for this book. The piece is entitled "if a black woman is afraid of the dark is she afraid of a shadow or herself" and features a commentary on colorism and the underrepresentation of Black women in popular media. She holds a BFA in studio art from the University of Nebraska at Lincoln (2018). Her work is a part of Nebraska History Museum collection as well as the Thomas P. Coleman print collection at the Sheldon Museum of Art. She was a 2018 nominee for the University of Nebraska Vreeland Howard Award and four-time award winner of the Kimmel Harding Scholarship for Emerging

Arts (2014–2018). Wiese has curated art shows across the state for the past four years with emphasis on sharing the work of artists of color. You can see/purchase her work at www.katwiese.com.

www.ingramcontent.com/pod-product-compliance
Lightning Source LLC
Chambersburg PA
CBHW022308280326
41932CB00010B/1021